Communication as . . .
Perspectives on Theory

Edited by
Gregory J. Shepherd
Ohio University

Jeffrey St. John
Ohio University

Ted Striphas
Indiana University

SAGE Publications
Thousand Oaks ▪ London ▪ New Delhi

For information:

Sage Publications, Inc.
2455 Teller Road
Thousand Oaks, California 91320
E-mail: order@sagepub.com

Sage Publications Ltd.
1 Oliver's Yard
55 City Road
London, EC1Y 1SP
United Kingdom

Sage Publications India Pvt. Ltd.
B-42, Panchsheel Enclave
Post Box 4109
New Delhi 110 017 India

Printed in the United States of America.

Library of Congress Cataloging-in-Publication Data

Communication as—: perspectives on theory / editors Gregory
J. Shepherd, Jeffrey St. John, and Ted Striphas.
    p. cm.
Includes index.
ISBN 978-1-4129-0657-9 (cloth) — ISBN 978-1-4129-0658-6 (pbk.)
   1. Communication—Philosophy. I. Shepherd,
Gregory J. II. St. John, Jeffrey. III. Striphas, Theodore G.
P90.C6292 2006
302.2′01—dc22

                            2005000648

This book is printed on acid-free paper.

              09   10   9   8   7   6   5   4

Senior Acquisitions Editor:	Todd R. Armstrong
Editorial Assistant:	Deya Saoud
Production Editor:	Tracy Alpern
Copy Editor:	Brenda Weight
Typesetter:	C&M Digitals (P) Ltd.
Indexer:	Juniee Oneida
Cover Designer:	Edgar Abarca

Communication as . . .

Contents

Acknowledgments

This book hinges on two main premises: first, communication is—or should be—a contested concept; and second, arguments over the meaning, value, and utility of communication ought to be generative. In our estimation, the 27 chapters that follow demonstrate just how productive arguments of this kind can be—for communication theory specifically and for the discipline of communication more broadly. And yet, these arguments have been generative of more than scholarly knowledge. They have helped to produce—inasmuch as they embody—a dense web of interpersonal encounters without which this book would not have been possible. Truly, what you are now reading and what you are about to read represent collaboration to the core.

As editors, we were struck again and again by the complementarity of our respective editorial strengths—the ease, equity, and egalitarianism by which the process of producing this book unfolded—and so, as colleagues and friends, each of us wants to thank the other two. Also palpable were the influences of the many teachers and students who have inspired our interest in communication theory, along with the support and goodwill of everyone who encouraged us to see this project through from beginning to end. The acknowledgments that pepper many of the subsequent chapters similarly bear witness to the generosity and comradeship that projects like this both foster and follow from.

Greg Shepherd would like to acknowledge his teachers at the University of Minnesota, Penn State, and the University of Illinois, but especially his mentors Barb and Dan O'Keefe, who taught him that ideas matter and so should be contended, and that best friends contest ideas with zeal and love. He also wants to thank all of his colleagues and students at the University of Iowa, the University of Kansas, and Ohio University, whose conversation allowed for the appearance of his articulation of theory, but especially three friends and colleagues, old and new: Eric Rothenbuhler, Autumn Edwards, and Bill Rawlins. Finally, he would like to thank Mary Shepherd for providing more than three decades of experiential proof that communication is indeed transcendence.

Jeffrey St. John wishes to express his gratitude to two extraordinary teachers—Kristin Langellier and the late Tom Puckett—for introducing him to the study of communication.

Ted Striphas would like to express his thanks—long overdue—to Cindy White, whose introductory communication class at the University of New Hampshire first inspired his interest in communication research and theory. He also would like to acknowledge John Nguyet Erni, Lawrence Grossberg, Joshua Meyrowitz, Mari Boor Tonn, and Julia T. Wood, whose mentorship and courses at the University of New Hampshire and the University of North Carolina strengthened that interest into a lifelong professional commitment. Finally, he is grateful to Phaedra C. Pezzullo for her ongoing support in all spheres of work and life.

Collectively, the editors would like to thank Todd Armstrong, our editor at Sage, for his interest and astute editorial guidance. Our gratitude also extends to Deya Saoud, Tracy Alpern, Brenda Weight, and to the entire production team at Sage with whom we have had the good fortune to work. Finally, our thanks to the following reviewers whose outstanding and incisive feedback, we hope, is reflected amply in the individual chapters and in the shape of this collection as a whole: Marianne Dainton, La Salle University; Thomas G. Endres, University of Northern Colorado; Sonja K. Foss, University of Colorado at Boulder; Bradford 'J' Hall, University of New Mexico; Peter Marston, California State University, Northridge; Patricia Rockwell, University of Louisiana at Lafayette; Lynn H. Turner, Marquette University; and Laura Drake Witz, University of Maryland.

Introduction:
Taking a Stand on Theory

Jeffrey St. John, Ted Striphas,
and Gregory J. Shepherd

The essays in this book are the flowering of a modest seed, one which has bloomed into a remarkably diverse set of claims about how communication theory should be understood and put into practice. In our view, that seed was (and remains) an irritant, or agitant, of the most productive sort. At its core, it entails an unapologetically stubborn suspicion that communication theorists have become a bit too open-minded with regard to perspectives on communication theory: we fear for the resulting draftiness. From the outset, one of our goals for this book has been to nudge, push, or openly cajole theorists and practitioners of communication toward a fundamental reappraisal of what is at stake when we think and write and talk and argue about our subject. In concrete terms, we are insisting that they—and we—start to think in exactly those terms: about what's at stake. In fact, a stakeholder model of contemporary theorizing is one that we believe might compel us to embrace what matters most about communication: the real-world repercussions of what we think, write, and do. We firmly believe that it *matters* whether we take communication to be one sort of phenomenon or process or idea . . . or another. Our theorizing and teaching influence how we and others live our lives, for the better or for the worse.

An affirmative way of saying all of this is to argue that a bracing dose of "now wait just a minute" would do wonders for the study of communication. That is precisely what we have asked for, and gotten from, the 27 contributors to this volume. They do not believe that it is important to accept every idea about communication that happens to show up in a book or a journal article or a classroom lecture. Some of them reject many of the notions that appear in one or more of those places, and others question the very ground beneath our collective feet. Is our ontology truly coherent? Do we have our epistemology down quite as pat as we think we do? Are there elements of theories—or theories entire—that just don't work? These questions and others like them typically are not tackled through negation, but rather through the forging of a remorselessly positive claim *for* one stance on communication theorizing. Each contributor to this volume has been encouraged to defy the quietly powerful decorum demanded by most forms of academic writing and has been freed up to take a stand. Each has been asked to think like this: *My* stance is the one most serviceable for the study and practice of communication. *My* metaphor, *my* analogy, *my* model. *This, not those, and for these reasons. Here is what I believe and why I believe it, and here is the difference it makes.* Thus, while the authors of these chapters are tolerant of other views, knowing as we do that there are a multitude of perspectives on communication, that perspectives are adhered to and applied for different purposes, and that communication can sensibly be defined variously, they also assert a particular stance as primary, or essential, or most important among the alternatives, if not forever, at least for now. In other words, though their stances are not cast in stone, neither are these authors' positions made of straw, subject to undoing at the slightest winds of disciplinary change. Each contributor holds a view, and each is unafraid to suggest that others would do well to hold it also, and for some very compelling reasons. It is important that the standard apologies for one's not having chosen another theory, or for not giving sufficient attention to the merits of those unchosen others, are not generally found in these essays.

Before going any further down this path, we should be clear about what this book does not do. First, this is not a book that mounts an impassioned defense of the intellectual relevance of communication. Communication *is* relevant; each of the chapters in this collection begins with that assumption, and not a single one concludes anything other than the same. We see this volume as evidence of the richness of contemporary thinking about communication, the breadth of communication's influence on intellectual endeavors of all sorts, and the significant weight of our collective theorizing. Please do *not* read these essays as evidence of our immaturity as a field of inquiry, or as contributing to some "crisis in the field" conversation; they are not exercises in hand-wringing, or public soul-searching for a disciplinary place in the world. Each of us stands convinced of communication's salience as a body of theory and an embodiment of praxis even as we author alternative readings of its manifestations and ambitions.

Second, this book is not an exercise in or example of theory pluralism, or the belief that all theories have equal merit if understood and appreciated on their own terms. We want scholars and students to appreciate differences, but to understand also that those same differences *make* a difference. We decidedly did not want to edit a volume of many perspectives that left readers with the impression that our theoretical and methodological choices are about as consequential as the choice of dishes at a potluck dinner—which is to say, of next to no consequence at all. Communicative choices are, or should be, something different in kind from mere consumer preferences. The extent to which such choices are relevant to the world of consequences, and so guided by sober judgment, is one reason why, we assume, almost all contributors to this volume so readily accepted our charge to excite and influence readers with these essays.

More than 25 years ago, B. Aubrey Fisher published his influential treatment of communication theory under the title *Perspectives on Human Communication* (1978). In the conclusion to that work, Fisher cautioned readers to avoid the position that there is only one "right way" to study communication, even as he urged people conscientiously to select one perspective over others—weaknesses, warts, and all. Don't be a "mugwump" (p. 324), he advised; don't think you can lump disparate perspectives together and thereby avoid the need to discriminate critically among them. Guided by a like-minded belief in the constructive uses of clear-eyed appraisal, we happily take up Professor Fisher's mantle and urge that after reading these essays, you take advantage of the invitation to rank one of them above all others, or at least rank some ahead of others. This invitation is a rather unfashionable one in contemporary theorizing. In making it, we open ourselves (as coeditors, and as individual chapter authors) up to just the kind of judgments that we (ourselves and our fellow theorists in the field) work so strenuously to evade.

Finally, this book is not primarily about communication practice; it's about communication theory. This is not, of course, to say that theory isn't practical. As we've already tried to make plain, we follow William James in believing that metaphysical beliefs of all sorts are the *most* pragmatic of beliefs, because they are broadly and deeply consequential for the living out of our lives. But that doesn't mean that this is a book devoted to empirical study, behavior, or skill. This is, proudly, a work of *theory* by *theorists*. By that, we mean that it is a collection of abstractions. This is not a book that analyzes speeches, conversations, performances, or media texts; it is a book that includes some of the thinking required *for* the analysis of speeches, conversations, performances, or media texts. We believe that such activities, or practices, only can be understood theoretically. What makes the act of two persons speaking to one another a conversation for them and a densely significant communicative "act" or "event" for communication scholars is, precisely, a theoretical disposition coupled with the conceptual overlay we apply to these ordinary, everyday actions. These acts or events cease to be ordinary and everyday for scholars because we are inclined to think and write about them in theoretically informed ways. To the extent that doing so helps us help people make their conversations more equitable, or more constructive, or more influential, then we're getting somewhere. To the extent that it does not, our overlay is stripped of its lone link to public relevance and the communicative "act" serves only a localized, instrumental purpose. The point here is that communication theory stands one critical step behind practice; it is neither several steps behind (as philosophy) nor fully present in the buzz of communication itself (as practice).

On now to what this book is. It is a collection of 27 freestanding arguments. It is an exercise in contrarian thinking. And it is a deliberate rejection of the tacit claim in contemporary communication that an undifferentiated plurality of theories is somehow a good thing. Frankly, we have grown both leery and weary of communication as buffet: that is, the uncritical presentation of theories in the absence of evaluative measures with which to recommend one over another or some over others, or, heaven forbid, *one* over *all* others. A guest at the potluck may prefer one dish to another, but he or she doesn't stand at the table audibly faulting other guests for their failure to share his or her tastes. But communication is different; it either amounts to something significantly more than a simple matter of preference or we are all wasting our time. We think just such a voice *should* stand at the buffet of communication theories—and maybe kick the whole thing over from time to time.

Imagine this. What would happen in (or to) communication inquiry if the appraisal of theories no longer were relentlessly horizontal, but were instead openly vertical? What would happen in an undergraduate or graduate communication theory course if students were encouraged to rank the theories under investigation from best to worst, or from most useful or persuasive to least? Theorists are quick to defend the practical dimensions of their study of theory, to argue that our accumulated knowledge of communication theories has traction "out there" in the real world. But the frustration that usually accompanies that defense, together with the vigor with which we tend to make it, gives us away more often than not. How can we say what we think is *best for* communication practice if we are unwilling to think about what is *best in* communication theory? Judgment, then, is an integral component of communication theory and practice and, in a larger sense, of maintaining a vibrant, socially relevant communication discipline.

This book also is an exercise in both theoretical and expressive creativity. In addition to asking authors to take a stand on theory, we have asked them to write in a minimally referenced, essayistic style. This style wears favorably, we think, in relation to the exhaustively researched and extensively citational writing customary of most scholarly books and journals. Our reason for making this request cuts against the grain of one of the key trends in the field, one that, in our estimation, constrains the imaginations of communication theory and theorists. Since at least the second quarter of the 20th century, a strongly empiricist orientation has guided much of academic research and writing, including that in communication. This orientation's principal legacy has been a stultifying set of expectations for what counts as "good" theory. Theories, empiricism tells us, must demonstrate a clear connection to an observable reality and must be grounded in an extensive scholarly literature to be viewed as credible. For a variety of complex reasons, a cluster of procedures (including rules for referencing, footnoting, and the like) came to determine whether an idea was worthwhile, good, believable, or true (cf. Gadamer, 1998). The powerfully humanist belief that the inherent sense of an idea—its place in a community, its emergence within an identifiable tradition, or its reflection of a way of life—is the strongest measure of an idea's worth was overwhelmed by method. In an astonishingly brief time, the new empirical paradigm began to declare that what made a theory "good" was whether it could be proven, where proof was confined to normative and potentially limiting rules of measure and referral. That's what we hoped to avoid in this collection. Our idea has been to give a diverse grouping of accomplished thinkers the kind of free reign that scholars of an earlier century had, and that nonacademics still do.

In response to the long shadow now cast by empiricism, we contend that more space for theoretical speculation and stylistic experimentation must be carved out in the discipline of communication, and must be met with a corresponding generosity and patience on the part of readers, reviewers, and editors. Openness of this sort should not preclude our making judgments, however, but should move us to scrutinize the very terms by which we judge the worth of theories. More to the point, it may be less helpful to evaluate a specific theory or stance against empiricism's cherished norm of verifiability, for instance, than it would be to consider a theory's capacity *in the long term* to provoke new research, insight, and response.

There are, of course, costs associated with a blunt call for emancipation from the narrow confines of empiricism. For example, as editors of a collection committed to encouraging such freedom, we have struggled with the question of how heavy a hand to take in the editorial process. Often, editors of volumes such as this exert considerable influence over the formatting, style, pitch, and organization of individual essays, in part to ensure a high degree of consistency or uniformity across chapters. Our commitment to allowing expressive freedom to our contributors made us reluctant to exert such a leveling influence. We have given our authors a precise set of guidelines for tasks to address in their essays and a severe page limitation, and have otherwise left them to their own creative devices. Though we did request revisions from most authors and offered suggestions for improvement, even then we tried more or less to preserve the expression they already had made. For the most part, then, here was our approach: we gathered together a terrific assembly of thinkers, gave them a detailed charge, and let them have at it. The result is a collection of very strong and irreducibly diverse chapters that offers far less thematic consistency on the surface (from essay to essay) than may be typical of such works.

Our Contributors and Their Stances on Theory

This book encompasses an extraordinary range of stances on communication theory. A quick glance at the table of contents will show the diversity of metaphors by which the contributors as a whole understand—and would like you to understand—the idea of communication. And yet, these metaphors are more than just figurative language. Embedded within each are deeply held ontological, epistemological, and axiological orientations—choices that have guided each contributor in formulating her or his own stance. Each author, in other words, not only advances a specific argument about communication, but also (and often implicitly) makes broader claims about human agency, knowledge and reality, and the importance (or not) of making judgments. Thus, we want to raise the stakes for what it means to adopt a particular theoretical stance. This may be a book about communication and communication theory, but also, and just as important, it is about the intellectual, political, and ethical consequences of making the very choices that lead us to form and enact particular conceptions of communication.

While the range of stances on communication theory represented in these pages is extensive, it is by no means exhaustive. This book project originated in the 2002 National Communication Association annual convention, at which a small group of us briefly shared our thoughts on "What we take communication to be." These short presentations spurred a lively conversation with the audience, who, in addition to engaging with the substance of the papers, offered some views about what *they* took communication to be. One person, for instance, insisted that communication be conceived of as democracy and was as resolute in his position as the panelists were of their own. A second asked us to recall James Carey's work on communication as culture. And still another framed communication as performance, or performativity. Their responses are proof positive that a volume such as this one, however broad, at best can encompass only a fraction of possible stances on communication. The stances you do *not* find here, in other words, may well provoke as much thinking about communication as those you *do*. If you do not see your preferred stance in these pages, then by all means, go formulate it yourself.

Some authors in this volume are explicit about what they take to be the academic and/or "real world" consequences of choosing a particular stance (or stances). Other contributors offer relatively little comment on the subject. There are good reasons for this difference. Some in the latter camp, for instance, reject the distinction many people draw between institutions of learning and the so-called real world, as though formal education somehow fundamentally stood apart from daily life. (Ask anyone who works at a university: It's work!) These authors tend to foreground theoretical gains more than concrete outcomes for their chapters. Many would reject the idea that you must be able to "cash in" on a given theoretical stance at the end of the day (or upon graduation) for that theory to be relevant and useful. On the other hand, several authors in these pages believe just as strongly in those concrete outcomes—and argue for them accordingly. This divergence is telling. Clearly, it speaks to a rift in how communication scholars imagine both the purposes and consequences of their theorizing. Yet it also speaks, implicitly, to how the *nature* and *import* of the consequences that flow from adopting a particular stance cannot be assumed in advance, but follow from the complex theoretical, methodological, professional, pedagogical, and political choices each theorist must make prior to formulating a position. What's at stake theoretically in each of these chapters, in other words, is not only the *product,* or the specific theoretical stance, but the very *process* of theorizing itself.

In some cases, that is to say, the job of determining both the choices that went into formulating, and the consequences of adopting, a particular stance may fall on your shoulders. In all cases, you should consider what choices each author needed to make in crafting that stance. Out of what theoretical tradition or traditions is this person working? What role does this person think theory ought to play, and in what context(s)? With whom does this person side or identify politically, and how might that have influenced his or her decision making? We already have mentioned, moreover, how our desire to include a broad range of theoretical stances in this volume has meant that the authors needed to remain as concise and focused as possible in their remarks. At times, unfortunately, this brevity has resulted in the authors' including fewer, or less developed, examples than they (or we) would have liked. We encourage readers to respond to these formal constraints and perceived absences by generating more elaborated examples where you think they are needed. All this work might seem unnecessarily burdensome, but we hope that any frustration you may feel will be generative of classroom exercises, collegial debate, and scholarly publications: the very stuff that keeps communication (both the field and the activity itself) going.

Structure of the Present Work: A Unity-in-Difference

We have constructed an organizational framework that cuts across the divisions that usually pattern the institutional lives of communication scholars and their students (e.g., cultural studies, health, intercultural, interpersonal, journalism, media, organizational, performance, rhetoric, and so on). We have done this for two primary reasons. First, rather than relying on existing divisions within the field, we have opted instead to acknowledge that scholars and students routinely and increasingly work across them. This productive spirit of fusing and mixing, borrowing and adapting, improvising and extending also is in keeping with the history of our field, a field forged from such seemingly disparate disciplines as anthropology, history, linguistics, literary studies, philosophy, political science, psychology, sociology, theater, and more. We have organized this book, in other words, in a manner intended to push more than to reproduce the shape of the field of communication. Second, it became clear to us in reading over the chapters that, despite their differences, some commonalities in how the authors approached or thought of the idea of communication drew groups of them together. Some authors hold fast to its creative or constitutive capacities; others resist the idea that communication consists of ephemeral, insubstantial symbols and insist instead on its material dimensions; still others believe that communication cannot be understood apart from the affiliations and social networks that both produce and are produced by it; some contributors see communication as inherently political and politicizing; and some, finally, want to problematize the idea of communication entirely.

Just because a given set of chapters may cluster together, however, does not mean that, together, they constitute anything approaching a unified position, perspective, or school of thought. Far from it! The consonances between and among chapters, while important, are less crucial ultimately than their dissonances. Again, a key question driving this book is, *What's at stake in adopting this stance over another, or perhaps over all others?* Some authors cite fellow contributors to this volume, for instance, sometimes even claiming their work as foundational to their own. And yet, in all cases, these authors go on to articulate a different position, one that may differ only by degree or that may depart quite radically. Either way, theoretical differences of even a small degree can influence profoundly how we think about the purpose, value, and consequences of communication, theory, and communication theory. Each of the sections of this collection, as well as the collection as a whole, thus are best imagined as a unity-in-difference; they are complex wholes that are held together, tensely, contingently, and more or less uneasily, in what the cultural theorist Stuart Hall once called a "teeth gritting harmony." The structure by which we've organized this book in turn begs three final questions that we hope readers of this volume will consider: in what ways do seemingly consistent or compatible stances differ; why do they differ; and what's the larger significance of those differences?

On Not Having the Last Word

We have tried our best in this introduction not to ensnare ourselves in the worst of all possible ironies: that is, of unintentionally foreclosing on the chance that you, the reader, might take up our offer and stake a claim for a particular way of theorizing and enacting communication. How could we fall into that trap? Easy: We could overplay our hand. Remember, we have argued that communication as buffet—an uncritical theory pluralism—should be replaced with a model of theorizing in which the possibilities of evaluation and an insistent awareness of what is at stake are kept fully in mind. But to argue too strongly for our way of looking at theorizing—even if that way might allow you to grab hold profitably of one stance and jettison some, maybe even all the rest—would be to commit the same offense that prompted us to put this book together in the first place. If we unwittingly adopt a stance that says that the act of adopting one stance over all others is the *only* legitimate approach to communication theorizing, then we're right back where we started—and we're as guilty as anyone else of limiting the choices that we think should be available to theorists and practitioners of communication. Put differently, dogmatism is as undesirable and deadening to creative theorizing as is theory pluralism—and it's far meaner in the end.

You might have read that last sentence and concluded that we've completely contradicted ourselves, but we do not think that we have. We are just as wary of the "one-and-only-way" approach to communication as we are of the "all-roads-are-equally-good" approach—*and for the same reason.* Both approaches handcuff theorists unnecessarily; both try to set arbitrary and unproductive limits on what ideas or examples or metaphors or analogies or typologies or schemas could be used in the production of good, compelling theory. To take a stance and reject all others is one thing, but to take a stance and then reason that whatever is left is unworthy of existence operates in bad faith and at cross-purposes with everything we have labored to say in this introduction. To adopt a stance is to stake a claim, but it is not the same as denying the validity of other claims—nor should it be. It is, rather, to partake in the broader barter of ideas, to move in a realm of thinking and enacting in which we believe no participant should apologize either for making tough intellectual choices or for standing firm on the ground of his or her theoretical and praxical convictions.

References

Fisher, B. A. (1978). *Perspectives on human communication.* New York: Macmillan.

Gadamer, H. G. (1998). *Truth and method* (2nd rev. ed.). New York: Continuum.

PART I

Making

1

Communication as Relationality

Celeste M. Condit

Communication is a process of relating. This means it is not primarily or essentially a process of transferring information or of disseminating or circulating signs (though these things can be identified as happening within the process of relating). Instead, communication is the weaving and reweaving of visible and invisible four-dimensional webs, which constitute and reconstitute matter and ideation as humans, discourse, and other beings within a dynamic field of many forces. Such a conceptualization helps us out of the now stale debates of Western philosophy about the nature of communication.

Western philosophy from Plato through Derrida has repeatedly made the mistake of focusing studies of communication on the status of the word, sign, or symbol. The stream of conversation participated in by the likes of Plato, Aristotle, Bacon, and many others asked what and how signs mean, by asking how a particular sign or sentence "referred" to the "reality" for which it presumably stood. This line of inquiry assumed that communication was about referring to things, and it therefore focused attention on how isolated signs or propositions were related to real (i.e., nonlinguistic) things.

This idea that signs represented some naturally ordered reality was challenged first by the structuralists and then by the poststructuralist intellectual revolution. These critiques have been substantive, so that no one should any longer hold to a simplistic theory that words just refer to things. But the dominant strain of poststructuralism has, by its obsessive attention to negating the referential character of signs, reinforced the primacy of the sign and therefore has continued to focus theorization around signs (even while portraying signs as destabilized).

Signs and symbols, however, are merely components in the process of communication, which is better understood as a process of relating. Two people talking about a tiger in the jungle are not interested in a full and precise definition of *tiger*. Nor are they generally interested in denying that there is an essence to *tiger*. They are interested in maintaining certain relationships (me/my children) instead of other relationships (children/tiger's food). The referential properties of language are useful in such contexts, but only in a rough fashion, and any referentiality is always subordinate to the maintenance or reshaping of the web of relationships.[1] Even practices such as science, which appear to be heavily referential, are better conceptualized through the notion of relationships. The periodic table of the elements is a set of relationships, and any one cell of the table is vastly less informative than the relationships among the parts of the table (a fact highlighted by a comparison of the classic physics version of the table to the new earth scientists' version of the table; this is available at http://www.gly.uga.edu/railsback/PT.html).

The concept of relationship is unlike poststructuralist philosophy because relationality turns our attention away from the question of the sign. Nonetheless, the notion of relationship does have the key features of a poststructuralist concept. That is, it presumes fluidity and is nonessentialist. No relationship is static; relationships cannot be precisely and fully enumerated as to their qualities and boundaries. Indeed, even when laws try to stabilize relationships (e.g., "marriage"), the groups of relationships thereby constituted are nonetheless manifold and leaky. No two marriages are the same; no marriage is the same from moment to moment. No marriage can be summed up in any sentence or paragraph. A marriage is like two stars forming in proximity to each other: the gravity and energy of each centered collection of energy/matter influences the other, but the relationships between them are constantly changing. Relationships that are not legally codified are even less essentializable: think of the difficulties teenagers and twentysomethings experience in classifying the various degrees and types of relationships among their romantic/nonromantic "friends."

Yet relationship is not pure difference. It is not merely change. Relationship is interdynamic *force*. Like gravity, a relationship is diffuse, invisible, perhaps immaterial, and yet it pushes and pulls. Relating or relationships exert influence. Communication constitutes relationships and, in so doing, it reconstitutes the entities that are related. Perhaps, however, the idea of relationship contains a fatal flaw, because it presumes that some "thing" (a person, a class, a place) exists as a discrete and stable entity, and such things are then brought into relationship. Indeed, people often talk in this fashion about relationships. But this should be understood as a strategic essentialism.

Every thing that exists is in itself nothing more than a particularly, and perspectivally, constituted set of relationships. *Perspectivally constituted* means that it is understood as a thing, as something that can be named for a purpose, from a particular, time, place, and socially bound viewpoint. So one might talk about two nascent twin stars as being related to each other. But the "stars" do not exist as such. From a distance, one might imagine them as discrete entities, taking into account a long-term time scale that projects a "life history" for each aggregation of matter/energy by analogy to the life history of other such aggregations of matter/energy. But, the particular dynamics of the matter and energy in the area that is being called the star are influenced by the relationship of each atom to each and every other atom in the universe and the life history of all. There are no clear boundaries, no thing (no star) that has a discrete existence separate from the web of relationships of all to all.

For particular purposes, people isolate and name the aggregations. That is, speakers highlight particular lines of force and interaction. Moreover, there are some regularities in what human beings highlight and name as *things*. Indeed, aggregations of matter/energy with certain properties tend to strike humans as nameable or even name needing. In space, we tend especially to name areas with high densities of matter and energy and treat them as differentiated from areas of low density of energy and matter.[2] In the immediate human arena, we tend to name areas with high density of matter and/or unified mobilities (people, races, classes, towns, families), and we think about and thus emphasize relationships among these named entities for convenience. For many purposes, we concentrate on the more intense and immediate interactions among things that are closer in physical or social space rather than the more distal interactions, and so our notion of relationship is dominated by intense interactions around which we draw borders and which we then identify as discrete entities. But this is simply a convenience and a matter of particular interests (even if it turns out that evolution has sedimented this tendency in our nervous system). Nonetheless, these proclivities do not override a fundamental duality: that each collection of energy/matter that we treat as a distinct thing is constituted as it is by a particular framework that sees it as such *and* by an infinite set of relationships spiraling outward through the universe and all time.

The parent-child relationship is a powerful example. Children are initially not physically discrete from their biological parents. The United States has had difficulty deciding legally at what point a child becomes (should be treated as) an independent person. Even after birth, a child is not biologically discrete from its parents; it shares a connected lineage of genes and signaling substances from the ovum. In most cases, it also continues to augment its own body from that of its mother. Even more obviously, children are not socially discrete. They are not only under the care of their parents, but the parents shape the child by how much they feed it and hold it and hit it. But parents are only parents in relationship to the child, and the child shapes the parents as entities as well. Relationships are always multiway streets. As the experience of the American South proved, you can't have slaves if you don't want to be a tyrant, and the slaves control you even as you control them. Likewise, you can't be a master if you don't want to create slaves. All the same, in most contexts, people are able usefully to distinguish between parents and children, masters and slaves.

Individuals do not, of course, control relationships consciously and fully. Whether or not a child consumes lead and hence stunts his or her brain is as much a product of where the parent is in the social environment (and hence their possible placements in the physical environments) as it is of the parent's desires for the child or the relationships with the child. So when thinking of relationships among entities, this should be done fractally. That is, within each level of relationship is embedded another, similarly constituted by a set of dynamic interactions. Unlike fractals, however, every level interacts with every other. Perhaps using the term *relationality* will help remind us that a relationship is not a discrete, static entity but rather a process of the inter-action of forces.

Thinking about communication as a process of relating is superior to either of the two dominant frameworks of thinking in the academy today—the referentialist school or the deconstructive strand of poststructuralism. Relationality captures the force that is exerted by language and all other modes of material being, but it does not create a metaphysics of presence. That is, it does not privilege the isolated things created by words over the *processes* of creation and disassembly which make for the constant changes in beings. Relationships are about both presence and absence, about both similarity and difference. The forte of the classical tradition was to emphasize and understand the creation of presence. The forte of Derridean-led post-structuralism (Derrida, 1974) has been to challenge—to erase—presence: to show the limits of positivist/presentist concepts. Understanding both of these traditions enables us to avail ourselves of a metaphysics or ontology and epistemology that grasps the interplay of presence/absence but in a form that exceeds simple choice between two opposed poles.

Relationships are innately constituted by degrees of similarity and differ-ence, presence and absence. Let us confine ourselves to humans for a while.

To be a human is to be related to all other human beings. But this is not solely a set of identities or of differences. Every single living human being is biologically related to every other human being who has ever lived or will ever live. We are all the same, the same species. But this relationship is not identity. Every human is unique, different from every other human who has lived or will ever live. But more than that, the difference is originary. That is, when human beings became human beings, we were already different from each other. For example, the A, B, and O blood groups are not something that has evolved among humans. Chimps have these blood groups too. Humans became humans with differences from one another. But in addition to that, the differences vary in degree: humans have differential degrees of relationship to each other, just as the relationship of humans to chimpanzees is different in degree from humans to other animals.

The same pattern of inherent and gradational similarity and difference pervades our social being. Human beings are members of families, classes, races, and nations. A family is obviously constituted by both what is shared and what is different among its members. So, too, with a nation. But the concepts of race and class used in the United States have been flawed by the assumption that race or class must constitute an essential similarity. Black feminist thought has recently shaken up that idea, emphasizing the way in which race is always fractured by gender (and by class, among other factors; Collins, 2004). Scholars and activists are just beginning to describe a path for dealing with race and class as relationships of simultaneous difference and similarity, and only by seeing them as relationships with these qualities will U.S. society escape the current essentializing traps without reverting to a false universalism. Insisting on the gradational qualities of relationality will also augment that reenvisioning.

So, fine, perhaps conceiving of communication as relationship instead of as reference or dissemination is a better theory on the plane of "high theory" because it is more comprehensive: It accounts for more of the ways of being. What difference would it make for our "lower" theories: for generating predictions or giving accounts of the thousands of settings, genres, and types of human communication? A theory of relationality does not mean taking the relationship between two human beings as a model for all communication, though perhaps what has been called *relational* communication may have some greater utility and centrality to the discipline within such a paradigm shift. Instead, taking a relationality perspective on communication would mean always asking, "How are the interesting entities being constituted and related by this communication?" A few examples may help.

Begin with our pedagogy. Scholars studying communication apprehension (CA) have demonstrated that high levels of anxiety about communication

(CA) inhibit a person's success in life and that some people can, to some degree, be helped to overcome CA but that some people will always have more CA than others (Allen, Hunter, & Donohue, 1989). Moreover, they have shown that some CA is differentially tied to particular contexts (state CA) and other CA (trait) is tied to individual human beings (Ayres, 1990). A relationality approach would refocus the discussion around the question, "What is the nature of the relationship in a given communication context such that it would generate arousal that would be experienced as debilitating fear or avoidance?" Instead of treating people with high trait CA or who respond to a particular context with high state CA as aberrant, a relationally oriented scholar would inquire as to why a person might find a particular context of communication to be an aversive stimulus. What kind of relationship does a single speaker standing in front of a group of other people delivering a monologue presume? Often it presumes a relationship of knowledge, superiority, authority, or credibility. Why do some people feel unable to inhabit such a position? Why has a given society developed the norm of such relational encounters? Thinking about CA in this way leads to different pedagogy about it.

In the first place, relational theorists would describe CA in a different, more full and accurate, fashion to students. Current textbooks talk about the biological arousal involved in CA and prescribe as cures things like practice and visualization of success. Honesty about the underlying relational assumptions in the way public speaking (and other) situations are constructed may or may not help people cope with their fears. Methods for approaching that account need to be developed and experimentally tested. But being honest with the students has its own merits. Moreover, it will help instructors be honest about what is being asked of the students and reveal the extent to which our suggestions for coping with CA are Band-Aids on an inherently problematic, or at least challenging, context. It may even reportray those who are low in CA as arrogant. Perhaps arrogance is a key to personal success, but perhaps celebrations of such arrogance should be tempered. Or, perhaps one might find that people with low CA simply have a different set of expectations for the goals and relationships in a public speaking setting. In any case, the relational perspective may urge direction of some research efforts to understanding the relational expectations of low-CA persons and making some comparisons, perhaps using the understandings of low-CA individuals as models to help high-CA individuals. In other words, the relational perspective suggests that there is some substantial descriptive work that has not been done about CA. Good science requires good observation as much as it requires good experimental design, because the experiments need to take into account the important naturally occurring factors. Relationality provides a framework for that descriptive work.

Relationality as a framework could also restimulate and reorient work in persuasion. This applies equally to instrumentalist and invitational perspectives.[3] The instrumentalist approach has developed in psychology and the experimental side of communication studies, and it has focused on discovering techniques that produce higher levels of success in persuading others. The invitational perspective, launched by feminists such as Foss and Griffin (1995), has argued that all persuasion is inherently coercive, and therefore it is unethical to try to persuade other people of anything through any means.

The instrumentalist tradition of research on persuasion will have grave problems with a relational approach. Persuasion research that takes an instrumentalist focus has always had a greasy sheen. Such research has often been conceptualized as discovering nonrational approaches to getting what you want from someone. For the most part, the field has distinguished "good argument" from techniques of persuasion. At the most troubling end of the scale are techniques such as touching someone on the shoulder to increase the effectiveness of a sales pitch or such ploys as the "door in the face" and "foot in the door" techniques. Although social scientific research on such "techniques" can calm its conscience by taking an objectivist stance that says "we are merely seeking to understand how people are persuaded," when these results enter the textbooks as examples of how to persuade, the ethical questions cannot be avoided. Even findings that dictate the use of visual images or the advantages of attributions of particular form, which on their face make us less nervous, stem from an orientation that presumes that the persuader has a superior ability to control the thoughts, values, beliefs, or feelings of the persuadee.

Although not a panacea, the relational perspective brings into the open the assumptions of the relationships presumed in such an instrumentalist context. In health communication, these issues have been more explicitly broached. Scholars have asked to what extent cultural differences in health values, for example, need to be respected rather than simply overwritten with high-tech norms. But even here, the relational perspective allows greater explicitness. For example, one might ask, when does a high-literacy person have a right, perhaps even a responsibility, to attend to issues such as the use of natural numbers instead of percentages to communicate health risks to a low-literacy person of a different race, culture, gender, or class? What the relational perspective does is to contextualize "technique" *within* a relationship. Thus, the technique of selling cars by touching a customer on the shoulder gives us the ethical queasies because what is happening is that the context of one relationship (closeness, mutual care, trust) is being overlaid by one party unilaterally upon another relationship (selling a car). This is different from saying merely that one person is manipulating another person, because the fault lies in the fact that the manipulator doesn't really intend to establish the relationships of trust, closeness, and mutual care implied by the touch on the shoulder. It is therefore not sufficient to say that the buyer is responsible for not being duped. Rather, the seller is responsible for imitating or initiating a relationship he or she does not really want to enact.

Such techniques can rarely be said to be ethical because they rely on relational qualities that the initiator does not really wish to follow through. If one teaches that these techniques work, one should do so in the context of teaching students about the fluidity and defense of relationships as valuable entities with particular qualities, benefits, and obligations. But not all persuasion techniques will be of the character to falsely manipulate relationships. In contrast, techniques of risk communication will be appropriate adaptations to particular relational dynamics in some contexts and inappropriate manipulations in others. The standard of the advancement of mutual care serves as one important key to making such judgments (Noddings, 1984; O'Brien Hallstein, 1999).

The concept of relationality offers a different sort of challenge to those such as Foss and Griffin (1995), who have denied the appropriateness of persuasion altogether. These denials have been based on the belief that persuasion and coercion were impossible to distinguish. But that argument would invalidate any effort at communication whatsoever, because it is as difficult to distinguish when talking to someone becomes persuasion as it is to distinguish coercion from persuasion. As rhetoricians from both the right and left have emphasized, all symbol use is inherently persuasive, because all symbol use brings a host of loadings, interests, ambiguities, and entailments with it. It is impossible simply to mirror someone's own ideas to him or her and, to the extent that one is not a mirror, one introduces change in those ideas (even mirroring would introduce change by reinforcement).

The idea that one could forego persuasion rests on the belief in an autonomous self, and the relational perspective insists that there are no such things. Any two persons are always in some relationship to each other, and any relationship presumes ineradicable lines of influence, usually carried in part through the communicative flows of meaning and confusion that constantly remake the persons involved. So one cannot not persuade. Instead, the ethic of mutual care sets standards for a relationship and for communication in relationships. The older ideas of respect for the other and openness to changing one's own ideas are part of these standards (Ehninger, 1970), but additional criteria reside in attention to the sustainable quality of the relationship and to support for the other's needs/desires where that does not violate the quality of the relationship or any of one's own needs/desires that might be substantially greater. The concept of relationality thus rewrites the agenda for persuasion ethics in fundamental ways and opens a new kind of discussion about goals and standards.

I hope that these examples have provided a sufficient set of hints as to how thinking of communication as a process of relating should reshape the field of communication studies. Other examples are ready at hand. The study of nonverbal communication should cease focusing on sets of universal gestures, facial expressions, or categories of distance and instead begin to be a full-bodied analysis of how nonverbal factors establish and maintain relationships in different contexts. Small-group and organizational communication already have much of the relational about them, but reorienting to relationality as a fundamental quality will allow expansion and deepening of these tendencies.

In a crucial way, the call to relationality is a statement that it is well past time that communication studies came into its own. For more than two generations of scholarship, communication has been dominated by the Western vision of the individual. In experimental studies, communication studies is still a poor relative to psychology because the discipline's leading researchers continue to follow the models and assumptions of psychology—which focus on the individual rather than the relational system in which communication happens. In rhetorical studies, scholars have continued to frame studies around the liberal individual—or around bashing the liberal individual—but there has been no alternative framework for thinking about how public or cultural communication constitutes human being (only that it should not do so, theoretically speaking). Taking seriously the concept of communication as relating will allow us to take seriously communication as a process with a distinctive ontology and unique methods. It will thereby allow us to better understand communication, which means to better understand the human animals who relate, and thereby constitute their being, through such incessant communication.

Notes

1. Wittgenstein (2001) initiated this line of thinking of language in terms of use, but his unfortunate choice of the "game" metaphor obscured the more fundamental property of relationality and prevented further development of the concept.

2. The nature of the four basic forces of the universe is consonant with such a view because each of the forces acts over a different distance with a different amount of force, but this merely accounts for why matter is differentially dispersed in the universe rather than being a uniform soup.

3. A third, communitarian, perspective dominates rhetorical studies of persuasion. This perspective is the closest to the relational perspective. There is insufficient space to deal with the differences with enough detail to be satisfying.

Additional Readings

McGee, M. C. (1975). In search of "the people": A rhetorical alternative. *Quarterly Journal of Speech, 61,* 235–259.

Rogers, R. A. (1998). Overcoming the objectification of nature in constitutive theories: Toward a transhuman, materialist theory of communication. *Western Journal of Communication, 62,* 244–1272.

Shepherd, G. J. (2001). Community as the interpersonal accomplishment of communication. In G. J. Shepherd & E. W. Rothenbuhler, *Communication and community* (pp. 25–35). Mahwah, NJ: Lawrence Erlbaum.

Wittgenstein, L. (2001). *Philosophical investigations* (G. E. M. Anscombe, Trans.). Malden, MA: Blackwell.

Wood, J. T. (1998). Ethics, justice, and the "private sphere." *Women's Studies in Communication, 21,* 127–149.

References

Allen, J. P., Hunter, J. E., & Donohue, W. A. (1989). Meta-analysis of self-report data on the effectiveness of public speaking anxiety treatment techniques. *Communication Education, 38,* 54–76.

Ayres, J. (1990). Situational factors and audience anxiety. *Communication Education, 39,* 283–291.

Collins, P. H. (2004). *Black sexual politics: African Americans, gender, and the new racism.* New York: Routledge.

Derrida, J. (1974). *Of grammatology* (G. C. Spivak, Trans.). Baltimore: Johns Hopkins University Press.

Ehninger, D. (1970). Argument as method: Its nature, its limitations, and its uses. *Speech Monographs, 27,* 101–111.

Foss, S. K., & Griffin, C. L. (1995). Beyond persuasion: A proposal for an invitational rhetoric. *Communication Monographs, 62,* 2–19.

Noddings, N. (1984). *Caring: A feminine approach to ethics.* Berkeley: University of California.

O'Brien Hallstein, D. L. (1999). A postmodern caring: Feminist standpoint theories, revisioned caring, and communication ethics. *Western Journal of Communication, 63,* 32–57.

Wittgenstein, L. (2001). *Philosophical investigations* (G. E. M. Anscombe, Trans.). Malden, MA: Blackwell.

2

Communication as Ritual

Eric W. Rothenbuhler

The reality-constituting effects of ritual and ceremony are well known. Saying "I do" in the right circumstances at the right moment, to take a familiar example, makes it done and it cannot be undone without a different ceremony in a different time and place. The effective mechanism of such rituals is formal communication—people performing symbols according to normative forms to achieve social ends. This structure, familiar from special communication in special events, is also ubiquitously present in routine communication. The nod, the handshake, and the greeting are all small rituals; conversation, television watching, and news reading also have their underlying ritual structures. In this sense, communication is ritual. In all the small ways that form has consequences and propriety matters, communication is ritual.

"Ritual is the voluntary performance of appropriately patterned behavior to symbolically effect or participate in the serious life" (Rothenbuhler, 1998, p. 27). The "serious life" is a phenomenological category designating those things treated as more important, more morally freighted, and more obligatory than others within any given context (the term and its uses derive from Durkheim, 1912/1995; see also Pickering, 1984, pp. 352–361; Rothenbuhler, 1998). It is useful to use the term with a degree of relativity, allowing it to designate different things appropriately in different contexts. Compared to sickness and death, for example, who sits where is not the most serious thing. At the funeral, though, or in a board meeting, who sits where is a serious thing. There are right and wrong ways to do it, and seating orders will be taken as signs—people will talk about what it means.

The analytic category of ritual can designate both formal rites and ceremonies, set aside in special places and times and receiving special degrees of attention, and the relatively more formal elements and characteristics of otherwise ordinary, everyday activities—all of the little ways in which how you do it matters: a handshake or an introduction well-given or not, for example, or all of the examples of facework, deference, demeanor, and politeness studied by Goffman and others (e.g., Goffman, 1959, 1967).

The study of ritual communication thus requires attention to both the explicit use of communication in formal rites and ceremonies and to the often-implicit communicative consequences of the formal elements of everyday activities. This latter category is very broad and thoroughly entangled in the meaning and morality of life. Wherever serious things are at stake, people will read observables as signs; little or nothing will be dismissed as accidental and the details will have meaningful or moral implications, whether or not they were intended. Engagement with the serious life, then, renders the world a communicative experience. Just as the animist may see the natural world as a text of spiritual activities, the modern man or woman is inclined to engage the social world as a communicative text—as if it were written to be read.

Ritual communication, in both of its aspects, is consequential. This is most explicit in formal rites and ceremonies, which are usually conducted for the explicit purpose of bringing about some of their consequences. Oaths, promises, and rites of transition such as bar and bat mitzvahs, weddings, or baptisms establish obligations, often through defining new social roles. Citizens of one country can be turned into citizens of another; citizens can become soldiers, holders of office, or imprisoned felons; single individuals can become married couples; and children become adults. In the ritual aspects of everyday communication, too, people's selves are constructed and conveyed, their identities are at stake, their hopes are invested. In short, the ritual communication aspect of everyday life constructs the realities in which we live.

The study of ritual communication, then, including the reality-constructing consequences of communication in both formal rites and ceremonies and in the ritual aspects of everyday activities, requires a broad focus on "the communicative." This is a larger category than messaging behavior, larger than activities designed to communicate; it includes all of the ways in which things are done in the saying and said in the doing (Rothenbuhler, 1993).

It is useful to think of communication as ritual for empirical, theoretical, and moral reasons. More often than we usually think, it is empirically true that communication is ritual. Thinking of communication as ritual is a useful theoretical strategy because it draws our attention toward the social consequences of communication. Thinking of communication as ritual reminds us, finally, of the importance of communication in moral life, of our roles in life as moral agents.

Empirical

"Communication is ritual" may be an overgeneralization, but not by as much as it might appear. We tend to overlook how often our communication is primarily ritualistic, and nearly all communication has at least some ritualistic character or function.

The term *phatic communication,* designating relatively contentless greetings and formulaic questions and answers such as "How are you today?", "Fine, how are you?" is well known (Malinowski, 1923/1949, pp. 313–316). Goody (1972); Coupland, Coupland, and Robinson (1992); and others have demonstrated how important this apparently empty communication is. These are aspects of greeting and leave-taking that maintain the reality of two people in social relation (Firth, 1972). Bateson's (1972/1987) concept of meta-communication has been used to draw attention to a functionally similar relational aspect of all communication (Watzlawick, Beavin, & Jackson, 1967). In intimate relations, families, and organizational life, these relational aspects of communication and ritual forms for conducting them are that much more important (e.g., Bossard & Boll, 1950; Knuf, 1989–1990; Sigman, 1991; Wolin & Bennett, 1984). Identity as couple, family, or organization is implicitly threatened by the multiple roles and time apart required by modern life. Rituals of greeting, parting, boundary maintenance, and reunion thus are developed to manage those multiple roles along with time and space in relational terms.

Ritual also appears in a variety of forms in mass communication. Starting at the most micro and prosaic, newspaper reading, television viewing, or music listening are important parts of many people's daily lives. To count as a ritual, this media use must be more than a habit or routine; there must be an element of the serious about it. The serious life, the realm of oughts and ought-nots, enters into daily media use in a range of ways. One typical pattern is that media use comes to be associated with a family or household ritual. Watching the evening news together, along with food and talk, for example, and irrespective of the content of the news, can be a way to reintegrate the family after work, school, and other activities. Similarly, watching *David Letterman* or putting some music on the stereo after the kids are in bed can become the anchor for an important time of adult conversation and intimacy. These are not the most serious things in the world, but they are activities that one would regret missing, and that, if neglected, could impact family happiness. (See Lull, 1988; Morley 1992; and others for studies of family television watching that are rich in examples.)

Another way the serious life enters everyday media use is as a means of contact with more serious things beyond the individual's immediate experience. This is a (ritual) version of the classic vision of what the media are supposed to be good for: they connect center and periphery; they help integrate the social whole, even in massive modern societies; and they broaden the lifeworlds of their audience members. There is no reason, really, to believe all that, especially given the cheap amusements and commercial manipulations to which today's media industries have dedicated themselves, but the idea is there in the culture for a reason. It is not unusual for media audience members to experience obligation. Some things should be watched, some news is more important, some events require further reading. There are people who feel out of sorts if they are not caught up on the news. Similarly, some media use has a sense of propriety about it: some music listening requires undivided attention, favorite shows have to be watched in the TV room, Mom or Dad can't be interrupted, and so on. When media use is more than a habit or a circumstantial choice, when there is a sense of obligation or propriety, then that media use may well be ritualistic, providing a means of contact with the serious life.

A third way that daily television use, in particular, may be ritualistic is based on implications of the program schedule. The program schedule is a structure that viewers more or less must accept; it is an order that is imposed on their lives. That might mean relatively little, but it also can be built into more. More than a clock, the program schedule can regulate other activities and can be used as a way of marking time. Children and adults alike are prone to eat and sleep, among other things, at moments that fit the schedule at much higher proportions than would be predicted by the relevant biological processes. The progress of the day and the flow of the week can be noted and, modestly, celebrated with attention to the television. This often involves setting aside a certain time for television viewing: the week is almost over and we relax with Thursday-night TV, for example.

Most of these examples would fit in the category of family rituals, but I raise them here because of another intriguing question. What does it do to our experience of communication when we must fit ourselves into program flows? Was there something more important about watching television, in a quasi-ritual way, when there were only three channels and one had to watch it when shown or not at all? When one accepts the program schedule and arranges one's life (in whatever small ways) to view a certain thing at a certain time, is there something slightly ritualistic about that, something that is absent with time-shifted videotaping or on-demand pay-per-view? Is there something slightly ritualistic about getting news from a TV program available to everyone at a certain time and no other, more so than searching for the news on the Internet?

Another approach to media rituals has recently been delineated by Couldry (2003). He points out that the media have come to be seen as important social institutions because of the idea that they are in touch with important things that happen at the centers and tops of nations; he calls this the myth of the mediated center. He analyzes media rituals as all of those activities that mark "the media" as a distinct category and valued institution, and that protect the myth of the mediated center. Media rituals, in this light, include not only many of the activities of media organizations and their production staffs, but also those aspects of the content of the media that portray a sense of the importance of being *in* the media or that recruit audience members to these ideas. Celebrity systems, talk shows, advertising, and the most important of news events all work together, in this view, to maintain the idea of the media and its ritual importance.

Finally, the most obvious form of ritual communication in the media is ceremonial television. Certain special events on television require a kind of dressed-up viewing. They interrupt the normal schedule flow; are broadcast live; may attract huge audiences who plan their viewing and make special arrangements (perhaps to view in groups or with food and drink); and are proclaimed to be historic by their participants and the media. These events, such as state funerals, royal weddings, some of the Pope's trips, and former Egyptian President Anwar Sadat's visit to Jerusalem, were dubbed "media events" by Katz and Dayan in a series of articles in the 1980s and later in their book of the same name (Dayan & Katz, 1992). For the French translation, Dayan engaged in some revisions, and the new title was translated into English as "ceremonial television." On these occasions, television viewing has an obvious ritual element that can be identified in a variety of empirical indicators (e.g., Rothenbuhler, 1988, 1989).

So, from face-to-face interactions through organizational life and everyday media use to the most special of mediated events, nearly all communication has at least some ritual characteristics. A substantial proportion of communication is primarily ritualistic, having little other content or function. Very often, then, it is in a general sense true that communication is ritual. Even if it is, strictly, an overgeneralization, it is a reasonable estimate and a good starting presumption for a theory of communication.

Theoretical

Thinking of communication as ritual draws our attention toward the social consequences of communication. Theories of communication as ritual are concerned with the construction, regulation, and change of roles, norms, definitions, orientations, values, and meanings by the use of symbols. This draws our attention usefully away from physical metaphors of cause and effect thinking. Why is this important?

There is a tendency to expect amounts of exposure to messages, for example, to correlate with amounts of effects: more violent television could produce more violent behavior; more frightening television could produce more frightened thoughts; more repetitions of positive images or prosocial messages could produce more positive attitudes or prosocial behaviors. This is reasoning about communication by analogy to physical processes, where the effect of one moving object on another is a product of mass and energy. Biological metaphors also show up in concepts such as inoculation, contagion, or addiction. When the oath of office obligates the holder of the office, though, or a violation of protocol produces indignity that damages a social relation, it is not because of the amount of communication or because of a germ or other biological process. It is because of the myriad and mysterious logics of symbols in use and their human interpreters.

Do not misunderstand. There are physical and biological aspects of the human world that are relevant to communication. They need to be included in communication studies, and the proper concepts and methods to some extent have been developed in the physical and biological sciences. The same is true of the various infrastructural issues relevant to communication, such as economics, organization, law, and technology. These need to be studied for what they are and their constraints on communicative possibilities well understood. But the meaningful and moral aspects of the communicative world need to be theorized as meaning and morality.

The internal world of communication is constructed of signs in use, deployed by people who are trying to accomplish goals within physical, biological, economic, legal, and other constraints, while, among other complications, the goals, interpretations, and consequences will vary with the point of view of different actors. Communication is conducted in a world constructed of communication, in response to communication, in anticipation of communication. Take this sentence describing a potential empirical reality: Bob and Sue's work relationship has been damaged because he is indignant over her rudeness and she thinks he is petty. There is hardly a word there describing a thing that exists in nature. All of the elements, factors, causes, and consequences are social realities that exist only in the realm of the communicative.

Cause-effect logic, physical metaphors, and instrumental reason thus are misleading tools for the study of communication. The ritual model draws our attention, instead, to social practices with social consequences—which is what communication is. With our focus in the right place, we can then draw concepts and methods from elsewhere in the human sciences and develop new ones of our own tuned to the purpose at hand. We may find, for example, that understanding how a shaman uses text and performance to effect cures may be more useful to the study of persuasion than the rational actor model that dominates Western life and philosophy (e.g., Lévi-Strauss, 1958/1963).

Moral

Theoretical positions have moral implications, and when we teach them, advocate their use by others, or promote policies based upon them, they have moral consequences. Thinking "communication is ritual" has healthy moral implications, for it reminds us that communication is a moral activity, as is our theorizing about it.

In ritual, we are careful what we say because we recognize that the consequences are serious; that is a useful model for communication in general. What a nicer world it would be if we always stopped to think before we spoke, "I will create a new reality, do I want to live in it?"

It could be useful to teach that communication skills are like a loaded gun. Why not teach communication safety? The handful of individuals who produced and distributed the notorious Willie Horton ad that aired during the 1988 U.S. presidential campaign had a permanent effect on American politics. We cannot go back to a world in which such strategies would not be used, in which no one knew what effects they could produce. Why should speaking skills, writing, or video production ever be taught without communication ethics? Among those who make a living by communicating—such as professors, politicians, lawyers, managers, and executives, as well as journalists and media producers—who has reached midcareer without some trouble caused by communication? Why isn't that a field of study? Why don't we have classes devoted to avoiding bad consequences of communication?

Because we live in realities created by our communication, we must think about what ought and ought not to be done by communication. We should think about our capacities to produce consequences that are good or bad, happy or not, right or wrong, and the according realities we live in. We should be teaching that communication is terribly important, powerful, and dangerous.

Thinking "communication is ritual" thus draws our attention to its role in a serious world, where form and conduct are as consequential as substance and intention. In ritual communication, we constitute the moral realities in which we live together, for better or worse, till death do us part.

Additional Readings

Bell, C. (1997). *Ritual: Perspectives and dimensions.* New York: Oxford University Press.

Bloch, M. (1989). *Ritual, history, and power: Selected papers in anthropology.* London: Athlone Press.

Marvin, C., & Ingle, D. W. (1999). *Blood sacrifice and the nation: Totem rituals and the American flag.* Cambridge, UK: Cambridge University Press.

Rappaport, R. A. (1979). *Ecology, meaning, and religion.* Berkeley, CA: North Atlantic Books.

Turner, V. (1977). *The ritual process: Structure and anti-structure.* Ithaca, NY: Cornell University Press. (Original work published 1969)

References

Bateson, G. (1987). *Steps to an ecology of mind: Collected essays in anthropology, psychiatry, evolution, and epistemology.* Northvale, NJ: Jason Aronson. (Original work published 1972)

Bossard, J. H. S., & Boll, E. S. (1950). *Ritual in family living: A contemporary study.* Philadelphia: University of Pennsylvania Press.

Couldry, N. (2003). *Media rituals: A critical approach.* London: Routledge.

Coupland, J., Coupland, N., & Robinson, J. D. (1992). "How are you?": Negotiating phatic communion. *Language in Society, 13,* 327–343.

Dayan, D., & Katz, E. (1992). *Media events: The live broadcasting of history.* Cambridge, MA: Harvard University Press.

Durkheim, É. (1995). *The elementary forms of the religious life* (K. E. Fields, Trans.). New York: Free Press. (Original work published 1912)

Firth, R. (1972). Verbal and bodily rituals of greeting and parting. In J. S. LaFontaine (Ed.), *The interpretation of ritual: Essays in honour of A. I. Richards* (pp. 1–38). London: Tavistock.

Goffman, E. (1959). *The presentation of self in everyday life.* New York: Anchor Books.

Goffman, E. (1967). *Interaction ritual: Essays on face-to-face behavior.* New York: Anchor Books.

Goody, E. (1972). Greeting, begging, and the presentation of respect. In J. S. LaFontaine (Ed.), *The interpretation of ritual: Essays in honour of I. A. Richards* (pp. 39–71). London: Tavistock.

Knuf, J. (1989–1990). Where cultures meet: Ritual code and organizational boundary management. *Research on Language and Social Interaction, 23,* 109–138.

Lévi-Strauss, C. (1963). *Structural anthropology.* New York: Basic Books. (Original work published 1958)

Lull, J. (Ed.). (1988). *World families watch television.* Beverly Hills, CA: Sage.

Malinowski, B. (1949). Supplements I: The problem of meaning in primitive languages. In C. K. Ogden & I. A. Richards (Eds.), *The meaning of meaning: A study of the influences of language upon thought and of the science of symbolism* (10th ed., pp. 296–336). New York: Harcourt Brace. (Original work published 1923)

Morley, D. (1992). *Television, audiences, and cultural studies.* New York: Routledge.

Pickering, W. S. F. (1984). *Durkheim's sociology of religion: Themes and theories.* London: Routledge & Kegan Paul.

Rothenbuhler, E. W. (1988, Autumn). The living room celebration of the Olympic Games. *Journal of Communication, 38,* 61–81.

Rothenbuhler, E. W. (1989). Values and symbols in public orientations to the Olympic media event. *Critical Studies in Mass Communication, 6,* 138–157.

Rothenbuhler, E. W. (1993, Summer). Argument for a Durkheimian theory of the communicative. *Journal of Communication, 43,* 158–163.

Rothenbuhler, E. W. (1998). *Ritual communication: From everyday conversation to mediated ceremony.* Thousand Oaks, CA: Sage.

Sigman, S. J. (1991). Handling the discontinuous aspects of continuous social relationships: Toward research on the persistence of social forms. *Communication Theory, 1,* 106–127.

Watzlawick, P., Beavin, J. H., & Jackson, D. D. (1967). *Pragmatics of human communication: A study of interactional patterns, pathologies, and paradoxes.* New York: Norton.

Wolin, S. J., & Bennett, L. A. (1984). Family rituals. *Family Process, 23,* 401–420.

3

Communication as Transcendence

Gregory J. Shepherd

C ommunication is *the simultaneous experience of self and other*. That's
what I mean by *transcendence*. Communication is the experience of
transcending one's (current) self, overcoming one's (current) self, to become
more than what one was through connection with another. This is a definition born of the American pragmatist tradition, and it owes much to the
classical thinkers in that tradition, especially William James, John Dewey,
and George Herbert Mead, as well as contemporary pragmatist writers,
notably Richard Rorty, Cornel West, and Hilary Putnam. The definition is
deceptively simple; its implications are complex. Thus, I will proceed carefully, articulating each of the main terms of the definition before turning to
some of the consequences of holding this definition of communication.

Defining Terms

Communication Is an Experience

The word *experience* is, perhaps, the most important term in this definition.
I mean by it something akin to William James' radical empiricist notion of

The author would like to thank Bill Rawlins and Ted Striphas for helpful readings
of an earlier draft of this chapter.

pure experience—something that is nothing less than concentrated experience, an undiluted totality. And experience is always *of* something, but it is never only either thoughts about the thing or the thing itself. Imagine you say to someone, "I experienced the most amazing sunset last night." What would you mean by the use of the word *experienced?* You would, with the use of that word, be suggesting the fullness of what you felt and thought, what you sensed and imagined, what both you and the sun were doing, and what both you and the sun were being, in that moment. In short, you would be suggesting all that was captured in what James called "the immediate flux of life" that was you and the sun last night.

So when I define communication as an experience of self and other, I am trying to suggest that communication is a particular occasion of experience, one which happens when you experience, in all the fullness of life, your self and someone else.

Now let me introduce a second example. Suppose you say to me, "I had the worst dining experience of my life last night." What is different about that expression from saying, "I had the worst dinner of my life last night"? Well, you probably used the word *experience* to suggest a totality larger than simply the meal itself. I suspect, in fact, you are likely to go on and tell me maybe about the awful service *and* the crying baby at the next table *and* the freezing cold temperature in the restaurant *and* the hostess who put you in the nonsmoking table right next to the smoking section *and* the ridiculously high price of the food *and* the meagerness of the wine list *and* who knows what else in addition to some dishing about the dishes. The point here is that an experience is something whole, something uncontained and unrestrained, something much more than a simple, narrowly proscribed, representation.

As the sunset and restaurant examples may suggest, experiences can be good or bad, colorful or dull, rewarding or punishing, memorable or forgettable, and the like, but they cannot be right or wrong, accurate or inaccurate, or true or false. This makes my conception of communication quite different from the most commonly held ones, because communication is typically thought to occur only when people accurately interpret one another, or only when my meaning of/for something corresponds to your meaning of/for something. By defining communication as an experience, I am doing away with that requirement of accuracy or correspondence, and that is very important.

My definition urges an examination of the *quality* of the experience of communication: Was it full and moving, or degraded and anesthetizing? Was it honest and joyful, or insincere and unhappy? Communication, by my definition, is not something that is either accomplished or not, depending upon whether a message was accurately received, but rather a certain sort of opportunity or possibility realized, an experience of self and other, however good or bad (see also Shepherd, 2001b).

Communication Is an Experience of Self

In defining communication, in part, as an experience of self, I intend to call to mind George Herbert Mead's definition of individuals as social, or communicative, products: "All selves are constituted by or in terms of the social process, and are individual reflections of it" (1934, p. 201). We are not born with senses of self. Rather, selves arise in interaction with others. I can only experience myself in relation to others; absent interaction with others, I cannot be a self—I cannot emerge as someone.

It is important to understand that this experience of self, as an *experience,* is not a process of getting in touch with a pregiven entity. Remember, this definition does away with correspondence as a criterion. "Knowing" yourself is not, by my definition, a psychological process of uncovering your inner or "true" self, but rather a communicative process of always-becoming who you are. This *always-becoming* implies the sense of transcendence as the overcoming of self that I mentioned at the beginning of this chapter. Communication allows for the continual making, or building, of self, always providing an expanded sense of self (which is not to say a "better sense of self," because that would imply a given self to be more accurately sensed).

Communication Is an Experience of Other

Just as I become myself in interactions with you, you become yourself in interactions with me. And as we are always-becoming only when together, these interactions offer us the opportunity to experience one another. I am tempted to say here that communication allows for understanding one another, as long as everyone agrees that the banishment of correspondence from my measure of communication means that understanding one another has nothing to do with accurately interpreting one another. Rather, by this definition, understanding has to do with the adoption of a certain stance or attitude toward one another and the entering of a particular orientation—an orientation of sympathetic awareness (a common secondary definition of *understanding*). When we experience another in communication, we come to be in sympathy, or in common feeling, with that other. This common feeling is the sense of sharedness we often assume in engaging with others. But it is not "meaning" that we technically share with others when we interact, as is commonly said, but rather our significances, or our always-becoming selves. It is, in other words, the significance of the experience of one another that we share—each of us becoming more, not by our actions alone, but because of our *inter*action.

Communication Is the Simultaneous Experience of Self and Other

The term in my definition needing least explication, I suppose, is *simultaneous*, yet it is the term that best signals the rather wondrous nature of communication's accomplishment. In the experience of communication, I experience your presence and mine at once. Communication, in this way, is the experience of being-together. I express that as one word, *being-together*, in an attempt to capture both the togetherness of the experience as well as the "becomingness" or "being-ness" of the experience—the processual sense of always-becoming, and always-becoming more, together.

Perhaps another way of getting at the special nature of this simultaneity is to say that communication is the desirable (even if sometimes unhappy) experience of attending not just to me, at the ignorance of you, nor just to you, at the loss of me, but the sympathetic awareness of and attendance to both you and me in simultaneous regard. This definition hearkens to the Latin root of the word communication, *munia,* gifts and services. By my definition, communication is the mutual giving of selves and, so, serving of others. This should also point to the strong connection between my definition of communication and the associated term, and experience, *community* (see Shepherd, 2001a).

Definitional Consequences

The danger in defining communication as transcendence—as the simultaneous experience of self and other—is that it may make communication sound more mystical, more fantastic, possibly more weird, and probably more rare than it really is. This danger is also a legacy of the definition's pragmatic roots. Dewey rather famously characterized communication as "a wonder by the side of which transubstantiation pales" (1925, p. 138), but he also intended communication to be understood as a sort of usual experience, regular, highly significant, but unremarkable in its normalcy. Communication may be a miracle, but it is a rather mundane one, and the oxymoronic character of this mundane miracle is what lends this particular conception its definitional power. This pragmatic definition allows us to see how special, significant, necessary, and needed communication is in our lives, but also how, as a result, everyday it is. This will become clear through consideration of the various "consequences" to follow.

A Hopeful Definition

The common definition of communication that assumes the transmission of information, thoughts, or meanings to be the defining purpose of communication, with accuracy of receipt, or correspondence of content, held to be the measure of communication's success, rather quickly leads to the realization of communication's impossibility (see Shepherd, 1999). Can we ever, exactly, share information, thoughts, or meanings? But believing that we can never really know another as we know ourselves has rather severe consequences. It is a depressing knowledge with often antisocial implications. At worst, this view implies that we are doomed to isolation, forever apart from all others. Why try to understand others when understanding, defined as accurate reflection of another's knowledge, thoughts, or meaning, is impossible? At best, as Richard Rorty points out, this view suggests that we converse in order to make further conversation unnecessary (1982, p. 170). After all, once I "get" your message, or meaning, the task of communication has been accomplished and we have no further need to talk. Isn't it more uplifting to think of communication as an experience of being in sympathy with another and yourself at the same time? To me, that definition explains the aching need most of us have to be with others, the seeming naturalness of togetherness and what we know to be the aberrant character of isolation (think here of the hermit or monk, who, through sacrifice, assumes a position of isolation from others.) This need for being-together cannot be explained by a definition that equates communication with the simple transfer of thoughts, ideas, information, or even meaning.

It is important here to point out that my definition does not guarantee that being-together in communication will necessarily prove to be either easy or satisfactory—it is oftentimes hard and dissatisfying, but it does hold out hope for the possibility of something good. The definition captures James' "meliorism": something that is neither optimistic nor pessimistic, but full of possibility.

An Empowering Definition

This definition of communication implies the importance of voluntary participation; there can be no communication without the giving of selves, and the act of giving is always, by definition, voluntary (which is not to say that there may not be times when we are forced to speak, but communication is something more than mere speaking, and it requires volition). Similarly, a gift requires voluntary acceptance to count as a gift (a gift refused is, by definition, no gift). In other words, the possibility of communication and its potential promise is always dependent upon each individual's will. You may choose to shut yourself off from others, close down the expansion project of the growing self, stagnate and keep your gift from the world, or you may choose to leap into engagement with others, trusting, as James said, that others will meet your leap and allow for the experience of communication to take place. It is, in very large part, within your power. Communication is not something that happens in spite of you, but because of you. This definition implies the fundamental freedom of individuals.

This empowering sense of communication also implies an associated responsibility. Without your gift of self, the possibilities of communication cannot be realized. Without your gift of self, others will miss the opportunity to expand their senses of self. Without your gift of self, the potential sense of community that lies waiting to be accomplished will always be limited. Without your gift of self, the need for relationship that all of us have will be to some degree unmet. Without your gift of self, we will all be smaller, less than we could have been. Thus, as much as freedom is implied by this definition, so too is the fundamental interdependence of individuals.

An Ennobling Definition

This definition suggests that being together is as natural a condition as being apart, perhaps more so, because there can be no sense of self absent a sense of other. What Hilary Putnam said of the mind and the world is synonymous with what this definition of communication implies about the self and other: "The mind and the world jointly make up the mind and the world" (1981, p. 11). You and me jointly make up you and me. My understanding and your understanding jointly make up my understanding and your understanding. And the "making up" part is communication. That suggests the naturalness of association (Dewey, 1927), a rather comforting thought.

Consider this: a self cannot feel alone unless it has already experienced togetherness. The experience of aloneness is an experience of absence, suggesting, necessarily, a prior experience of presence. How can you know something's missing if you've never experienced whatever it is you now miss? This suggests what Dewey always argued: Care for others is every bit as natural as concern for self (e.g., Dewey, 1916, especially Chapter 26; see also Ryan, 1995, p. 359). This definition reminds us of the fundamental unselfishness of the social world.

This definition in turn raises us up—it defines communication as *transcendence*. The definition also suggests a certain ideal and an associated implied morality. There is a reason why we sometimes say to those who are too full of themselves, "get over yourself!" We believe that being-together, or understanding others in the sense of being in sympathy with them, is better than being-apart, or refusing to be in common feeling with others. We know it is not possible to experience sympathetic awareness with everyone, but, as Alan Ryan noted in defense of John Dewey's hope for peace prior to the Japanese attack on Pearl Harbor, this "suggests the difficulty of the task, not the foolishness of the ambition" (1995, p. 27).

Defining communication as the simultaneous experience of self and other implies not that we can experience others outside of our experience of self but that we nonetheless may strive through this experience to understand others as others. This is an enlarging notion, an ennobling idea.

A Democratic Definition

"Communication as transcendence" is a definition made for a democratic way of life. Transcending your self and being able to experience another as you experience your self are notions needed for a society built on the idea that there are no essential selves. This position contends that I don't know you because of who you are (by race, religion, ethnicity, sex, etc.), but by who you are becoming in an experience of communication. This is a definition for a people who understand that identities are never fixed, but are rather under constant re-creation—the kind of folks who people democracies, with their embrace of potential, change, and experimentation.

John Dewey wrote, "A democracy is more than a form of government; it is primarily a mode of associated living, of conjoint communicated experience" (1916, p. 87). People are conjoined, united, or made common through the experience of being-together in communication. The sense of togetherness that communication as transcendence provides is necessary to a democratic way of life because we have nothing in common, nothing really to unite us, other than the significance of shared experience. Those of us who live in liberal, pluralistic societies live in communities of strangers. As such, our democracy demands not simple tolerance of difference, and the fractionating that causes, but the transcendence of our essentially different selves—the getting over your self that communication allows (St. John & Shepherd, 2004). We need a definition of communication to embrace, and a definition in which to hold faith, that preaches this possibility and offers this opportunity. Communication, in this sense, fosters the associated living that is democracy, allowing for the coordination of activity necessary to full participation in the constant construction of our social selves and the society we are making.

Conclusion

Of all human desires, two are especially heartfelt: (a) that we have some say in the future, some measure of influence on our destiny—that we are not mere puppets of fate, cogs in wheels, or unanchored buoys at sea; and (b) that we are not alone. Defining communication as transcendence speaks to these desires. It allows for the possibility of both becoming what we were not and are not now, as well as being-together with others. This is the promise of pragmatism and its conception of communication. As Ryan noted in the conclusion to his biographical study of John Dewey, "We are not, in Heidegger's phrase, 'thrown into the world,' and we are not doomed to cosmic loneliness. We may find ourselves as individuals disappointed in all sorts of ways, may find ourselves lonely and frustrated, bored in our work, and much worse, but these are *problems,* not fate" (1995, p. 365, italics in original). And, of course, I believe that these are problems that can be overcome, and perhaps only overcome, through the simultaneous experience of self and other.

Additional Readings

Gadamer, H. G. (1998). *Truth and method* (2nd ed.). New York: Continuum.

James, W. (1991). *Pragmatism.* Buffalo, NY: Prometheus.

Shepherd, G. J. (2001). Community as the interpersonal accomplishment of communication. In G. J. Shepherd & E. W. Rothenbuhler, *Communication and community* (pp. 25–35). Mahwah, NJ: Lawrence Erlbaum.

Shepherd, G. J. (2001). Pragmatism and tragedy, communication and hope: A summary story. In D. K. Perry (Ed.), *American pragmatism and communication research* (pp. 241–254). Mahwah, NJ: Lawrence Erlbaum.

St. John, J., & Shepherd, G. J. (2004). Transcending tolerance: Pragmatism, social capital, and community in communication. In P. J. Kalbfleisch (Ed.), *Communication yearbook, 28* (pp. 167–187). Mahwah, NJ: Lawrence Erlbaum.

References

Dewey, J. (1916). *Democracy and education.* New York: Free Press.

Dewey, J. (1925). *Experience and nature.* Chicago: Open Court.

Dewey, J. (1927). *The public and its problems.* New York: Henry Holt.

Mead, G. H. (1934). *Mind, self, and society.* Chicago: University of Chicago Press.

Putnam, H. (1981). *Reason, truth, and history.* Cambridge, UK: Cambridge University Press.

Rorty, R. (1982). *Consequences of pragmatism.* Minneapolis: University of Minnesota Press.

Ryan, A. (1995). *John Dewey and the high tide of American liberalism.* New York: W. W. Norton.

Shepherd, G. J. (1999). Advances in communication theory: A critical review. *Journal of Communication, 49,* 156–164.

Shepherd, G. J. (2001a). Community as the interpersonal accomplishment of communication. In G. J. Shepherd & E. W. Rothenbuhler, *Communication and community* (pp. 25–35). Mahwah, NJ: Lawrence Erlbaum.

Shepherd, G. J. (2001b). Pragmatism and tragedy, communication and hope: A summary story. In D. K. Perry (Ed.), *American pragmatism and communication research* (pp. 241–254). Mahwah, NJ: Lawrence Erlbaum.

St. John, J., & Shepherd, G. J. (2004). Transcending tolerance: Pragmatism, social capital, and community in communication. In P. J. Kalbfleisch (Ed.), *Communication yearbook, 28* (pp. 167–187). Mahwah, NJ: Lawrence Erlbaum.

4

Communication as Constructive

Katherine Miller

A bout 6 years ago, I was asked to contribute a chapter to a handbook in the organizational behavior discipline. This handbook—somewhat like the one you're reading now—was planned as a series of short essays imparting the insights of academic experts on codifying the received wisdom about behavior in the workplace. I was excited to be able to contribute "the" chapter about communication—I'd have the opportunity to reach an audience outside our own discipline and share some of the things we've learned in communication theorizing and scholarship. I thought long and hard about how to package my ideas, and eventually came up with the title "Communicate Constructively." Let me quote here the opening two paragraphs of my essay for a flavor of the arguments I made in the chapter. I wrote:

> Communication processes often serve as a scapegoat when things go wrong in organizations. A "failure to communicate" (or at least a failure to communicate well) is often fingered as a causal factor in interpersonal, group, network, and interorganizational problems. And often, when communication is blamed, it is critiqued in terms of its "constructive" nature. Consider a few examples. Performance appraisals are typically seen as deficient if the feedback wasn't "constructive" enough. Meetings are criticized if they do not serve a "constructive" purpose. An organization's web page might be derisively labeled as all fluff with no "constructive" information.
>
> Thus, in everyday organizational parlance, and in a variety of situations, we think that effective communication is "constructive." But what does it mean to

be constructive? How can we unpack this colloquialism to make sense of it in terms of organizational communication scholarship? In this chapter, I will "deconstruct" the notion of "constructive" by exploring a broad sampling of research from organizational communication and from the communication discipline in general. In doing this, I will consider the concept of constructive communication at two distinct levels. The first of these levels will consider three principles to guide constructive communication in organizational settings. The chapter will then conclude with a brief look at the broader philosophical issue of communication as a constitutive (i.e., "constructive") process through which organizational behavior is both enabled and constrained.

I really thought I was quite clever in this chapter. In offering the notion of constructive communication, I could first talk about very specific research within organizational communication by proposing principles that might not be obvious to those in organizational behavior or practicing managers. These principles ("Constructive Communication Frames the Message for the Audience," "Constructive Communicators Recognize the Tension Between Openness and Ambiguity," and "Constructive Communicators Select Communication Media With Care") were solidly supported by theory and research within our discipline and were illustrated with interesting case studies of the principles in action. But my cleverness entered, I thought, when I could also contend that communication should be seen as constructive at a more abstract level, arguing for defining communication and organizing as mutually constraining and enabling processes—organizational communication as constitutive. As I noted:

> In a sense, then, the dictum to "communicate constructively" is one that we cannot help but obey, for our communication necessarily *constructs* the organizations in which we live and work. . . . However, these "constructed" structures also serve as powerful constraints on interactions. These reified structures (e.g., "the way we do things," "the proper channels," the old boy network," "red tape") make it clear that these organizations that have been socially constructed through communication can be very resistant to change.

Sadly—but perhaps predictably—the editor of this volume was not as impressed by my cleverness as I was. His first response opened as follows:

> Dear Kathy: Thanks for sending the chapter. I have to admit that I have problems with it. 1) I see somewhat of an infection from postmodern (PM) philosophy (the view that people create reality in their minds), in your use of the term "deconstruct" and other places where framing seems to be more real than reality itself. Also you talk of communication as a constructive process. Isn't its essence to convey information? I think PM is a very pernicious philosophy, both

in general and in business where an objective judgment of the facts is essential to success and survival. I do not mean to say framing isn't useful, but only within the context that reality is real.

My initial response to this critique was dismay mixed with a bit of amusement. Amused because I'd never been accused by any colleagues in communication of being postmodern—quite the opposite, in fact. But dismayed that my ideas about communication in organizations—cultivated over many years of scholarship and immersion in the field—were rejected out of hand because they did not reflect, as the editor stated, "the most important or fundamental things people in organizations need to know about communication (e.g., be clear, be objective, listen, use multiple sources)." The editor and I then engaged in a spirited round of e-mails, me wanting to stick to both my level-one principles and level-two metatheory and the editor concluding that "we are at loggerheads here because no matter what else we have learned, I still believe that clarity and objectivity are the core of good communication in real organizations." I eventually withdrew the chapter and it has languished in my file drawer and hard drive ever since.

These events were very distressing to me at the time. It wasn't just that I had worked hard on a chapter that wasn't showing up in print or on my vitae. Rather, I was most disturbed that I had made what I thought was a convincing argument and failed miserably in the process. However, with the passage of time, I've come to view my experiences with this editor as just so much more evidence that my arguments were on target. His communicative experiences had constructed one world—a world in which "clarity and objectivity and just plain exchanging of information are critical," and my communicative experiences had constructed another—a perhaps more nuanced world of symbolism, meaning, and dialectical tensions regarding relationships, communication channels, and communication content.

Further, in the years since my experience with that editor, several highly regarded communication theorists have made arguments very similar to the one I made in that ill-fated chapter. Indeed, within weeks of the withdrawal of my essay, a now well-known article by Robert Craig was published in *Communication Theory* (Craig, 1999). Craig's arguments regarding "communication theory as a field" have been influential in helping us sort out various approaches to communication theory. Perhaps the most contentious of Craig's claims, though, paralleled the argument I presented in very brief form in the chapter I've described here. In this argument, Craig contrasts a transmission model of communication with a constitutive model of communication. The transmission model sees communication as "a process of sending and receiving messages or transferring information from one mind to another" (p. 125), whereas the constitutive model sees communication as a "process that produces and reproduces shared meaning" (p. 126). Craig then provides a case not for choosing between these models but for recasting the constitutive view of communication as a "metamodel" that allows for a variety of ways of conceptualizing communication. Craig argues:

> The constitutive model does not tell us what communication really is, but rather implies that communication can be constituted symbolically (in and through communication, of course) in many different ways, including (why not, if it is useful to do so for some purpose?) as a transmission process. (p. 127)

This view of communication was also recently set forth by Robyn Penman in her book *Reconstructing Communicating: Looking to a Future* (Penman, 2000). Penman talks about various views regarding meaning as ways of "imagining" communication, and she, like Craig, acknowledges that a "transmission" imagining often dominates everyday life. In most organizations, for instance, communication is seen as "a relatively straightforward activity that we use to achieve effects—sending messages or controlling others" (p. 3). However, like Craig, Penman invites us to move up a level of abstraction and consider an alternative imagining, one that "requires us to inquire into communicating and not communication; to treat communicating as the essential problematic of concern; and to recognize that we construct our reality in our communicating" (pp. 6–7). Penman then spends much of her book looking at several case studies in which taking a constitutive or constructive view of communication provides a window into the ways in which context and lived experience shape communication experiences.

These views of communication as best conceptualized through a constitutive or constructive metamodel have been criticized. For example, Myers (2001) critiques Craig for providing few criteria for adjudicating among various communication models and sees the constitutive metamodel as problematic because it doesn't allow for fundamental differences among those supporting various first-order models. That is, Myers sees the constitutive model as blurring and downplaying essential and deep-seated differences between, for instance, those adhering to a critical view of communication and those adhering to a psychosocial model. Craig, however, responds that the constitutive metamodel does not impose a grand unified theory but instead "seeks, by turning to the practical life world that all of us share, common ground on which to discuss some of those differences" (Craig, 2001, p. 235).

My experiences with the handbook editor provide some support for both of these views. In one sense, these events clearly support the notion of a constitutive or constructive metamodel of communication in which varying views of communication (e.g., the editor's and mine) could reside. As I noted above, we had clearly constructed different communicative worlds. However, my interaction with this editor also provides support for Myers' concerns about the incommensurability of lower-order models. The editor and I never resolved our differences. We were, as the editor said, "at loggerheads." And though I could use these experiences to support my view of a constructive conceptualization of communication, the "fundamental differences" between his view of communication and my view of communication remained. Because he viewed a constructive metamodel as a pernicious and dangerous manifestation of contemporary academic theory, a constitutive view did not provide any grounds from which productive discussion was likely.

So where does this leave us? Well, it leaves me first with an even stronger allegiance to my view of communication as constructive. Through communication in a large array of contexts—relational, organizational, public, mediated—we construct social worlds. We can see these communicatively constructed worlds on a variety of levels—the difference in the cultural worlds of fundamental Islam and Western capitalism, the differences in the educational worlds of a private academy and an inner-city high school, the unique matrimonial worlds created through years of intimate interaction with a spouse. However, I don't believe this allegiance to a social constructionist view of communication leaves me in danger of slipping into solipsism (or even that pernicious postmodernism of so much concern to my editor!). For the processes through which these social worlds are constructed are patterned, regular, and—quite often—highly predictable. In my editor's context of business school, bottom lines, and benchmarking, it is little surprise that his constructed world is one that values clarity and a belief in a hard and fast reality. It is also not a shocker that my life in the discipline of communication—a discipline that draws on a wide range of classical and contemporary intellectual currents—has led me to a different communicatively constructed world. Thus, an important challenge for communication scholars is to more fully explore the tension between change and stability that a constructive view of communication entails.

A second related challenge for communication scholars is, following the tenets of Giddens' structuration theory (Giddens, 1984), to understand that a view of communication as constructive requires an appreciation of both agency and constraint. To consider the more commonplace use of the term *construction,* many homeowners can vouch for the mind-boggling number of choices that must be made in building a new house. What kind of floor plan will be functional? Wood, tile, or carpet? Wallpaper or paint? Gas or electric appliances? Track lighting or chandeliers? Stainless steel or brass bathroom fixtures? What to do about landscaping? Indeed, many individuals and families going through this arduous task would beg for a little *less* agency in the construction process. However, the other side of the dialectic must be considered—that is, our constructed abode is constraining as well. At the most basic level, the house we construct is the house we then live in, and this is a constraint in and of itself. But there are also constraints in the construction process. Our early choices limit future choices in a variety of structural and economic ways. Blueprints are difficult to revise, and financial considerations may make it impossible to have both the granite countertops we covet and the hardwood floors that we dreamed about.

So it is with a view of communication as constructive. This metaphor brings with it agency—the power and freedom to use communication to create the social worlds we desire. But those social worlds are cages, as well. Our constructed communicative world leads us to perceive others in particular ways and to frame events with a specific spin. Our constructed communicative world also structures our communicative choices in terms of lexicon, media, style, and a host of other variables. Our constructed communicative world leads us to interact most frequently with those who have built in the same neighborhood. But, in spite of these constraints, there are times when worlds connect or collide and we are given the opportunity to understand another's construction or perhaps to change our own. As I learned in my interaction with the editor from the organizational behavior discipline, these times can be challenging. But it is during those times that one begins to appreciate the insight that can be gained from a constructive view of communication.

Additional Readings

Banks, S. P., & Riley, P. (1993). Structuration theory as an ontology for communication research. In S. A. Deetz (Ed.), *Communication yearbook 16* (pp. 167–196). Newbury Park, CA: Sage.

Craig, R. T. (1999). Communication theory as a field. *Communication Theory, 9,* 119–161.

Holstein, J. A., & Gubrium, J. F. (2000). *The self we live by: Narrative identity in a postmodern world.* New York: Oxford University Press.

Leeds-Hurwitz, W. (1992). Forum introduction: Social approaches to interpersonal communication. *Communication Theory, 7,* 1–28.

Penman, R. (2000). *Reconstructing communicating: Looking to a future.* Mahwah, NJ: Lawrence Erlbaum.

References

Craig, R. T. (1999). Communication theory as a field. *Communication Theory, 9,* 119–161.

Craig, R. T. (2001). Minding my metamodel, mending Myers. *Communication Theory, 11,* 231–240.

Giddens, A. (1984). *The constitution of society: Outline of the theory of structuration.* Berkeley: University of California Press.

Myers, D. (2001). A pox on all compromises: Reply to Craig (1999). *Communication Theory, 11,* 218–230.

Penman, R. (2000). *Reconstructing communicating: Looking to a future.* Mahwah, NJ: Lawrence Erlbaum.

5

Communication as a Practice

Robert T. Craig

A stance on "communication as a practice" serves communication theory by transforming our understanding of the theory-practice relationship. Before elaborating this point, I will first define the term *practice* and defend the theoretical claim that communication is a practice.

In one common usage, practice is what basketball teams do between games, or what public speakers do when they rehearse a speech in front of a mirror before delivering it. That is not, however, the sense of practice I am primarily using in this chapter. In the sense I am using, the entire sport of basketball is *a practice*—a coherent set of activities that are commonly engaged in, and meaningful in particular ways, among people familiar with a certain culture. Public speaking is also a practice in that sense. There are many kinds of practices—dietary practices, marital practices, scholarly practices, political practices, religious practices, business practices, and so on—and practices can be described at different levels of specificity. We can talk about "the practice of sports" or "sports practices"—either way meaning the whole, broad set of activities that come under the general heading of sports in our culture. At a more specific level, we can talk about the practice of club soccer, spectator practices at professional sporting events (such as booing), and collegiate athletic recruiting practices. Returning to the basketball example, I should point out that "basketball practice practices"—the things basketball teams do at practice sessions—are also practices. Basketball practice is a practice.[1]

Practices involve not only engaging in certain activities but also thinking and talking about those activities in particular ways. Practices have a *normative*—sometimes, even, an *artistic*—aspect. They can be done well or badly, and people tend to evaluate the conduct of practices in which they participate or take an interest (e.g., that was a great game, or that was an awful speech). By the same token, practices also have a *conceptual*—sometimes, even, a *theoretical*—aspect. In learning a complex practice, we learn a set of verbal concepts that we use for practical purposes such as planning, coordinating, instructing, praising, criticizing, telling stories, or otherwise talking or writing about the practice. Dancers and dance aficionados, for example, in their endless talk about dance, learn words for various forms of dance, movements, styles, performance qualities, and so on.

In short, as a practice develops, a normative discourse about the practice develops along with it. The normative discourse is characterized by specific *discursive practices,* or ways of using language for practical purposes (e.g., ways that critics, teachers, and dancers talk and write about the practice of dance). The normative discourse is a constitutive part of the practice. It is this ongoing communication about the practice—as standards of excellence, ethical norms, techniques, styles, and so forth, are continually conceptualized and disseminated through a culture—that makes the practice meaningful and regulates its conduct.

Although most of the normative discourse goes on informally among people interested in the practice, certain parts of it may become so technically sophisticated that only professional experts such as trainers, media commentators, or academic scholars can fully master them. As the discourse becomes more elaborate and specialized, scholars may begin to study the practice, write books, and offer courses in the history, theory, and philosophy of the practice as well as practical courses in how to do it. In this process, an academic discipline can evolve to become a constitutive element of a cultural practice, so we have academic dance related to the practice of dance, political science to practices of politics and government, literary studies to the practice of literature, and so on. In my view, that is essentially how the academic discipline of communication studies came into existence and how it relates to the practice of communication (Craig, 1989, 1993, 1996a, 1996b, 1999a, 1999b, 2001a; Craig & Tracy, 1995).

In the modern culture familiar to the writers and most likely readers of this book, however culturally diverse we may be in other respects, communication is a practice. In that culture, the term *communication* (or its equivalent in some other languages) is used to refer to a range of activities—communication practices—that involve talking and listening, writing and reading, performing and witnessing, or, more generally, doing anything that involves "messages" in any medium or situation. Coffee shop conversation is a communication practice, and so is mobile text messaging. Employee appraisal interviews are a communication practice, and so are community public participation meetings. Reality TV, letters to the editor, pop-up ads, political campaign rallies, praying, talking to one's kids about drugs, and calling home on weekends—all are communication practices.

Communication practices are not necessarily "good" ways of communicating, although, as practices, they must be recognizable activities and topics of critical discourse *as* ways of communicating. Pornography is a communication practice. Political terrorism is a communication practice (a way of sending a message). The ethical legitimacy of these forms of communication can be debated, but they are clearly communication practices, recognizable as such in our culture.

That it now makes perfect sense for us to list such a diverse range of activities all under the general heading of communication reflects an interesting cultural development of fairly recent historical vintage. The idea of communication has a long history, but only in the last century has it become such a prominent way of talking about social practices (Cameron, 2000; Craig, 2001b; Mattelart, 1996; Peters, 1999). If communication is now a practice, as I am claiming, then communication, according to my definition of a practice, must be a coherent set of activities that are commonly engaged in and meaningful to us in particular ways.

How do we know that communication is a practice? We might think we know that communication is a practice because everyone communicates, but the mere fact that everyone does something does not necessarily make it a practice. Everyone breathes, for example, but breathing per se is a sheer biological function, not a social practice. For the most part, we do not practice breathing as members of a culture, we simply breathe. There are notable exceptions. Students of yoga, for instance, learn specific breathing exercises that are integral to the practice of yoga. In the culture of yoga, therefore, breathing is more than just a biological function; it is a meaningful practice.

Communication can be a sheer biological function like breathing. At the most basic level of information exchange, all organisms communicate, if only by replicating their DNA. Complex species have evolved elaborate signaling processes such as mating rituals. Distinctive forms of human communication, ranging from pheromones (chemical signals emitted by the body) to gesture, speech, and language, have evolved biologically and occur universally in all human societies. By itself, the mere fact that these basic communication capacities occur universally does not prove that communication is a practice. Just as breathing is a meaningful practice in yoga, however, ethnographers of communication tell us that all human groups have particular, culturally meaningful *ways* of communicating that are, in fact, practices (Hymes, 1974; Philipsen, 1992).

We might, then, think we know communication is a practice because all cultures have communication practices, but this still does not prove that communication per se is a practice (a coherent, meaningful set of activities) in any culture. For communication per se to be a practice, there must be a *cultural concept of communication* referring to the general kind of practice that people are engaged in whenever they communicate. It is not a foregone conclusion that every culture has such a normative concept of communication or that people everywhere are "practicing communication" when they engage in activities that we, in our highly communication-conscious culture, might regard as communication practices. What people in particular cultures (and particular corners of "our culture") actually think they are doing when they communicate is a key ethnographic variable. Philipsen opened his classic article on "Speaking 'Like a Man' in Teamsterville" with the observation that "talk is not everywhere valued equally" (1975, p. 13). In the urban neighborhood Philipsen studied, communication was not an appropriate way for men to resolve problems. Instead, men were expected to use other modes of action such as "silence, violence, and nonverbal threats" (1975, p. 13). Although silence, nonverbal threats, and even violence can all be regarded as forms of communication, the upshot of Philipsen's analysis is that communication per se was not a meaningful cultural practice among Teamsterville men.[2]

So, in claiming that communication is a practice in our culture, my point is not simply that we communicate a lot or that we have communication practices. My point is that communication per se has become a meaningful practice for us. We regard communication in general as an important kind of activity that can be done well or badly in all of its many forms. We are "particularly self-conscious and reflexive about communication" and generate "large quantities of metadiscourse about it" (Cameron, 2000, p. viii). The term *metadiscourse* (discourse about discourse) refers to a variety of common *metadiscursive practices* or ways of talking about communication for practical purposes (e.g., "they are getting their message out" or "we need to sit down and talk"). These ordinary ways of talking about communication give the practice of communication the specific range of meanings that it has for us. In our culture, this normative discourse about communication has developed to such an extent that an academic discipline of communication studies, with its technically sophisticated metadiscursive practices (comprising what we call communication theory), has been instituted and now plays an active role in cultivating the practice of communication in society (Craig, 1989, 1999b).

What, then, are the consequences of this stance on theory? My claim is that a stance on communication as a practice transforms our understanding of the theory-practice relationship. Traditional understandings of theory and practice tend to be of two kinds. One is the "practical" perspective that theory is useless ("it may work in theory, but . . ."). The other is the "scientific" perspective that valid theory, by explaining causal processes in nature, forms a basis for technological applications ("knowledge is power"). The perspective of communication as a practice suggests an entirely different way of understanding theory and practice. Although that transformed understanding cannot be explained fully in this short essay, the following paragraphs briefly summarize three essential points:

1. Theory is a practice.

2. Theory provides ways of interpreting practical knowledge.

3. Theory is fundamentally normative.

1. *Theory is a practice.* Whatever else communication theory may be from other scientific or philosophical perspectives, it is also a kind of metadiscursive practice, a set of expertly designed ways of talking about communication that are available to be used in everyday discourse (Craig, 1999b). Theoretically informed ways of talking about communication (for example, using concepts like information overload, online community, personal space, conflict styles, team collaboration, or media literacy) disseminate through society insofar as people are exposed to them and find them practically useful for their own purposes. Some of that dissemination goes on in college classrooms, when teachers and students use theoretical concepts in discussions of realistic examples. Participants may find themselves thinking and talking about communication in new ways, with a more sophisticated awareness that influences their practice of communication in situations outside the classroom. We, as both scholars and practitioners, all participate in this ongoing activity—this *practice*—of cultivating the practice of communication. As we have become more aware that we are engaged in this practice, some of us have naturally begun talking and writing about it. A normative discourse has emerged, and scholars have begun to refine and formalize it. This chapter is an example of normative discourse about the practice of cultivating the practice of communication. Here, and in other theoretical writings, scholars are attempting to create useful new ways of talking about communication theory. For example, I have suggested that we use the term *practical discipline* to refer to academic disciplines, such as communication studies, that are engaged in cultivating particular social practices (Craig, 1989), and several scholars have suggested methodological approaches to practical communication theory (e.g., Barge, 2001; Craig, 2001b; Craig & Tracy, 1995; Tracy, 1995).

2. *Theory provides ways of interpreting practical knowledge.* Practical knowledge—the basis of our ability to perform successfully as participants

in a social practice—is largely tacit and unconscious (Schön, 1983). Imagine trying to explain to someone everything you know that enables you to carry on a successful conversation with another person. Although you might come up with a few general rules (use eye contact, listen, be relevant), no amount of explanation could more than scratch the surface of the complex habits, skills, background information, and situational awareness that even a simple conversation requires, much of which cannot be articulated verbally. As every novice user of cookbooks or computer manuals knows, even the most explicit instructions can be useless to someone who lacks the skills and background knowledge required to follow them. No theory can tell us everything—or, in a sense, anything—we need to know to participate in a practical activity. Practical knowledge comes only with the accumulation of direct experience.

Is theory, therefore, useless? The largely tacit nature of practical knowledge does limit the role of theory to some extent; however, it does not warrant the extreme conclusion that theory and practice are unrelated (see Craig, 1996a, in reply to Sandelands, 1990). Theory contributes to "discursive consciousness" (Giddens, 1984), our conscious awareness of social practices and ability to discuss them knowledgeably. Discursive consciousness enables activities such as reflection, criticism, and explicit planning, thereby shaping practical conduct. A theory of a practice provides a particular way of *interpreting* practical knowledge, a way of focusing attention on important details of a situation and weaving them into a web of concepts that can give the experience a new layer of meaning, reveal previously unnoticed connections, and suggest new lines of action. Classroom communication, for example, can be discussed in terms of information processing, group dynamics, or ritual, among other theories. Each theory illuminates a different aspect of the situation and suggests a different approach to practical problems.

3. *Theory is fundamentally normative.* In the traditional scientific perspective, the application of theory to practice is technological. Scientific theory describes underlying mechanisms that explain how things work, and practice, using theory-based tools and techniques, can exploit that scientific understanding to produce desired outcomes. As applied to communication, this scientific-technological perspective cultivates an "effects" orientation such that, for example, the application of theories of persuasion in advertising should produce measurably more persuasive ads, and theories of conflict should lead to measurably more efficient conflict resolution.

A stance on communication as a practice is not opposed to using communication techniques or trying to improve communication outcomes by applying scientific theory and research. Those are perfectly legitimate practices.

However, it is important to see those practices within a bigger picture. Contrary to a narrow scientific-technological view, practice involves much more than using conscious techniques to achieve predetermined goals. The discourse about a practice is fundamentally normative, fundamentally about defining elements that constitute the practice, coordinating and regulating activities, deciding what goals are important, making evaluative judgments, and the like. As MacIntyre wrote, a practice derives its value from more than just the "external" goods or pragmatic outcomes it produces. More essential to a practice are its "internal" goods, the "standards of excellence which are appropriate to, and partially definitive of, that form of activity, with the result that human powers to achieve excellence and human conceptions of the ends and goods involved, are systematically extended" (MacIntyre, 1981, p. 175). On this view, becoming an excellent communicator means more than just learning how to get results. It means growing as a person, appreciating the values that underlie good communication, developing the skills and character traits that naturally emerge from serious engagement in the practice of communication, and thereby contributing to the cultivation of those communication-based values, skills, and traits in society.

MacIntyre's theory of practice is idealistic, to be sure, and the idealism of his theory is precisely what makes it practically useful as a spur to critical reflection. Applied to communication, it invites us to reflect on the standards of excellence that underlie our everyday choices and judgments about communication. All theories are potentially useful in that way. Every theory, considered as an interpretation of practical knowledge, presents an idealized normative standard for practice. How useful a theory is depends on the relevance and validity of the ideal forms of practice that it implies. As we use theory in talking about a practice, therefore, it is equally important to reflect critically on the ideals implied by the theory we are using.

Normative ideals should not be taken for granted in theory or in practice. Cameron (2000) has argued that beliefs about good communication currently ascendant in mainstream British and American culture reflect middle class, feminine stereotypes and questionably imply that men, working class people, and ethnic minorities are deficient in communication skills. Related ideological biases in communication theory have been pointed out by other scholars (Carey, 1989; Deetz, 1994; Grossberg, 1982; Mattelart, 1996; Schiller, 1996).

The practice of communication theory thus contributes to the normative discourse that constitutes and regulates the practice of communication in our culture. As scholars and practitioners, we cannot be uninvolved observers. We are engaged in that ongoing communication about communication and have the responsibility of active participants. Or so it will be, if our stance on theory is that communication is a practice.

Notes

1. For other views on the concept of practice, see Bourdieu (1992), Gadamer (1981), Giddens (1984), MacIntyre (1981), Schatzki (1996), Taylor (1985), Turner (1994), and Wenger (1998).

2. A version of the Teamsterville article was reprinted in Philipsen (1992). Philipsen did not explicitly conclude that communication was not a meaningful practice among Teamsterville men. He did, however, observe that communication had a different and relatively less important role in the "code of honor" that characterized Teamsterville culture than in the "code of dignity" that characterized other American sites he studied (see Philipsen, 1992, pp. 101–121, 124).

Additional Readings

Gadamer, H.-G. (1981). *Reason in the age of science* (F. G. Lawrence, Trans.). Cambridge: MIT Press.

Perry, D. K. (Ed.). (2001). *American pragmatism and communication research.* Mahwah, NJ: Lawrence Erlbaum.

Schön, D. (1983). *The reflective practitioner: How professionals think in action.* New York: Basic Books.

Tracy, K. (1997). *Colloquium: Dilemmas of academic discourse.* Norwood, NJ: Ablex.

Wenger, E. (1998). *Communities of practice: Learning, meaning, and identity.* Cambridge, UK: Cambridge University Press.

References

Barge, K. J. (Ed.). (2001). Practical theory [special issue]. *Communication Theory, 11*(2), 5–123.

Bourdieu, P. (1992). *The logic of practice.* Stanford, CA: Stanford University Press.

Cameron, D. (2000). *Good to talk? Living and working in a communication culture.* London: Sage.

Carey, J. W. (1989). *Communication as culture: Essays on media and society.* Winchester, MA: Unwin Hyman.

Craig, R. T. (1989). Communication as a practical discipline. In B. Dervin, L. Grossberg, B. J. O'Keefe, & E. Wartella (Eds.), *Rethinking communication: Vol. 1. Paradigm issues* (pp. 97–122). Newbury Park, CA: Sage.

Craig, R. T. (1993). Why are there so *many* communication theories? *Journal of Communication, 43*(3), 26–33.

Craig, R. T. (1996a). Practical theory: A reply to Sandelands. *Journal for the Theory of Social Behaviour, 26*, 65–79.

Craig, R. T. (1996b). Practical-theoretical argumentation. *Argumentation, 10*, 461–474.

Craig, R. T. (1999a). Communication theory as a field. *Communication Theory, 9*, 119–161.

Craig, R. T. (1999b). Metadiscourse, theory, and practice. *Research on Language and Social Interaction, 32*, 21–29.

Craig, R. T. (2001a). Communication. In T. O. Sloane (Ed.), *Encyclopedia of rhetoric* (pp. 125–137). New York: Oxford University Press.

Craig, R. T. (2001b). Dewey and Gadamer on practical reflection: Toward a methodology for the practical disciplines. In D. K. Perry (Ed.), *American pragmatism and communication research* (pp. 131–148). Mahwah, NJ: Lawrence Erlbaum.

Craig, R. T., & Tracy, K. (1995). Grounded practical theory: The case of intellectual discussion. *Communication Theory, 5*, 248–272.

Deetz, S. A. (1994). Future of the discipline: The challenges, the research, and the social contribution. In S. A. Deetz (Ed.), *Communication yearbook 17* (pp. 565–600). Thousand Oaks, CA: Sage.

Gadamer, H.-G. (1981). *Reason in the age of science* (F. G. Lawrence, Trans.). Cambridge: MIT Press.

Giddens, A. (1984). *The constitution of society: Outline of the theory of structuration.* Berkeley: University of California Press.

Grossberg, L. (1982). The ideology of communication: Post-structuralism and the limits of communication. *Man and World, 15*(1), 83–102.

Hymes, D. (1974). *Foundations in sociolinguistics: An ethnographic approach.* Philadelphia: University of Pennsylvania Press.

MacIntyre, A. (1981). *After virtue: A study in moral theory.* Notre Dame, IN: University of Notre Dame Press.

Mattelart, A. (1996). *The invention of communication* (S. Emanuel, Trans.). Minneapolis: University of Minnesota Press.

Peters, J. D. (1999). *Speaking into the air: A history of the idea of communication.* Chicago: University of Chicago Press.

Philipsen, G. (1975). Speaking 'like a man' in Teamsterville: Culture patterns of role enactment in an urban neighborhood. *Quarterly Journal of Speech, 61*, 13–22.

Philipsen, G. (1992). *Speaking culturally: Explorations in social communication.* Albany: SUNY Press.

Sandelands, L. E. (1990). What is so practical about theory? Lewin revisited. *Journal for the Theory of Social Behaviour, 20*, 235–262.

Schatzki, T. R. (1996). *Social practices: A Wittgensteinian approach to human activity and the social.* New York: Cambridge University Press.

Schiller, D. (1996). *Theorizing communication: A history.* New York: Oxford University Press.

Schön, D. (1983). *The reflective practitioner: How professionals think in action.* New York: Basic Books.

Taylor, C. (1985). *Philosophy and the human sciences: Philosophical papers 2.* Cambridge, UK: Cambridge University Press.

Tracy, K. (1995). Action-implicative discourse analysis. *Journal of Language and Social Psychology, 14,* 195–215.

Turner, S. (1994). *The social theory of practices: Tradition, tacit knowledge, and presuppositions.* Chicago: University of Chicago Press.

Wenger, E. (1998). *Communities of practice: Learning, meaning, and identity.* Cambridge, UK: Cambridge University Press.

PART II

Materializing

6

Communication as Collective Memory

Carole Blair

C ollective memory is an increasingly important area of inquiry in a number of academic fields, including communication. Contemporary communication scholars have studied memory in relation to political speeches, feature films, music, television newscasts, museum display, public policy debates, images on postage stamps, iconic photographs, commemorative monuments, scrapbooks, theatrical performances, nursery rhymes, and social protest demonstrations. They have understood memory as significant to virtually all forms of communication practice.

Indeed, students of communication have long understood memory to be important, at least in the context of message production. The ancient Greeks and Romans are credited with inventing and developing memory systems that enabled public figures to speak at length without consulting notes. As Frances Yates (1966) argued,

> The first basic fact which the student of the history of the classical art of memory must remember is that the art belonged to rhetoric as a technique by which the orator could improve his memory, which would enable him to deliver long speeches from memory with unfailing accuracy. And it was as a part of the art of rhetoric that the art of memory traveled down through the European tradition. (p. 2)

Public speakers were instructed to associate ideas they wished to recall for their speeches with specific geographical images—physical landscape features or buildings—so that they could remember their ideas concretely and in sequence. This early art of memory was systematic and teachable, and its value was demonstrated by the commitment of a speaker to learn, practice, and cultivate it. In time, with the development of communication technologies—from the printing press to the teleprompter—this art fell into disuse because nearly everyone, including public speakers, had memory aids ready at hand.

Today we understand memory and its relationship to communication quite differently, particularly in recognizing that memory is not simply a mental operation that a person uses or that she or he can refine and improve. It is, instead, a phenomenon of community—hence the notion of *collective* memory. As Barbie Zelizer suggests (2001, p. 185), memory may be lodged in a number of kinds of groups—ethnic groups, families, nation-states, or professional organizations. This collectivized understanding of memory goes by a number of monikers, including public memory, cultural memory, and social memory. These different names should not be ignored; they signal some significant differences of intellectual assumption and emphasis. However, what the perspectives represented by these different names have in common is their focus on memory as a collective or communal phenomenon, rather than as an individual, cognitive function. Perhaps the simplest example is the idea of a generation's memory. We worry about what will happen when the World War II generation passes away. Who will remember the reasons for entering that conflict? Its battles and turning points? The conduct of citizens at home? The ravages of the Holocaust? The continued racial segregation of the U.S. military? More important, *how* will these aspects of wartime be remembered? Whatever their particular emphases, these different perspectives on collective memory also take one of the most basic predicates of communication—representation—to be at the heart of how groups of people remember. As Andreas Huyssen (1995) suggests, memory is based on the capacity to *re-present* an event, a place, a person, or an idea that one has already encountered: "The past is not simply there in memory, but it must be articulated to become memory" (p. 3).

The example of the World War II generation's memory should not lead us to equate collective memory and history. Although memory and history are related, they are very different, as Pierre Nora (1989) points out:

> Memory is life, borne by living societies founded in its name. It remains in permanent evolution, open to the dialectic of remembering and forgetting, unconscious of its successive deformations, vulnerable to manipulation and appropriation, susceptible to being long dormant and periodically revived. History, on the other hand, is the reconstruction, always problematic and

incomplete, of what is no longer. . . . Memory insofar as it is affective and magical, only affects those facts that suit it. . . . History, because it is an intellectual and secular production, calls for analysis and criticism. . . . Memory takes root in the concrete, in spaces, gestures, images and objects; history binds itself strictly to temporal continuities, to progressions and to relations between things. Memory is absolute, while history can only conceive the relative. . . . (pp. 8–9)

One might say simply that history is the production of historians, while memory is a performance of social collectives. History claims for itself a legitimacy based on research norms. Collective memory, by contrast, is an overtly political and emotionally invested phenomenon. The most basic assumption of memory studies, under whatever name, and in whatever field it is practiced, is that collective memory serves interests of the present.

There are at least six senses in which communication may be said to be collective memory, or, at least, to be inherently and intricately related to collective memory.

First, communication depends on people's preunderstandings of language or other social codes or symbol systems. We are born into language; it predates and prefigures us. Our native language, whether Hmong or American English, allows us to participate in communicative exchanges with others who speak that same tongue. But our languages carry with them vestiges of the past and very partial understandings of the world they allow us to give voice to. The "truths" we are able to utter about the past are shaped by the language we have available to utter them. Friedrich Nietzsche (1873/1989) put the matter directly in suggesting that it is "the legislation of language [that] enacts the first laws of truth" (p. 247). He continued:

What is truth? A mobile army of metaphors, metonyms, anthropomorphism, in short, a sum of human relations which were poetically and rhetorically heightened, transferred, and adorned, and after long use seem solid, canonical, and binding to a nation. Truths are illusions about which it has been forgotten that they *are* illusions, worn-out metaphors without sensory impact, coins which have lost their image and now can be used only as metal, and no longer as coins. (p. 250)

Nietzsche's focus here on forgetfulness is telling. Perhaps it is a necessary, amnesiac fiction to take language as a neutral and transparent instrument for representing experiences to others, but it is still a fiction. Our language comes to us preowned, and what we represent of our past in language is thus also, in a sense, preowned. If we remember by means of language, we remember selectively and partially, according to the resources and constraints of our language. And, it is important to note, we remember collectively, by means of our inheritance of the languages and other symbol systems we use to communicate.

Second, communication depends on shared background assumptions. It is a commonplace that any two or more participants in a conversation must share at least some assumptions. For example, even a couple engaged in a relational shouting match probably shares at least the belief that it is good to air their differences, the understanding that verbal combat is better than physical struggle, and the idea that it is better to argue than to break up. These shared assumptions are a product of how we learn from and understand the past, whether they are assumptions about interpersonal relationships or national identity. Communication always makes claims on the past at least implicitly. We must assume that our understandings of the past are shared by others to some extent. Indeed, we depend heavily upon such understandings whenever we form communicative messages. A number of communication scholars have noted that we are strongly genre-dependent (e.g., Campbell & Jamieson, 1977). That is, we seek counsel for how to deal communicatively with a particular problem by looking toward similar challenges of the past, how others dealt communicatively with such challenges, and how we can adapt their communication solutions to the particulars of our current situation.

Third, communication is cumulative. In other words, a message refigures what has gone before it. This claim is one of the most central to collective memory studies in its emphasis on the reconfiguration of understandings of the past based on the interests and resources of the present. Michel Foucault (1972) made the argument for this position succinctly:

> Every statement involves a field of antecedent elements in relation to which it is situated, but which it is able to reorganize and redistribute according to new relations. It constitutes its own past, defines, in what precedes it, its own filiation, redefines what make it possible or necessary, excludes what cannot be compatible with it. And it poses this enunciative past as an acquired truth. (p. 124)

In other words, each message that enters a communication context changes our understandings of that context and of the messages that have come before it. Every message presumes particular relationships with other messages that have preceded it. Each message defines what has come before it in relation to legitimacy, astuteness, ethical defensibility, soundness, or their opposites. So, the interests marked in communication of the present moment intervene in contexts, defining and assessing, redefining and reevaluating those contexts and their elements. For instance, as Zelizer (1995, p. 222) notes, the term *World War I* did not enter common parlance until long after the war was over. Until the mid-20th century, it was commonly referred to as "the Great War," or even sometimes as "the war to end wars." Both names became untenable, largely because of World War II. Most obviously, the First World War had not ended war. Nor could it be referred to as "great" in terms of scope (the military engine of war or the number of casualties) or of just war doctrine, in comparison to its successor.

Fourth, communication constructs and refigures identities according to "membership" in collectives or social groups. Those collectives often have strong, narratively constructed memory associations. For example, during the recent war with Iraq, American reporters often interviewed soldiers from the unit they referred to repeatedly as "the storied 101st Airborne Division" of the U.S. Army. The temptation to think of the interviewee as a fearless, heroic paratrooper, based upon memory associations, would be strong for anyone knowledgeable about the 101st's role in past wars. An example closer to home might be the changes we see (or think we see) when the first of our high school friends gets married. In Western culture, we tend to think of marriage as a primary determinant of identity, based upon our society's inherited ways of understanding the institution. Persons with spouses are typically considered more socially stable, more mature, more responsible, more attractive job prospects, and so forth. To their immediate social group, newly married persons also may be considered more aloof, less social, more sedate, or less spontaneous than before. Regardless, our viewpoint is shaped by collective residues of tradition and what we are *supposed to think,* given cultural norms, about marriage.

Fifth, communication depends upon material supports or technologies. That is, we make use of various "technologies"—understood broadly—to communicate with others: e.g., language, ritual behavior, visual symbols, electronic or virtual media, and so forth. This material dimension of communication has a number of implications for collective memory (for elaboration, see Blair, 1999), the most obvious of which is the capacity for some material supports to preserve our communicative messages. Even oral language has the capacity for preservation. Consider societies that depend on what we call "oral traditions" to maintain cultural mores and beliefs or even their religious doctrine. Those societies have well-developed narratives by which to remember and maintain stories of heroes and religious figures, periods of war and peace, standards for civilized behavior, and rules for living. The invention of alphabetic and symbolic written languages allowed our ancestors—and will allow us—to record our thoughts on paper and to preserve them long after our own demise. Film and videotape revolutionized the possibility of maintaining not only a verbal but also a visual record of events wherever a camera was running. Such material preservation, of course, enhances the possibilities that our representations of the present will be picked up, appropriated, accepted, revised, rejected, or reviled at some point in the future. They may, of course, still be forgotten despite their preservation. But they are available at least for collective memory work.

A second implication of the materiality of communication technologies is the *deliberate* attempt to shape collective memory by means of particular kinds of communicative messages. For example, we are used to thinking about the objects in a museum or other historic preservation site as being definitively precious, worth our time and trouble to pay a visit and observe the objects. But museums, like other communication modalities, impart very partial understandings of the cultures and pasts they represent. Not everything from a culture, or art historical period, or technological era, is collected, retained, or displayed by a museum. Only those objects that are valued for particular reasons in the ongoing present are displayed in their collections. So, for example, why are Judy Garland's ruby slippers from *The Wizard of Oz*, Indiana Jones's hat, Michael Jordan's jersey, and Archie Bunker's chair displayed in the National Museum of American History in Washington, DC, as opposed to the hundreds of millions of other possible choices from American popular culture and social history? Why is the giant but tattered flag that flew over Fort McHenry displayed and so carefully preserved there? What is the museum attempting to impart to its audience about U.S. history by displaying these items and not others?

A third implication is an interesting return—with a twist—of the theorized connection between memory and place. Recall that ancient rhetoricians advised speakers to associate their ideas with physical places, for clarity of recollection. More recently, communication scholars, as well as memory scholars in other fields, have built on the assumption of thinkers like Gaston Bachelard (1958/1994) that people already, *naturally*, associate ideas with places, and have begun to study places—domestic architecture, museums, pubs, and memorials, for example—as themselves representing important communicative messages, rather than simply serving as backdrops, contexts, or scenes in which communication occurs.

Sixth, directly related to the notion of materiality is the idea that communication often involves struggles over power. Communication is not just something we do; it is a highly valued practice or "commodity," particularly in some forms and with some specific outcomes. As a result, sometimes communicators compete for—among other things—the means to represent the past in their own ways for the purpose of serving particular interests in the present. Note, for example, the venomous conflicts over the public display of the Confederate battle flag in the American South during the past fifteen years. The proponents of flag display argue that they are simply honoring their "heritage," paying tribute to a way of life represented by the "Old South." Opponents suggest that such proud displays create traumatic memories for those whose ancestors were enslaved in that culture, and that to honor the Old South is to eulogize the historical practice of slavery. Needless to say, the outcomes of the various skirmishes in this war of symbolism have everything to do with the present. African Americans argue that honoring the system that embraced slavery is an overt symbolic means of reinforcing white supremacy in the present moment. Their counterparts suggest, rather disingenuously, that removing the battle flag from civic sites (like state capitol buildings) violates their civil rights. The point is that the struggle over symbolism of the past is just as surely a struggle over power in the present. It has long been held in various aphorisms and anecdotes that to the cultural "victor" belongs the privilege of writing history. With little adaptation, it seems fair to suggest that struggles for power in social groups often are waged under the sign of memory—what the group will choose to remember, how it will be valued, and what will be forgotten, neglected, or devalued in the process.

The study of communication as collective memory, like any other theoretical position, may have some drawbacks. For example, it would be problematic to place a stronger emphasis on popular renditions of the past—how we would like to remember—than on historical accounts that seek for a more neutral rendition of what happened in the past (Zelizer, 1995). The dangers of presentism also have been remarked and investigated productively (Cox, 1990). However, if we think of history and memory not as competitive but as mutually enriching, memory studies can serve our understanding of communication in a number of ways.

They do so most generally by urging us to consider what is at stake when a communicator refers to or invokes the past. The past, from the perspective of collective memory studies, is not a dry, neutral record of what went before but an ideologically inflected cultural resource that communicators draw upon in their interactions with others. Most important, when some version of the past is invoked, it is all too often marked as "true," as an unquestioned or obvious matter of facticity, despite its inflections and what has been left out or forgotten.

Understanding communication as collective memory also invites analytic access to a broad range of communicative phenomena, from interpersonal exchanges to media programming to popular culture products. In fact, it transforms what we would usually take to be a context for communication— a museum, a park, a preservation site, or other place—and implores us to see it as a mode of communication in its own right.

A collective memory perspective also allows us to probe a communicative message at a number of levels of abstraction, from the basics of its language and assumed genre to the identities it constructs and the ways in which it enacts power. It reminds us to think about how any message alters its context and speaks back to messages that have come before. And because of its focus on what and how we remember, it prompts us to think clearly about what is not said, as well as what is, for forgetfulness is a central operation in the process of constructing coherent and communicatively powerful memories.

Additional Readings

Halbwachs, M. (1992). *On collective memory* (L. A. Coser, Ed. & Trans.). Chicago: University of Chicago Press.

Huyssen, A. (1994). *Twilight memories: Marking time in a culture of amnesia.* New York: Routledge.

Lipsitz, G. (1990). *Time passages: Collective memory and American popular culture.* Minneapolis: University of Minnesota Press.

Nora, P. (Ed.). (1996–1998). *Realms of memory: The construction of the French past* (Vol. 1–3). (A. Goldhammer, Trans.; L. D. Kritzman, Eng. Trans. Ed.). New York: Columbia University Press.

Zelizer, B. (1998). *Remembering to forget: Holocaust memory through the camera's eye.* Chicago: University of Chicago Press.

References

Bachelard, G. (1994). *The poetics of space.* Boston: Beacon Press. (Original work published 1958)

Blair, C. (1999). Contemporary U.S. memorial sites as exemplars of rhetoric's materiality. In J. Selzer & S. Crowley (Eds.), *Rhetorical bodies* (pp. 16–57). Madison: University of Wisconsin Press.

Campbell, K. K., & Jamieson, K. H. (1977). Form and genre in rhetorical criticism: An introduction. In K. K. Campbell & K. H. Jamieson (Eds.), *Form and genre: Shaping rhetorical action* (pp. 9–32). Falls Church, VA: Speech Communication Association.

Cox, J. R. (1990). Memory, critical theory, and the argument from history. *Argumentation and Advocacy, 27,* 1–13.

Foucault, M. (1972). *The archaeology of knowledge* (A. M. S. Smith, Trans.). New York: Pantheon.

Huyssen, A. (1995). *Twilight memories: Marking time in a culture of amnesia.* New York: Routledge.

Nietzsche, F. (1989). On truth and lying in an extra-moral sense. In S. L. Gilman, C. Blair, & D. J. Parent (Eds. & Trans.), *Friedrich Nietzsche on rhetoric and language* (pp. 246–257). New York: Oxford University Press. (Original work published 1873)

Nora, P. (1989). Between memory and history: Les lieux de mémoire. *Representations, 26,* 7–25.

Yates, F. A. (1966). *The art of memory.* Chicago: University of Chicago Press.

Zelizer, B. (1995). Reading the past against the grain: The shape of memory studies. *Critical Studies in Mass Communication, 12,* 214–239.

Zelizer, B. (2001). Collective memory as "time out": Repairing the time-community link. In G. J. Shepherd and E. W. Rothenbuhler (Eds.), *Communication and community* (pp. 181–189). Mahwah, NJ: Lawrence Erlbaum.

7

Communication as Vision

Cara A. Finnegan

C ommunication theory suffers from iconophobia. In a field whose oft-stated reason for being is to teach people how to communicate better, our ideas about what constitutes "good communication" depend heavily upon a fear of images. Indeed, communication theory seems to subscribe to John Dewey's infamous dictum, "Vision is a spectator; hearing is a participator" (1927/1954, p. 219). We tend to assume that the purest, best communication is talk (or, second-best, its verbal stepsister, text). Talk is imagined as conscious, face-to-face, participatory, deliberative, engaged. Vision, by contrast, is imagined as unconscious or misleading; images are framed as dangerous, and audiences in this scheme can only be passive, unengaged, or duped. At best, the field of communication ignores vision; at worst, it excoriates it.

Such an orientation is particularly problematic when communication scholars study visual communication. Political communication decries a culture of "media spectacle" that substitutes images for "real debate" about ideas in the public sphere. Rhetorical studies positions talk and text as superior to vision, because—as many, from Plato on, have argued—appearances lie, distort, and make "pure" communication impossible. And, arguably, the media effects research tradition would not exist at all were it not for the tacit assumption that the effects of visual media are, well, *bad*.

These are broad caricatures, of course, but my point is this: Communication has done little to interrogate its own iconophobia, even though many of our theories of communication actually depend upon it. If we pursue the consequences of this polemical claim, then an important set of questions emerges. How might our understanding of communication be different if our metaphors for communication were less fearful of images and more friendly toward them—that is, less *iconophobic* and more *iconophilic*? What would a communication theory grounded in iconophilia look like? And how might it translate to richer scholarship on the visual? This last question is of particular importance to me. As a visual communication scholar, I am bothered by the extent to which vision, when it figures in our scholarship at all, is framed as inherently flawed. I want to set aside negative caricatures of the visual that undergird particular orientations toward communication and attempt instead to think in new ways. Following art historian James Elkins's suggestion that we "become irritated at our favorite theories" (2003, p. 201), I suggest that this rethinking of our metaphors for communication is a good way to begin.

Like *communication, vision* is itself a term that invites many metaphors. We routinely discuss our scholarly "insights," tell our friends that "I see what you mean," and argue about whether politicians are "blind" to the consequences of their actions. However, not all visual metaphors are created equal. It is not enough to argue that we should frame "communication as vision"; as the quotation from Dewey hints above, some metaphors for vision may actually be iconophobic. In this essay, I take up three potential ways to frame communication as vision: surveillance, spectacle, and analogy. In the spirit of taking a stance and seeing it through, what follows is not an extended treatment of the metaphors but a brief, opinionated discussion that recognizes the benefits and drawbacks for communication of each. Of these three, I argue that analogy best enables us to theorize "communication as vision" without falling into the trap of iconophobia. If communication scholars were to adopt the more iconophilic orientation to vision offered by analogy, they would be better prepared to embrace the richness and complexity of visual communication.

Communication as . . . Surveillance

The metaphor of vision as surveillance frames communication as a dialectic of power relationships. In the language of surveillance, someone (usually someone more powerful) is watching, and someone else (usually less powerful) is being watched. Film and television scholars, for example, productively have employed the metaphor of "the male gaze" to explore how the viewing experience is based upon a gendered (and raced and sexed and classed) kind of surveillance. The "dominant gaze" is the male gaze, the white gaze, the straight gaze; those who enact the dominant gaze are those who possess the most power in a given culture. Framing communication as surveillance emphasizes the disparities between those who have the power to gaze and those who do not.

Beyond the gaze, surveillance can also be imagined more broadly as visual practices of control. We are subjects of surveillance in many aspects of our everyday lives, yet we often internalize these practices without a thought. Think about the video camera in the corner of the local convenience store, or the number of visual documents we are required to carry: driver's license, passport, student ID card. In communication theories of surveillance, vision and the technologies of vision exist to produce and reproduce institutional control.

Imagine a documentary photograph of hundreds of poor, scruffy-looking men in an unemployment line—a common image from our collective memory of the Great Depression in the United States. They wait to enter an employment agency under the watchful gaze of a tight-lipped, stiff-looking officer of the law. An analysis of such an image from the perspective of surveillance would pay attention to the power dynamic enacted in the picture. It would encourage us to think about the "haves" and "have nots." We might remark upon how the unemployed men are subjected to the gaze of both the police officer and the photographer. We might argue that the police officer, as a representative of the state, embodies the institutional power that both provides and limits opportunities for these men. And we might consider how the photographer, and by extension the viewer, participate in the subjection of this group of unemployed men simply through the act of viewing and photographing them. Thinking about communication in terms of surveillance encourages us to think about power and requires us to pay attention to the technologies of that power, such as the camera. It reminds us that society is often organized to reinforce these power dynamics despite our individual attempts to transcend them.

But we lose much if we theorize communication as vision solely in terms of surveillance. Returning to the hypothetical photograph, might we not imagine the relationships among the photographer, the police officer, and the unemployed men differently? Might it not be possible that the photographer and the unemployed men are in fact complicit in the act of photographing this scene, both interested in displaying the misplaced nature of the uptight police officer's anxiety? Focusing solely on traditional definitions of the gaze might impede our ability to imagine these relationships in different ways. And, treating the image itself as a product of state surveillance might blind us to other interpretations, such as the use of the camera to create conditions for social justice. If we overemphasize the culture of surveillance, we miss the opportunity to explore modes of communication apart from those dictated by the inevitable influence of institutional power. The metaphor of communication as surveillance is, then, ultimately iconophobic. It frames vision and the products of vision as a dangerous one-way street of domination and does little to account for the countless ways in which people may step outside the boundaries of (albeit very real) power dynamics to enact their agency creatively.

Communication as . . . Spectacle

Many cultural critics suggest that we live in a "society of spectacle." Indeed, spectacle seems an appropriate metaphor for exploring communication in a visual, digital culture that relies more on surface appearances than on the substance of rational argument or the intensity of emotional engagement. Guy Debord defines spectacle as "a social relationship between people that is mediated by images" (1967/1995, p. 12). Spectacle acknowledges the fast-forward culture in which we live. It reminds us that not all communication is thoughtful, precise, and engaged. In fact, most of it is just the opposite: we hurtle through our multimedia universe absorbing images and information at a glance, scarcely able to reflect on what we see and hear.

One byproduct of framing communication as spectacle, however, is that audiences tend to be figured as passive viewers of the spectacle; they absorb but do not engage. Consider again our hypothetical photograph. From the point of view of spectacle, the photograph is not an image of *poverty*, but an *image* of poverty; that is, the metaphor of spectacle turns our attention away from materiality. The photograph in this view becomes a constructed set of social relationships displayed through the medium of photography; the *experience* of poverty is replaced by its *image*. No longer a material condition, the poverty of the unemployed men leaves viewers of the photograph with nothing to do but watch. As Debord observes (eerily echoing Dewey), spectacle "is the opposite of dialogue" (p. 17). One problem with the metaphor of spectacle, then, is that it disempowers the audience for communication. It constructs audiences as passive or helpless in the wake of omnipresent, ever-circulating messages.

The metaphor of spectacle itself is not necessarily iconophobic. In fact, it might even be viewed as idolatrous, or uncritically accepting of all images; after all, they are "only" representations, nothing to be afraid of. But framing communication in terms of spectacle promotes iconophobia because the metaphor serves as a foil for those who wish to reveal the spectacle's inadequacy. If we frame communication as spectacle, we are inevitably left with two uncomfortable choices. Either we uncritically embrace the spectacle, its surface representations, and the audience's passive role, or we step outside the metaphor entirely to critique it. Either way, the metaphor of spectacle offers little to an iconophilic communication theory of the visual.

Communication as . . . Analogy

Analogy is a core feature of human cognition. We think in analogies. For small children first acquiring language, every round object is a "ball" until they learn to discern the differences amid the similarities: baseball, basketball, orange. Analogy may be defined variously as the search for similarity amid otherness, the quest for proportion between objects that are different, or the practice of making the strange familiar. Analogy has much to offer an iconophilic communication theory. In *Visual Analogy: Consciousness as the Art of Connecting,* art historian Barbara Stafford describes analogy as "a general theory of artful invention" and "a practice of intermedia communication" (1999, p. 8). She suggests that analogy does not uncritically emphasize similarity to the exclusion of differences, but rather it teaches *discernment* (such as learning to tell the difference between a baseball and an orange). We treat visual communication analogically when we recognize connection even in the midst of disjuncture.

Consider one last time our hypothetical photograph. What would it mean to engage this photograph from a point of view that frames communication as analogy? It would mean searching for connections amid the differences we might locate within the image, as well as between the image and our experience of the world. Unlike an orientation to surveillance that emphasized the disconnection of the police officer from the unemployed men, attention to analogy might entail recognizing how all the men (as well as the photographer and the viewer) are implicated in broader questions about poverty. Attention to analogy might entail recognizing the unemployment line as something more than an image; it might even remind the viewer of a similar place located near where he or she lives. It might entail making associations with ways that poverty and state power have been illustrated in other media, both past and present. Ultimately, attention to analogy opens up, rather than closes off, avenues for interpretation because it leaves space for the agency of the viewer. The viewer is neither the suspicious or oppressed viewer of the surveillance metaphor, nor the passive viewer of the spectacle metaphor. Instead, the analogical viewer is an engaged viewer who sees connections, who uses her or his own knowledge and experiences to make sense of what he or she sees and to put things together. Unlike surveillance or spectacle, the metaphor of analogy does not dictate the parameters of the viewing experience but rather makes it possible for the viewer to construct the viewing experience for herself or himself.

While the other metaphors I have discussed construct a disempowered or passive audience for communication, analogy requires active, discerning, creative audiences. Framing communication as analogy does not ignore aspects of surveillance and spectacle, but it is not limited to (or by) them. As a practice of "intermedia communication," analogy offers communication theory a way to liberate itself from the iconophobia often found in communication scholarship on the visual. Visual communication conceived analogically is not something that happens *to* audiences (surveillance) or apart from them (spectacle), but rather in communion with them. To paraphrase Dewey, analogy is a "participator."

Indeed, analogy is more than a mere metaphor for communication. It is a perceptual process tied directly to how humans come to know and learn. It is a core part of what communication scholar Ann Marie Seward Barry (1997) has called "visual intelligence":

> We must also understand that the principles of perceptual process are the keys to creative thinking as well—to reaching out beyond our past and into the future, and in doing so to recognize in relationships implied in analogy, metaphor, and symbol the means to penetrate the mysteries of the universe. (p. 67)

The editors of this volume understand the foundational role of analogy, for the very desire to explore diverse metaphors for communication is analogical: an implicit search for connection amid difference.

Perhaps the biggest drawback to relying upon analogy as a metaphor for communication is its potential misapplication. Typical views of analogy treat it solely as the search for similarity. Arguably, one danger of emphasizing communication as analogy might be that our communication theories could devolve into pie-in-the-sky quests for positive connection at the expense of understanding difference, disjuncture, and dissimilarity. Yet, such interpretations are based upon misreadings of the function of analogy rather than a problem inherent in analogy itself. Analogy does not have to ignore difference or disjuncture, or seek to "overcome" it. Rather, it recognizes difference and attempts creatively to negotiate it by juxtaposing it with points of connection and similarity: "Seeing is about being struck that something is, or can be, connected to something else" (Stafford, 1999, p. 138). If we are to have a communication theory that allows us to "see," that accommodates the full range of communicative phenomena, then we need theories that offer richer conceptions of the visual. Of the three metaphors for vision that I have presented here, analogy best allows for such a conception.

Communication as . . . Iconophilic

My ultimate wish is for a theory of the icon that does not depend upon icono-phobia. As currently conceived, communication theory cannot deliver. I have suggested here that analogy may be one way to frame a noniconophobic theory of communication. An iconophilic theory of communication as vision would neither uncritically "worship" images (idolatry) nor approach them out of fear (iconophobia). Rather, it would make space for communication scholars to embrace visual communication as analogy, as an "artful invention" to be engaged openly by active viewers.

Additional Readings

Barry, A. M. S. (1997). *Visual intelligence: Perception, image, and manipulation in visual communication.* Albany: SUNY Press.

Elkins, J. (2003). *Visual studies: A skeptical introduction.* New York: Routledge.

Jay, M. (1993). *Downcast eyes: The denigration of vision in twentieth-century French thought.* Berkeley: University of California Press.

Mitchell, W. J. T. (1994). *Picture theory: Essays on verbal and visual representation.* Chicago: University of Chicago Press.

Stafford, B. M. (1999). *Visual analogy: Consciousness as the art of connecting.* Cambridge: MIT Press.

References

Barry, A. M. S. (1997). *Visual intelligence: Perception, image, and manipulation in visual communication.* Albany: SUNY Press.

Debord, G. (1967/1995). *The society of the spectacle.* New York: Zone Books.

Dewey, J. (1927/1954). *The public and its problems.* Athens, OH: Swallow Press.

Elkins, J. (2003). *Visual studies: A skeptical introduction.* New York: Routledge.

Stafford, B. M. (1999). *Visual analogy: Consciousness as the art of connecting.* Cambridge: MIT Press.

8

Communication as Embodiment

Carolyn Marvin

Lies written in ink can never disguise facts written in blood.

—Lu Xun, 1926

This chapter will be a discussion of two powerful instruments of communication, body and text, and their long and difficult embrace. By *body,* I mean our biological *res extensa,* the heat-seeking skin packages that all living human beings inhabit. By *text,* I mean whatever detaches the body from its message. We chiefly think of texts as graphic representations of spoken language or numbers from which the living body is extracted. Visual images, too, can be thought of as texts that keep bodies at a distance, distilling them as analog or digital lines or dots set into a receptacle medium such as stone, cellulose, celluloid, or electrical current. The long process of displacing and concealing bodies by texts that characterizes modernity has been virtually unplumbed by communication scholars, a remarkable omission in our efforts to understand how human societies develop and engage media. But perhaps this is not very surprising at all. The cultural reflex that regards text as mind's trace divorced from any corporeal origins reflects an aspiration to transcend bodies that has been centuries in the making. In the modern social imaginary, the body is at best superfluous to communicative exchange, at worst a moral impediment to thought.

A much different view regards bodies as the stubborn, ineradicable foundation of human communication and a powerful underlying subject of all mediated communication. It proposes that bodies have modified texts in significant ways and have been importantly modified by them in return, notwithstanding a conventional narrative that assigns them a gradually disappearing role in the history of media. This more complicated view takes seriously the fundamental corporeality that undergirds communication and challenges a dominating ethos in which only what is textually expressible is socially valued. In the worldview of textual dominance, the activity of bodies is often presented in extreme terms—beyond notice on the one hand, pathological on the other. Bodies are brushed aside as ineffectual and decorative until they surface too insistently and become ominously threatening. The notion in both views, that bodily absence is a virtue, is a central assumption of contemporary communication and greatly influences how we think about and organize social relations.

By contrast, text is presumed to have only strong effects. A tradition that extends from Eric Havelock (1963) to Elizabeth Eisenstein (1979, 1980) and Ernest Gellner (1983) attributes tectonic cultural shifts to the assimilation of texts, especially written ones. In broad strokes, these include the destruction of customary social life, rearrangements of the sensory "mix," and the origins of individualism. Printing, writing's industrial handmaiden, is given credit for launching and sustaining the Renaissance and for laying the foundations of modern science and nation-states. The fate of communicating bodies is generally taken for granted in these stories. How texts have refashioned the deportment and appearance of communicating bodies; how bodies have been mystified, segregated, banished, buffered, and positioned; and how they have accommodated, resisted, and fought back *as bodies* rarely have been explored. Nor has the evolution of structures of feeling that organize relations among embodied persons in a textualized world.

We certainly think we know about text, the medium scholars swim in. It is, oddly, the body that needs anchoring. Since incarnation is the very condition of human life, this seems startling. Gesture, the set of observable signals that coordinate bodies with one another, is our original communication, however unthinkingly we may dismiss it. Gesture, which is harder to ignore because it is gloriously exaggerated in dancing, military drill, group festivity, music making, religious ceremony, and public assembly, is treated as embellishment if we think of it at all. Classic insights about the communicative dimensions of gesture—Marcel Mauss's notion of a social repertoire of "body techniques" and George Herbert Mead's (1934) account of language as "vocal gesture" are two—have lain dormant and undeveloped.

But these are stubborn ideas. Robin Dunbar (1998) has argued that spoken language arose to improve the efficiency of social grooming, the gestural communication of solidarity that cements social bonds for the survival of primate groups. Dunbar's claims offer a useful frame for James Carey's

(1975) well-known distinction between ritual (which can be described as gesturally embodied) and transmission (which is textually disembodied) communication. Though widely admired, this distinction never has been seriously taken up in the field and, as we might say, fleshed out.

The standard historical narrative offers a story of technological and moral advancement that progressively strips bodies from the arenas of important communication and invests all past communication with the dream of bodilessness (Peters, 1999). Textualization is presented as overcoming the material and moral limitations of the human body. Of course, media can never eliminate bodies. In fact, though we are at pains to deny it, all media *ever* mediate are bodies (often in layered fashion by mediating media that mediate bodies). In this light, media history appears less as a chronology of textual innovations leaping across the finitude of bodies. It appears, rather, as an antagonistic encounter between bodies and texts in a high-stakes struggle to allocate purity, honor, and power. (See Marvin & Ingle, 1999; Marvin, 1994, 1995, 2004). If the arc of Western history looks like an unbroken string of textual triumphs from the first stirrings of bureaucracy in the 11th century, these victories have never been total nor secure. This is because the textual class requires bodily power to enforce its dominion, a point that will be developed.

Our own text-centric model of culture does seem provincially modern. In absolutist Europe, peasants were the feet and body of society, nobility its arms, the clergy its head, and the king the embodiment of the whole. Elsewhere and at other times, the communicating world has been a dream, a dance, a chain of being, or a battle. Every model of culture elaborates a relationship of the body to the society around it. To imagine culture as text is altogether different from imagining it as dance. In one, the body remains separate from culture, an ontologically distinct entity. In the other, culture is actively constituted in bodily participation.

It remains hard work to stake out a bodily focus for communication in a field that has its center in text-focused media régimes. Our first task is to reconsider mediation itself. Instead of implying a historical progression of textual artifacts on a one-way mission to leave the body behind, mediation is more accurately characterized as *any* packaging of the communicative body expressed in one of two modes. *Dramatization* works to enhance the potency of the communicative body. Clothes, ornamentation, masks, perfume, cosmetics, armor, dancing, singing, feasting, and oratory are dramatizing media that take the communicative power of the physical body seriously and amplify its aura, the sense of its communicative presence.

Textualization works by evacuating the body from communication and impoverishing this aura. It does not get rid of bodies (though this happens— as Henri Lefebvre says [1991], the text kills) so much as it covers up and disguises them, or attempts to turn them into texts. Print, musical notation, film, telephony, and video are textualizing media that fragment and reconstitute the body's message in simplified form. Sociologically, textualization gives rise to two great classes. One of these commands text; the other is commanded by it.

The textual class (it includes, no surprise, academics) is skilled at producing and using texts. It is also the class most entitled to shield and preserve the bodies of its members from physical hardship and danger. This is its privilege, to withdraw the physical body from the fray while deploying those for whom withdrawal is not an option. The body is the emblem of those who lack textual credentials, whose bodies are available to be used up by society, and whose powers of social participation derive from whatever value their bodies have for cultural muscle work, the most dramatic expression of which is war. In modernity, all bodies are disciplined by texts: some to use them, some to stay away from them (Marvin, 1994, 1995). Textualization is the indispensable act of modern power in which every aspect of our lives is implicated. It confers personhood and social status through textual identification and credentialing. It saturates the imaginative environment with information, advertising, and entertainment, all of which overwhelm the authority of bodily experience.

To portray the textual class as the seat of modern power may seem ludicrous to academics who find it difficult to imagine themselves in any such position. They are, of course, only handmaidens. In the social ecology of text-body relations, academics are textual functionaries who recruit and train new text-class members while convincing the body class to hold textual institutions in awe.

What does it mean, then, for the textual class to rule? Consider how U.S. presidents, who dress in the uniform of textual professionals and rarely display the emblems of combat familiar to traditional societies, wage war. A president goes to war not by raising his sword, but by signing a text. No guns move without signed orders, though the president's power lies in the readiness of these guns to respond and in the belief of those who stand behind them in the Constitutional text that authorizes the governmental system. Much cultural energy is devoted to concealing this absolute reliance of the textual class on its bodily substratum and to eliminating opportunities for it to move against the textual class. This antagonism toward the body class it depends on is the deep contradiction at the heart of textual sensibility and power.

The impoverishment and delegitimization of bodily experience generate nostalgia for the romance of face-to-face communication among some textual class members, but this nostalgia is more self-indulgent than serious. To privilege the body genuinely is to embrace its defining power, which is the exercise of physical force. The textual class abhors bodily force, its greatest threat and the enforcer of its authority. The remote object of textual class affections is more nearly constituted in mediated bodies, such as those disseminated in the romantic reconstructions of journalists and anthropologists and in glossy images of advertising and tourism. When, to the everlasting disappointment of guardians of text-based hierarchy, removing the body altogether from communication turns out to be impossible, whole campaigns are mounted to make it less visible. This is done by restricting and stigmatizing its actions, by making it more like text, by directing attention away from it. Yet bodies fight back, reasserting themselves in bodily spectacles, war, and contests of secular and religious morality.

Body and text are not absolute analytic categories but relative positions on a classifying continuum in which each may exhibit more or fewer attributes of the other. Bodies that speak in ways that defer to dictionaries and other artifacts of textually disciplined language present themselves as more text-like than bodies whose colloquial speech bears the oral impress of neighborhood origins. Pornography and popular novels are lower on the scale of cultural esteem than the theoretically driven, relatively more disembodied texts of physicists, lawyers, and engineers. In principle, images fall more often than written texts on the bodily end of the textual spectrum. The more texts float free of the bodies that produce them, the higher their cultural standing and that of the bodies associated with them. This variable classification calls to mind Mikhail Bakhtin's (1984) division between the grotesque body—overflowing, stinking, fecund, vulgar—and the body of classical sculpture—smooth, unorificed, decorous, self-contained. To smooth and cover the orifices of the grotesque body is to narrow its communicative channels, to make it more like text.

How are we to understand the obvious point that posttraditional societies, however awash in rapidly multiplying texts, are preoccupied with sex, fashion, sports, creature comforts, and sensational crime—bodily concerns, all? The bodily melodrama of popular culture constitutes a kind of rebel beachhead against the discipline and pace of contemporary textualization. In a textual world, of course, nothing is so simple. The popular bodies that command the greatest prestige are the very ones that have been most successfully transformed into texts. Extravagant social and cultural rewards flow to athletes and performers not for their corporeal virtuosity alone, but to those whose bodily achievements lend themselves to the widest possible dissemination through textual reproduction. This is the *licensed carnival* of the textual class.

An adequate account of the historical impact of textualization will not be a matter of grand theory. It is not subtle enough. Only extended and patiently detailed investigations can convey how body-based communities have textually reimagined themselves again and again. The conquest of the New World and the Inquisition are a part of that story. So are humbler, smaller-scale stories of drastically changed beliefs and expectations, uprooted and transformed social relationships, and status rearrangements bitterly struggled over. Grand theory can open up directions of inquiry and suggest provocative hypotheses. But, in the end, it only signals where to begin looking.

With that thought in mind, the Reformation offers itself as a seismic center of the shift from bodily to textual magic that so profoundly marks the modern West. Religion has always addressed bodily experience, especially its most deeply felt moments of suffering and death. The Church Universal, dominant in the West, is a shockingly corporeal faith, its central event the brutal sacrifice of a god who agrees to take on ultimate bodily pain. With the Reformation, the relationship of believers to the deity ceased to be mediated through the body of the priest and came to be mediated through individual Bible reading. This and accompanying text-body struggles (Muir, 1997; Duffy, 1992; but see Stock, 1983, who traces this process to the 11th century) over the magical bodily potency of icons; statues; and rituals of gesture, song, and dance profoundly transformed the West. (Capitalism, the cultural successor of the Reformation, appears as the most spiritually ascetic of arrangements, having evacuated material things of their meaningful connections with bodies while transforming both into an etherealized text stripped of experience, connection, love, and existential groundedness—the bottom line).

The 19th century was a great accelerator of textualization. Lawrence Levine (1998) has traced the division of high and low culture to the segregation of elite and popular bodies in opera, theater, and museum audiences. Where bodily improvisation had been the anticipated prerogative of performers and noisy evaluation the norm for audiences, high culture was reimagined as a sacred canon of inviolable texts of music, dance, and drama from which performers must not deviate. Audiences for the so-called high arts became progressively less sensuous and more intimidated, their responses less confident and less performed. The mutually constituted tasks of cultural judgment and participation were severed, the former surrendered to an emerging class of textual critics who took upon themselves the task of maligning the newly distinguished popular arts as well.

Concurrently, Progressives sought to break up urban political machines heavily dependent on the mobilization of bodies and to promote the notion of well-behaved "independent-minded" literates as the only fit civic participants (Marvin & Simonson, 2004). "Informed" and "deliberative" voters read newspapers and kept their voices down in political discussion, which they favored over an older notion of politics as a team sport. Poor, immigrant, African American, and other bodies that troubled textual elites were disenfranchised for failing to achieve the literacy levels of the educated middle class. Alcohol-laced, physically exuberant rallies; military marches; and bonfires were discredited and sometimes outlawed. These occasions of broad sensual appeal had regularly drawn the body class together to present itself as a political and physical force to be reckoned with. Increasingly deprived of political muscle and lacking textual credentials, the body class became ever more detached from the political process, which is its condition today.

There is an ominous saying that a regime's success can be measured by how many people survive it. Nothing demonstrates more clearly that bodies are the raw materials of society and incarnation of our core moral situation. To this end, the basic job of society is to reproduce, organize, deploy, and dispose of bodies. The job of culture is to justify, cope with, and teach those arrangements. Modern societies seek to sustain the burdens of child rearing, work, and war through a consensus that partly depends on collective denial and evasion of the inequities of any particular distribution of these sacrifices. Textualization is central in making this happen. It encourages the immaterial accounting of burdens in highly filtered words and images, and in statistics safely received in environments to which those especially burdened—the poor, diseased, unemployed, and imprisoned—have little access.

Textualization therefore creates the modern dilemma in which the textual class risks losing touch, and everything that term implies, not only with the real conditions that sustain their society but also with their own moral commitments as willing bodies, for which there is no substitute, to the survival of the group. The textual class encounters the world through vicariously distant representations and simplifying abstractions. It is challenged not only to empathize with the real condition of the body class on which it builds its power but by the temptations of a moral relativism that dilute its convictions. The body class places the bodies of those it loves on the line for community. In this sacrificial embodiedness, moral relativity is not possible. Moral dogmatism is the dilemma of the body class. Both views are responsible for their share of the world's horrors and its finest achievements. To understand the complexities that beset these two communicative worldviews, and the consequences of their entwined fate, is a grand and sober challenge for scholars of communication.

Additional Readings

Clanchy, M. (1993). *From memory to written record: England 1066–1307*. Oxford, UK: Blackwell. (Original work published 1979)

Caplan, J. (Ed.). (2000). *Written on the body: The tattoo in European and American history*. Princeton, NJ: Princeton University Press.

Thornton, T. P. (1996). *Handwriting in America: A cultural history*. New Haven, CT: Yale University Press.

Muir, E. (1997). *Ritual in early modern Europe*. Cambridge, UK: Cambridge University Press.

Torpey, J. (1999). *The invention of the passport: Surveillance, citizenship and the state*. Cambridge, UK: Cambridge University Press.

References

Bakhtin, M. (1984). *Rabelais and his world* (H. Iswolsky, Trans.). Bloomington: Indiana University Press.

Carey, J. (1975). A cultural approach to communication. *Communication, 2,* 1–22.

Duffy, E. (1992). *The stripping of the altars: Traditional religion in England, c. 1400–1580.* New Haven, CT: Yale University Press.

Dunbar, R. (1998). *Grooming, gossip, and the evolution of language.* Cambridge, MA: Harvard University Press.

Eisenstein, E. L. (1979, 1980). *The printing press as an agent of change: Communications and cultural transformations in early modern Europe* (Vols. 1–2). Cambridge, UK: Cambridge University Press.

Gellner, E. (1983). *Nations and nationalism.* Ithaca, NY: Cornell University Press.

Havelock, E. (1963). *Preface to Plato.* Cambridge, MA: Belknap Press, Harvard University Press.

Lefebvre, H. (1991). *The production of space* (D. Nicholson-Smith, Trans.). Cambridge, MA: Blackwell.

Levine, L. (1998). *Highbrow/lowbrow: The emergence of cultural hierarchy in America.* Cambridge, MA: Harvard University Press.

Marvin, C., & Ingle, D. W. (1999). *Blood sacrifice and the nation: Totem rituals and the American flag.* Cambridge, UK: Cambridge University Press.

Marvin, C. (1994). The body of the text: Literacy's corporeal constant. *Quarterly Journal of Speech, 80*(2), 129–149.

Marvin, C. (1995). Bodies, texts, and the social order: A reply to Bielefeldt. *Quarterly Journal of Speech, 81*(1), 103–107.

Marvin, C. (2004). Peaceable kingdoms and information technology: Prospects for the nation-state. In M. Sturken, D. Thomas, & S. Ball-Rokeach (Eds.), *Technological visions: The hopes and fears that shape new technologies* (pp. 240–254). Philadelphia: Temple University Press.

Marvin, C., & Simonson, P. D. (2004). Voting alone: The decline of bodily mass communication in presidential elections. *Communication and Critical/Cultural Studies, 1*(2), 127–150.

Mead, G. H. (1934). *Mind, self & society from the standpoint of a social behaviorist.* Chicago: University of Chicago Press.

Muir, E. (1997). *Ritual in early modern Europe.* Cambridge, UK: Cambridge University Press.

Peters, J. D. (1999). *Speaking into the air: A history of the idea of communication.* Chicago: University of Chicago Press.

Stock, B. (1983). *The implications of literacy: Written language and models of interpretation in the eleventh and twelfth centuries.* Princeton, NJ: Princeton University Press.

9

Communication as Raced

Judith N. Martin and Thomas K. Nakayama

Conversations about race in the United States at the beginning of the 21st century reflect the contradictory status of race in society. On the one hand, the conversations seem to be ubiquitous—discussions of affirmative action policies in hiring and education, equal access to voting during national and state elections, and persistent racial disparities are often in the news. On the other hand, conversations about race in workplace and social settings often are uneasy or simply absent. Examinations of the racial dimensions of our own discipline are no different. On the one hand, advertisements seek faculty of color and undergraduate and graduate programs seek students of color, but, on the other hand, there is little discussion about how communication is raced, what this means, and the implications of this racialization for students and faculty.

There are at least three ways to view the relationship between communication and race:

1. Racial histories and demographics inform and reflect communication behaviors.

2. The conceptualization and study of communication is raced—historically and contemporaneously.

3. The field of communication is raced.

In this essay, we'll first define what we mean by race and then describe these three approaches, focusing primarily on the third.

Scientists today largely have discredited traditional physiological/biological notions of race, noting that there is more genetic variation within racial groups than between them (Omi & Winant, 1994; Wells, 2002). They, along with communication scholars, emphasize instead the social construction of race and the fluidity of racial categories. For example, scholars have shown how the category "white" evolved over the years in the United States, expanding to include people of Irish, Jewish, and southern European descent— all previously excluded as not quite white (Brodkin, 1999; Ignatiev, 1995; Jacobson, 1998). Race, then, is a social construction, but it has a very real, material impact on our everyday lives. It is a fiction, but it is real—and it is this cultural contradiction that undergirds our conversations on race and its place in communication studies.

Communication Behavior Is Raced

A first view of communication as raced examines how racial characteristics inform communication habits. Stated simply, communication is an intensely racialized practice. With whom we communicate, when we communicate with them, and how much we communicate with others follows largely racialized formations. Communication scholars for years accepted that race influences the communication behaviors of "others," but only recently have we turned the spotlight explicitly on the communication of white people. This research exposes the underlying racial hierarchy and describes how the connection between race and communication for white people largely goes unrecognized (Nakayama & Krizek, 1995). Though people who are not white see that distinctness, dominance, normalcy, and privilege are characteristics of whiteness, and hence influence the communication of white people, white people themselves often do not recognize or see these connections (Bahk & Jandt, 2004).

In their study of student communication at a multiracial campus, Halualani, Chitgopekar, Morrison, and Dodge (2004) highlight the general features of this link between race and communication, reflecting larger societal patterns. That is, those students (like most individuals) largely communicate with others in their own racial group, despite living in an increasingly multiracial/multiethnic society. Individuals do not, however, simply *choose* to communicate with members of a particular racial or ethnic group. Instead, these communication patterns reflect larger social organizing about where racial groups predominately live and the kinds of workplace encounters they are likely to have, as well as the leisure aspects of our racialized society. In short, we argue that it is imperative to place our communication practices within the context of a highly racialized society in order to better understand everyday communication practices. Yet, to understand why the relationship between race, power, and communication is often obviated, we also need to examine the historical development of the study of communication.

The Study of Communication Is Raced

A second view suggests that the very study of communication itself is raced. From its origins in 5th century BCE Greece, the study of communication (then called rhetoric) focused almost exclusively on the communication patterns of those in power. Plato, Aristotle, Cicero, and others were interested in empowering Greek and Roman citizens, although ignoring the ways that communication might help slaves, women, and other noncitizens advocate for their interests, needs, and desires. The practice and study of communication was by and for those already empowered in society (Crowley & Hawhee, 1999; Dues & Brown, 2004).

This elitism was not easily translated into the development of communication studies in the United States. The drive for democratic participation in society was a major motive for the development of "speech" courses for those students who did not come from privileged backgrounds (Cohen, 1994). Even today, communication studies is largely missing from elite institutions such as Harvard, Yale, Princeton, Chicago, and Emory, but remains prominent at less elite ones.

We must note, however, that this democratic drive was marked by the racialized society in which it occurred. When the then-new land-grant institutions were established by the 1862 Morrill Act, public speaking was taught mainly to empower its white male students—largely from farming families and other nonelite backgrounds—to participate in democratic institutions; the study of communication (speech), meanwhile, remained in largely segregated contexts.[1] The Second Morrill Act established "1890s institutions," which are today known as historically black colleges and universities (HBCUs). These schools, though undoubtedly important, offered segregated and sometimes second-class educational opportunities for their students.

It is instructive, then, to examine how the study of communication continues to be raced today in our research, teaching, and practice. This examination follows a trend set by other disciplines as well as several subdisciplines within the field of communication. For example, anthropologists have recognized anthropology as currently one of the "least integrated or whitest professions" (Shanklin, 2000, p. 99). More important, Shanklin goes on to explore the implications of this whiteness—that anthropology delivers "inchoate messages about anthropological understanding of race and racism in introductory texts and that anthropologists do not participate actively in public discussion" (p. 99).

Similarly, the accrediting Council for Education in the field of journalism and mass communication notes that the standard failed most frequently in accreditation in this discipline—Standard 12—is that which calls for racial integration of faculty and students and the inclusion of women (De Uriarte, Bodinger-de Uriarte, & Benavides, 2003). The second most failed standard is Standard 3, which calls for diversity in curriculum. Where diverse curriculum exists, it is rarely a required course (pp. vii–viii). In 2000, minorities earned only 25% of all BA degrees and 10% of all MA degrees in U.S. journalism programs. Figures remain miniscule for PhDs, now almost universally required for a tenured position as a journalism educator (p. viii).

The Field of Communication Is Raced

Can the same be said for the field of communication? Are we largely a white profession, white in racial composition of faculty and students, white in curriculum, white in research interests and theorizing, and largely silent when it comes to the public debate on race and communication?[2]

Taking a quick look at institutional data on communication majors highlights the whiteness of our discipline and its attraction to white students out of proportion to their demographic numbers. We highlight the two institutions at which we currently work. At Temple University, 59.4% of the students are white, but 65.6% of the communications and theater students are white. At Arizona State University, 67.8% of the student body is white and 77.4% of the communication students are white (only 17.7% of communication students are minority students—the remaining are either unknown or international). Set against the number of minority students, the predominance of white students highlights the disparity. While we know of no national study on communication students, we speculate that this is a national trend. Yet, as a discipline, we remain unreflexive about the whiteness of communication studies. Our point is not simply that communication has many more white students than its general demographics would indicate, but to question *the ways in which the study of communication continues to empower white people, while at the same time unwittingly remaining unresponsive to the needs of the rest of society.*

Ashcraft and Allen (2003) argue that introductory textbooks are one important venue for understanding the ways that race functions in the communication discipline, in that they "disseminate a field's canon of knowledge"

(p. 7) and socialize graduate students and faculty members who teach from them. Thus, they not only reflect the discipline but also help reproduce it. Ashcraft and Allen's content analysis of organizational communication textbooks led to the identification of the following themes in the treatment of race:

1. Race is a separate, singular concept that is relevant only under certain circumstances.

2. Race is relevant insofar as it involves cultural differences, which can be identified, valued, and managed to improve organizational performance.

3. All cultural differences are synonymous with international variations.

4. Racial discrimination is a function of personal bias, interpersonal misunderstandings, organizational failure to manage cultural differences, and disproportionate demographics.

While these observations are specific to the field of organizational communication, they seem to hold true for theory and research in interpersonal communication, intercultural communication, and rhetoric—the areas we are most familiar with—and are likely to hold true in other areas as well. The common thread here is the focus on communication at the individual level, with little regard for the larger contexts in which power and historical relations might enter. In a reflection of Ancient Greek concerns about communication, we can see that contemporary communication concerns center around ways to help white people deal with racial difference, whether for organizational effectiveness, interpersonal effectiveness, or managing differences. Interpersonal communication skills (e.g., studies identifying components of communication competence) are presented in such a way that they seem to help white individuals deal with others who are assumed to be white.

Studies of intercultural contact reflect this same centering of whiteness (Cooks, 2001). Halualani et al. (2004) note that "the most glaring shortcoming in intercultural contact literature is the predominant focus on majority (or white/European American) attitudes toward interacting with minority groups" (p. 274). Again, communication studies clearly is in the service of white people at the expense of racial others.

Our call here is for communication scholars to begin taking our racialized history and contemporary context seriously, so that we can begin to service the diversity of U.S. society and its future outlook. As long as we ignore race or work primarily to serve the needs of white Americans, our undergraduate communication majors, graduate students, and faculty will become increasingly isolated from engaging contemporary social issues, whether in health care, education, business, or elsewhere. It is only "by examining the racial roots of our own field, we take a significant step toward understanding how organizing is deeply raced" (Ashcraft & Allen, 2003, p. 32).

And this conversation has started. Ashcraft and Allen's (2003) examination of the racial roots of organizational communication, Warren's (2001, 2003) examination of whiteness in the performance studies classroom, Cooks's (2001, 2003) and others' examination of the racial roots in teaching and research in intercultural communication have opened the conversation about the interwoven character of race and communication studies.

A recent discussion on CRTNET (Communication Research and Theory Network—the National Communication Association's [NCA's] daily electronic news service) illustrates the kinds of institutional issues we've reviewed. This particular discussion focused on travel grants provided to students of color to attend the NCA annual convention. Several discussants strenuously objected to these grants and questioned the ethics of awarding grants on the basis of race. Some even argued that these grants were morally indefensible. While this discussion seems to focus narrowly on the single issue of assisting students of color to travel to the NCA convention, it also provides an example of how and why communication studies remains a very segregated field of study. On the surface, those arguing against travel grants frame the issue in terms of equity and fairness—why should some conference attendees be awarded travel grants solely on the basis of ethnicity or race? However, viewed in the larger historical context of race relations within our discipline, this argument reflects a coded communication practice—termed "whitespeak" by Dreama Moon (1999)—which not only excludes by ignoring the larger issues, but also creates a community, through white bonding. The CRTNET exchange thus is one example of how communication (the practice, idea, and field) is raced: Long-standing racialized patterns of communication and the historical organization of the discipline empower some to speak on behalf of "fellow" white individuals who want to reproduce the discipline's structures of racial privilege by discouraging incentives to members of groups who historically have opted out of this discipline. This kind of community—as a scholarly, academic community—can only fail in its attempts to build itself on that racialized foundation.

The whiteness of communication is reflected in the most recent National Center for Education Statistics (U.S. Department of Education, 1993/1999) that show that 87.5% of communication faculty are white. In his study of the communication discipline, Ronald Gordon points to these statistics among others and argues that the composition of the field influences how we study communication: "The views that we have of 'communication' have, as a result, been skewed. They have not represented a sample of all possible conceptual positions and vantage points from which knowledge of communication can be constructed. Our American communication theorists have been an extremely homogeneous group" (1998/1999, p. 3). Yet, we are suggesting that the consequences of the whiteness of communication studies is not simply that this demographic has narrowed our ways of thinking about communication, but that it has also allowed discouraging barriers to be erected to keep the field the way it is.

Our call, then, is to envision communication studies in another way, with a different agenda and future. As we move toward living in a more racially diverse society, as well as a more globally oriented world, a discipline that remains racially segregated risks its own viability. We wish to avert the potential marginalization of communication studies and call for beginning the long process of taking race seriously in this discipline. It already is taken seriously in the everyday practice of communication.

As an academic discipline, we risk our profession and our field if we continue to ignore the significance of race and the role of race in society. The ongoing racial disparities in the United States in employment, housing, religion, and other institutions guarantee that race does matter. If communication scholars cannot or will not begin to contribute to a better understanding of the importance of communication in a racialized society, it will be increasingly difficult to argue that communication studies is central to the mission of most universities and colleges, as many emphasize serving social and community needs.

Indeed, as noted, some communication scholars, including Ashcraft and Allen (2003), Buttney (1997), Crenshaw (1997), Cooks (2001, 2003), Halualani et al. (2004), Jackson and Garner (1998), and Moon (1999), have begun the long process of reconfiguring our discipline's mission and vision. Yet, many more of us need to embrace a much more socially inclusive and responsible mission for our profession. In so doing, we can position communication in a way that addresses social needs, situates us well to seek external funding and grants, and offers universities a meaningful mission and vision—both now and in the future.

Notes

1. Some HBCUs, such as Tuskegee, emphasized the "industrial arts" (e.g., tailoring, masonry, carpentry) as more practical approaches to helping its students survive in a white-dominated society. See Conley (1990) for a more detailed history of communication.

2. We should acknowledge NCA's policy on diversity, at http://www.natcom .org/policies/External/Diversity.htm. It calls for inclusivity (which is good) and promotion of dialogue, but it fails to emphasize that dialogue has to be set within a context of unequal and hierarchal relations.

Additional Readings

Bernardi, D. (Ed.). (1998). *The birth of whiteness: Race and the emergence of U.S. cinema.* New Brunswick, NJ: Rutgers University Press.

Martin, J. N., Krizek, R. L., Nakayama, T. K., & Bradford, L. (1996). Exploring whiteness: A study of self labels. *Communication Quarterly, 44,* 125–144.

Nakayama, T. K., & Martin, J. N. (Eds.). (1999). *Whiteness: The communication of social identity.* Thousand Oaks, CA: Sage.

Shome, R. (1996). Postcolonial interventions in the rhetorical canon: An "other" view. *Communication Theory, 6,* 40–59.

Warren, J. T. (2003). *Performing purity: Whiteness, pedagogy, and the reconstitution of power.* New York: Peter Lang.

References

Ashcraft, K. L., & Allen, B. J. (2003). The racial foundation of organizational communication. *Communication Theory, 13,* 5–38.

Bahk, C. M., & Jandt, F. E. (2004). Being white in America: Development of a scale. *Howard Journal of Communications, 15,* 57–68.

Brodkin, K. (1999). *How Jews became white folks: And what that says about race in America.* New York: Rutgers University Press.

Buttney, R. (1997). Reported speech in talking race on campus. *Human Communication, 23,* 477–506.

Cohen, H. (1994). *History of the speech communication discipline: Emergence of a discipline 1914–1945.* Annandale, VA: Speech Communication Association.

Conley, T. (1990). *Rhetoric in the European tradition.* New York: Longman.

Cooks, L. (2001). From distance and uncertainty to research and pedagogy in the borderlands: Implications for the future of intercultural communication. *Communication Theory, 11,* 339–351.

Cooks, L. (2003). Pedagogy, performance, and positionality: Teaching about whiteness in interracial communication. *Communication Education, 52,* 245–257.

Crenshaw, C. (1997). Resisting whiteness' rhetorical silence. *Western Journal of Communication, 61,* 253–278.

Crowley, S., & Hawhee, D. (1999). *Ancient rhetorics for contemporary students* (2nd ed.). Needham Heights, MA: Allyn & Bacon.

De Uriarte, M. L., with Bodinger-de Uriarte, C., & Benavides, J. L. (2003). *Diversity disconnects: From class room to news room.* Retrieved December 15, 2004, from http://journalism.utexas.edu/faculty/deuriarte/diversity_disconnects.pdf

Dues, M., & Brown, M. (2004). *Boxing Plato's shadow: An introduction to the study of human communication.* Boston: McGraw-Hill.

Gordon, R. D. (1998–1999, Winter–Spring). A spectrum of scholars: Multicultural diversity and human communication theory. *Human Communication, 2,* 1–8.

Halualani, R. T., Chitgopekar, A. S., Morrison, J. H. T. A., & Dodge, P. S.-W. (2004). Diverse in name only? Intercultural interaction at a multicultural university. *Journal of Communication, 54,* 270–286.

Ignatiev, N. (1995). *How the Irish became white.* New York: Routledge.

Jackson, R. L., II, & Garner, T. (1998). Tracing the evolution of "race," "ethnicity," and "culture" in communication studies. *Howard Journal of Communications, 9,* 41–55.

Jacobson, M. F. (1998). *Whiteness of a different color: European immigrants and the alchemy of race.* Cambridge, MA: Harvard University Press.

Moon, D. (1999). White enculturation and bourgeois ideology: The discursive production of "good (white) girls." In T. K. Nakayama and J. N. Martin (Eds.), *Whiteness: The communication of social identity* (pp. 177–197). Thousand Oaks, CA: Sage.

Nakayama, T. K., & Krizek, R. L. (1995). Whiteness: A strategic rhetoric. *Quarterly Journal of Speech, 81,* 291–309.

Omi, M., & Winant, H. (1994). *Racial formations in the United States from the 1960's to the 1990's.* London: Routledge.

Shanklin, E. (2000). Representations of race and racism in American anthropology. *Current Anthropology, 41,* 99–103.

U.S. Department of Education, National Center for Education Statistics. (1993, 1999). Table 231: Percentage distribution of full-time and part-time instructional faculty and staff in degree-granting institutions, by program area, race/ethnicity, and sex: Fall 1992 and fall 1998 [National study of postsecondary faculty]. Available at http://nces.ed.gov/programs/digest/d02/tables/PDF/table231.pdf

Warren, J. T. (2001). On the performative dimensions of race in the classroom. *Communication Education, 50,* 91–108.

Warren, J. T. (2003). *Performing purity: Whiteness, pedagogy, and the reconstitution of power.* New York: Peter Lang.

Wells, S. (2002). *The journey of man: A genetic odyssey.* Princeton, NJ: Princeton University Press.

10

Communication as Social Identity

Jake Harwood

Conformity is bad. We should be ourselves and celebrate our individuality. Or, in the words of cartoonist Gary Larson's penguin, stuck in a flock of identical penguins, "I've just gotta be me!" So goes the mantra of the modern (Western) world, and so, often, goes our understanding of human communication. We study individuals, how they talk, why they talk. We examine relationships, to be sure, but often we are interested in inherently individualistic processes—satisfaction or feelings (personal feelings!) of intimacy. Perspectives such as social exchange theory have us performing mental calculations of the personal rewards and costs provided by our friends and lovers. Our *selves* tend to be understood as very "personal" selves, operating as autonomous units, either unconnected to others, or connected as a function of the rewards provided to the individual. In contrast, when people operate in terms of more collective interests, they are usually considered in deviant or pathological terms. Rioters throwing rocks at police, football hooligans on a rampage, and soldiers killing the enemy (without considering their individual characteristics) are often considered to be acting at a "less than human" level.

The social identity/self categorization approach offers a different take on our social experience (Tajfel & Turner, 1986; Oakes, Haslam, & Turner, 1994). This approach (put broadly) states that an individual self can be understood at different levels of abstraction. At the individual (personal identity) level, we are concerned with our difference from other individuals, and the things that make us unique as people. At the collective (social identity) level, we are concerned with our group's differences from other groups, and the things that make our group unique. When operating at the level of social identity, individuals act as group members, understand and judge the behaviors of self and others in terms of group memberships, and tend to *deindividuate* both self and others. It is crucial to note that this deindividuation is not regarded as a pathological or somehow more primitive mode of functioning. From this perspective, operating in terms of groups is an inherent part of being human (Turner, Hogg, Oakes, Reicher, & Wetherell, 1987). Such functioning makes institutions like families, governments, and teams possible, and allows us to enjoy the benefits that come from collective activity. However, it also has negative consequences in terms of, for instance, the ways in which deindividuating self and others can lead to prejudice and intergroup conflict. This general approach has been characterized as an *intergroup* approach, and the current chapter explains why this approach, and social identity theory in particular, is a useful way for us to approach human communication (see Harwood & Giles, 2005, for a review of social identity approaches to communication).

This intergroup approach provides some unique tools for understanding social behavior. For instance, Reicher (1986) has provided a number of insights into the behavior of crowds, particularly in riot situations. Understanding the behavior of the individuals in a crowd in terms of their operation at a superordinate level of identity provides a greater understanding of such behavior than does examining the riot as the work of a mass of lunatics hell-bent on destruction. Similarly, the intergroup approach also draws attention to the contribution of *both* sides in a crowd situation. Police or other authorities contribute to such situations, and yet the way in which they conceive of themselves in terms of identities and their perceptions of the rioters are rarely examined (Stott & Reicher, 1998). The one exception to this occurs when it serves our political purposes. For instance, when behaviors by authorities in other regimes conveniently can be characterized as repressive or anti-democratic, Western media feel comfortable in describing them as such (for example, think of how Western media covered the crackdown on democratic protest in China's Tiananmen Square in 1989). The focus on civil disturbances in the West, however, tends to be almost exclusively on the behavior of the "rioters" rather than on the authorities. Hence, an intergroup approach provides an understanding of the behavior of people in these situations, as well as the ways in which the situations are framed by observers.

Crowds and riots are not the primary fodder for communication researchers. Therefore, in the following sections, I provide some brief examples of how themes central to contemporary communication research can be reexamined (and perhaps revitalized) by adopting an intergroup perspective.

- *Mass Communication:* Social identification with a particular demographic group and portrayals of that group on specific television programs influence television viewing. For instance, Harwood (1997) shows that young people faced with a particular television show are more likely to watch it if the cast is young than if it is older. Harwood (1999) demonstrates that this preference is modified by the extent to which being young is important to a particular individual. Individuals who identify strongly with "youth" will be drawn to shows with casts and themes that reinforce their age identity. Traditional approaches to mass communication take a more individualistic approach to gratifications, and hence are less able to account for rewards sought and obtained at the collective level (see Harwood & Roy, 2005; Mastro, 2003).

- *Group Communication:* Group leaders are evaluated not only on their leadership traits and abilities, but also with regard to their group prototypicality (how similar are they to the "ideal member" of the group?). Leaders who conform to the group prototype more closely, for instance, are paradoxically able to "get away with" more nonprototypical actions as leaders (see Hogg & Tindale, 2005). Small-group scholars tend to focus on interpersonal dynamics. Neglecting the collective level of group identification results in ignoring a fundamental motivation for group participation and interaction. Research such as that described by Hogg and Tindale provides interesting illustrations of how the processes of "small groups" and "big groups" (i.e., large-scale social collectives such as ethnic groups) can be quite similar. Small-group researchers would do well to examine how and when individuals identify with their groups and how they evaluate their fellow members as conforming to the group prototype.

- *Family Communication:* Identification with the family as a group is a key element in determining family harmony and positive communication. For instance, in stepfamily relationships, the greater the extent to which members of both constituent families identify with the new family unit, the greater the harmony within the new unit (Banker & Gaertner, 1998). Of course, numerous other social categorizations (and hence identities) exist within the family. For instance, age is a defining characteristic of certain family relationships; grandparents are inevitably significantly older than their grandchildren. Thus, grandparents and grandchildren may identify with one another as members of the same family, and also differentiate from one another on the basis of age. As families increasingly become sites for other forms of intergroup contact (e.g., via interracial marriages, interfaith marriages), a social identity approach will be crucial in understanding when and how these individuals categorize as ingroup (family) versus outgroup (different races, faiths, ages, etc.) members, and the influence of such categorizations on family communication (Harwood, Soliz, & Lin, in press; Soliz, 2004).

- *Instructional Communication:* Within the classroom, students who perceive social group similarities between themselves and their instructors have a greater tendency to positively evaluate those instructors (Edwards & Harwood, 2003). This effect should be stronger for the students who strongly identify with the pertinent social group. Identifying with the collective may also be crucial in class or group assignments. For instance, it is conceivable that identification with the class collective might be a crucial determinant of in-class participation.

- *Intercultural Communication:* Language is a fundamental dimension of ethnic and cultural identity. Individuals use language to signal and defend their identities, and people respond to language in terms of their social identifications. This is apparent in conflict over the use of French in Québec, regional linguistic variation in Spain, the use of Spanish in U.S. public schools, and the preservation of Aboriginal languages in Australia. Work in Wales, for instance, has demonstrated that individuals whose Welsh identity is threatened will respond with increasingly "Welsh" language use (presumably to emphasize their group distinctiveness and bolster identity). Similarly, the differential use of English versus Welsh can result in very different levels of compliance with a request for help, depending upon the recipient's level of Welsh identity (Bourhis & Giles, 1977; Giles & Coupland, 1991). Intercultural communication cannot be understood fully without considering the extent to which the participants in that communication are invested in (identify with) the cultures under consideration.

- *Communication and Technology:* Individuals communicating through technological channels (e.g., e-mail), are often understood to be operating in an environment that is anonymous and hence free of traditional stereotyping processes. However, groups may become apparent in such contexts (e.g., via use of names indicating gender or culture, self-identification as a member of a particular group, or structural aspects of the context). Given that other cues in such contexts are restricted, when social categorizations do become apparent, they may gain more power and be more influential than in other contexts. Thus, online communication may be particularly characterized by group-level behaviors, collective identities, and group-based communication— quite the reverse of the scattered, dislocated, and isolated online experience sometimes imagined (Postmes & Baym, in press). Future work on technology should understand the positive and negative implications of collective identity salience in computer-mediated settings.

Conclusions

From the preceding examples, it should be clear that communication is influenced by group identities, and that even in close personal relationships, such identities can influence important dynamics of interaction. Likewise, it is clear that communication shapes identities, raising or lowering the salience of particular group identifications and constructing the meaning of groups for members and nonmembers. Attention to such issues has been cursory in the communication literature, yet it is clear, from issues of ethnic conflict to concerns with small-group dynamics, that group identifications have an important role to play in understanding behavior. Put in straightforward form:

- The salience of social identities varies based on systematically identifiable features of individuals and situations. Communication phenomena such as language use will raise or lower the salience of particular categorizations.

- When a particular identity is salient, our own communication and our interpretations and attributions about others' communication are made in terms of that identity. Choices about language, tone, and even whether to initiate interaction will be made on the basis of self- and other-categorization.

- Communication constructs the meanings of particular social identities. Social interaction and, indeed, all forms of socialization contribute to our understanding of the nature of groups, their characteristics, and their function in society. Our racist, sexist, homophobic, ageist (to mention a few!) attitudes are communicative constructions.

Attention to collective action and identity is important. Significant social problems (e.g., racism, war) are very clearly a function of individuals acting in terms of their group memberships and treating others in terms of those memberships. Counting American casualties in Iraq one by one while guesstimating Iraqi casualties to the nearest thousand only makes any sense if we work from an intergroup perspective and understand the relevance of those casualties for an ingroup versus an outgroup. Of course, an intergroup perspective also helps us understand (more positive) behaviors like social groups joining together to fight discrimination, families bonding at times of crisis, and even the broad environmental consciousness that has emerged in the last 20–30 years. Again, it is easy to treat group-based cognition and behavior as a pathological state that results only in hatred and destruction, but taking such a perspective ignores the positive outcomes from group-level identities, as well as the fact that we all operate in terms of our group identities much of the time.

More fundamentally, we need to understand collective identities as a key aspect of human behavior, and we need to think about incorporating this higher-level sense of self into our communication research as a more routine issue. We are not random individuals wandering the planet with no connections to others, and our connections to others cannot be understood purely as a function of individual-level phenomena. We don't celebrate a victory by our college alma mater because it will provide us with direct personal rewards, and we don't get a chill from singing a national anthem because we like the tune. The times when we communicate truly as individuals unencumbered by one group membership or another are actually fairly rare. To be a part of a group is to be truly human, and to ignore that is to sever ties that are very important to people. Even our closest interpersonal relationships are imbued with group identifications that both join us to those within our groups and separate us from those not in our groups. As we seek to understand how communication connects and separates us, social identity processes deserve considerably more attention than they have been afforded by communication scholars.

Additional Readings

Harwood, J., & Giles, H. (2005). *Intergroup communication: Multiple perspectives.* New York: Peter Lang.

Oakes, P. J., Haslam, S. A., & Turner, J. C. (1994). Stereotyping and social reality. Oxford, UK: Blackwell.

Reid, S., & Giles, H. (Eds.). (in press). Communication and intergroup contact [Special Issue]. *Group Processes and Intergroup Relations.*

Tajfel, H., & Turner, J. C. (1986). The social identity theory of intergroup behavior. In S. Worchel & W. Austin (Eds.), *Psychology of intergroup relations* (pp. 7–24). Chicago: Nelson-Hall.

Turner, J. C., Hogg, M. A., Oakes, P. J., Reicher, S., & Wetherell, M. (1987). Rediscovering the social group: A self-categorization theory. Cambridge, MA: Basil Blackwell.

References

Banker, B. S., & Gaertner, S. L. (1998). Achieving stepfamily harmony: An intergroup-relations approach. *Journal of Family Psychology, 12,* 310–325.

Bourhis, R. Y., & Giles, H. (1977). The language of intergroup distinctiveness. In H. Giles (Ed.), *Language, ethnicity and intergroup relations* (pp. 119–135). London: Academic Press.

Edwards, C. C., & Harwood, J. (2003). Social identity in the classroom: An examination of age identification between students and instructors. *Communication Education, 52,* 60–65.

Giles, H., & Coupland, N. (1991). *Language: Contexts and consequences.* Pacific Grove, CA: Brooks/Cole.

Harwood, J. (1997). Viewing age: Lifespan identity and television viewing choices. *Journal of Broadcasting and Electronic Media, 41,* 203–213.

Harwood, J. (1999). Age identification, social identity gratifications, and television viewing. *Journal of Broadcasting and Electronic Media, 43,* 123–136.

Harwood, J., & Giles, H. (2005). *Intergroup communication: Multiple perspectives.* New York: Peter Lang.

Harwood, J., & Roy, A. (2005). Social identity theory and mass communication research. In J. Harwood & H. Giles (Eds.), *Intergroup communication: Multiple perspectives* (pp. 189–212). New York: Peter Lang.

Harwood, J., Soliz, J., & Lin, M.-C. (in press). Communication accommodation theory: Applications in the family context. In D. O. Braithwaite & L. Baxter (Eds.), *Engaging theories in family communication.* Newbury Park, CA: Sage.

Hogg, M. A., & Tindale, R. S. (2005). Social identity, influence, and communication in small groups. In J. Harwood & H. Giles (Eds.), *Intergroup communication: Multiple perspectives* (pp. 141–164). New York: Peter Lang.

Mastro, D. (2003). A social identity approach to understanding the impact of television messages. *Communication Monographs, 70,* 98–113.

Oakes, P. J., Haslam, S. A., & Turner, J. C. (1994). *Stereotyping and social reality.* Oxford, UK: Blackwell.

Postmes, T., & Baym, N. (2005). Intergroup dimensions of the Internet. In J. Harwood & H. Giles (Eds.), *Intergroup communication: Multiple perspectives* (pp. 213–239). New York: Peter Lang.

Reicher, S. (1986). Contact, action and racialization: Some British evidence. In M. Hewstone & R. Brown (Eds.), *Contact and conflict in intergroup encounters* (pp. 152–168). Cambridge, MA: Basil Blackwell.

Soliz, J. (2004). *Shared family identity, age salience, and intergroup contact: Investigation of the grandparent-grandchild relationship.* Unpublished doctoral dissertation, University of Kansas, Lawrence, KS.

Stott, C., & Reicher, S. (1998). Crowd action as intergroup process: Introducing the police perspective. *European Journal of Social Psychology, 28,* 509–529.

Tajfel, H., & Turner, J. C. (1986). The social identity theory of intergroup behavior. In S. Worchel & W. Austin (Eds.), *Psychology of intergroup relations* (pp. 7–24). Chicago: Nelson-Hall.

Turner, J. C., Hogg, M. A., Oakes, P. J., Reicher, S., & Wetherell, M. (1987). *Rediscovering the social group: A self-categorization theory.* Cambridge, MA: Basil Blackwell.

11

Communication as Techné

Jonathan Sterne

B efore communication is intersubjective connection, coordination, ritual, meaning, culture, or anything else, communication is something that people do. At its core, communication is a special form of action. To use an antiquated phrase, it is a practical art, or rather a set of practical arts. This holds true no matter what favorite example we use for that massive and ambiguous thing we call communication: it is true in conversation, in large-scale media systems, in human-animal interaction, and in the most subtle dimensions of encounters with others. Communication is, above all else, a *techné*. In this chapter, I will outline what I mean by techné and then offer brief historical, political, and philosophical arguments for its use as a defining metaphor for communication. *Techné* is a Greek word, and it is addressed in the writings of many of the ancient Greek thinkers. To be fair, the word's connotation is somewhat ambiguous depending on whom you read and which text you choose (see, e.g., Parry, 1993). Hence, I will offer my preferred reading of the term, which is not to be mistaken with the single, historically correct definition. I want to argue about communication, not my interpretation of the ancient Greeks.

Aristotle most famously designated techné as practical art and practical knowledge. For him, techné meant both the process of producing things in the world (crafts, for instance) and the capacity or knowledge of contingency—practical knowledge—that allows and accounts for that production

---

Many thanks to Carrie Rentschler and Ted Striphas for their suggestions on this essay.

(Aristotle, 1962, Book VI, Ch. 3–4). As Heidegger wrote of this section in Aristotle's *Nicomachean Ethics,* techné "reveals whatever does not bring itself forth and does not yet lie before us, whatever can look and turn out now one way and now another" (Heidegger, 1977, p. 13). Creation and contingency are central to how we should understand techné. A simple example would be a musician's "technique," which describes the practical sense that she brings to her instrument and the actual process through which she plays it. A musician's technique encompasses both her actual movements and the practical, embodied knowledge she brings to the instrument.

Several things should be apparent from this definition and example. First, techné is embodied knowledge, not formal or logical knowledge. Techné is meant to be distinguished from abstract knowledge, which Aristotle called *epistémê.* Epistémê designates the realm of formal theory, scientific knowledge, of facts and ideas. So, to extend the musician metaphor, the ability to play a song that rocks or to perform a masterful interpretation of Bach's cello etudes is a form of techné, because it demonstrates the unfolding of a sensibility. To be sure, this sensibility is cultured. As countless ethnomusicologists have shown, the most basic ideas of "in tune" or "in rhythm" vary from culture to culture. At the same time, a musician's technique is also an irreducibly personal, embodied sense of what it means to make music. Thus, techné bridges the chasm between possibility and actuality: it indexes both what the musician actually does and what she or he might do, or even what she or he is capable of doing or willing to do. Techné refers both to action and the conditions of possibility for action.

Conversely, the ability to name from memory all the flats in the key of G-flat is a form of epistémê, as is an encyclopedic knowledge of the names and instruments of all the backup musicians who played with your favorite jazz soloist. Formal knowledge is also cultured, but it is knowledge that requires thought, memory, formal learning, action, or recollection. Epistémê has no necessary connection to what one does or can do. It is knowledge for the sake of knowledge. The object and purpose of epistémê are different from those of techné: the former is knowing about, the latter is embodied knowledge.

Techné has, in our time, given way to two terms that designate some of the most important aspects of communication: *technique* and *technology.* Both terms share with techné an ambiguity between the actual and the possible and the dual connotation of practical knowledge and practical acts. To consider communication as a technique or learned skill is uncontroversial. To use phrases like "good communicator" or "knack for getting her point across" implies that communication is an art about which people gain practical knowledge. In the domains of arts and media, this is even more clear. Language used to describe the work of a writer, an artist, a songwriter, or, for that matter, a chef, or someone who makes perfume, is often the language of skill, sense, and facility. But techné goes further than this, for it designates not only the skills of people who we might say have special talents, but rather the talents and styles of communication embodied in each person. The subtle gestures of casual conversation, the split-second decision of whether to meet a stranger's eyes on the street, the inflections of the voice—hundreds of different techniques of empathy and avoidance, closeness and distance—are in use at every moment of every day.

"One might say that arms and legs are full of numb imperatives," writes sociologist Pierre Bourdieu (1990, p. 69). He argues that social life is built up from "practical logics" that do not necessarily follow the rules of formal reason but rather have a logic of their own. For example, "a man who raises his hat in greeting is unwittingly reactivating a conventional sign inherited from the Middle Ages, when, as Panofsky reminds us, armed men used to take off their helmets to make clear their peaceful intentions" (Bourdieu, 1981, p. 305).[1] If we meet and I tip my hat as a greeting, it is not because I wish to indicate that I do not plan to kill you. It is simply out of habit, a technique of greeting. In this way, a tip of the hat exists as a sort of unthought, unconsidered "second nature." It is something people "just do." But this habit has a history and a social valence, as do all such gestures and habits. All this is to suggest that although the techné of communication is intensely personal and stylized, it is also intensely social. Scholars of interpersonal communication who examine distance and comportment in bodily action have made this point repeatedly, as has Erving Goffman (1963), who famously demonstrated that while norms and stigmas are intensely social, it is up to each individual to negotiate them effectively and creatively.

All this is well and good, but why use techné as a driving metaphor for communication in general? Techné has descriptive and political benefits for those of us who wish to develop an account of communication as a social phenomenon. Descriptively, an approach to communication as techné demands that we examine what people actually do when they are communicating—not what they *say* they are doing or what they *think* they are doing, but what they do. Here we return to Bourdieu and his notion of practical logic. In casual conversation, each gesture or turn of phrase is not consciously willed or considered. Rather, it comes out of a repertoire or sensibility developed by the people involved. If a musician had to think before each movement on an instrument, or, for that matter, if I had to think before each press of a key on this keyboard, we never would get anything done. Because the sensibility is embodied, and superficially spontaneous (that is, spontaneous after lots of practice), it does not necessarily conform to the rules of logic or the protocols of reason. In most examples of communication, the "communicative" part consists of actions taken by people or machines located in some kind of social network. The mechanical action is obviously unconscious and habitual, but so are much of people's actions. This is true whether we are talking about radio listening, movie making, or conversation. Personal action, thus, is tied inextricably to larger social sensibilities and relations; we must account for apparently spontaneous action as coming out of learned repertoires of possibility.

Indeed, it is the question of possibility that has so animated 19th- and 20th-century philosophers of interest to communication theorists. Marx's famous adage that people make history but in conditions not of their own making perfectly captures the relationship between possibility and concrete action in techné. Bourdieu's notion of *habitus,* the "nonspontaneous principle of spontaneity" (1990, p. 56), attempts to explain how apparently spontaneous action is rooted in learned, embodied social tendencies. Michel Foucault's notion of a "diagram" of social relations that makes possible the interactions in a prison, a school, or a confessional similarly partakes of Aristotle's useful ambiguity between an event and its possibility in techné (for a full discussion, see Deleuze, 1988; Foucault, 1977, 1991). Though they approach the question very differently, both Bourdieu and Foucault situate actual events within a broader terrain of conditions of possibility. To use a somewhat prosaic metaphor, they are both interested in the rules of the social game. Both sides of the language debate in linguistics also partake of the social question animated by techné. A sense of concrete action rooted in a range of embodied possibilities animates both Edward Sapir and Benjamin Lee Whorf's hypothesis that language makes possible understanding and Noam Chomsky's notion of a "generative grammar" that exists in people's minds prior to the acquisition of language (Chomsky, 2004; Sapir, 1949; Whorf, 1956). Both theories treat language as a techné, an art that produces something in the world and requires a practical sense (the debate, of course, is over the origin of that practical sense).

A concept of communication as techné also requires us to rethink the relationships we posit between bodies and technologies. Modern media are vast aggregates or assemblages of techniques, institutions, and technologies. Machines and technological systems are an extension of the logic of possibility, practical knowledge, and realized action hidden in techné because they are essentially crystallized sets of repeatable activities and relationships. Though the word *technology* has been around since the Middle Ages to refer to a treatise on practical arts, it came to mean "the practical arts, collectively" in 19th-century usage (*Oxford English Dictionary,* "technology," s.v.). Communication technologies are nothing more and nothing less than collectivized, amalgamated, and routinized techniques of communication.

Bruno Latour's famous example of the door-closer illustrates this well. Here, a whole set of social relations, practices, and assumptions are crystallized in the device to keep a door closed at the entrance to a sociology department. There are many reasons to keep a door closed: to separate inside and outside; to control passages, people, and noise; to demarcate space symbolically;

to control temperature; and so forth. There are also many ways to keep a door closed. The door-closer thus reinforces these structured tendencies and habits, even as it acts independently of people once it is built and set up, simply closing the door each time it is opened. When the door-closer works, it disappears from consciousness. Its function is forgotten. When the door-closer does not work the way it is supposed to, it has all sorts of new social significance, simply by virtue of closing the door a little too quickly (and batting passersby on the behind) or too slowly (Latour, 1988). Technologies, thus, are associated with habits and practices, sometimes crystallizing them, sometimes promoting them, and sometimes fighting them. They are structured by human practices so that they may, in turn, structure human practices. Technologies are crystallized bits of practical art and practical reason—they are techniques externalized and delegated to machines.

Often, these functions could be performed by people *or* machines. Whether we are talking about a person responsible for closing a door or a spring-loaded gadget, a door-closer controls the physical communication of bodies between a room and a hallway. Other technologies (and if you think about it, all modern technologies are really technological systems) ossify techniques of communication in other ways. On a simple level, people use cameras to see for them; telephones, microphones, and magnetic pickups to hear for them; speakers to sing, speak, and serenade for them; and electric lights to supplement their limited powers of sight. In some cases, a word encompasses both people and machines. An interesting contemporary example is *computer*. Computers were once individuals or groups of people employed to make calculations. Now the term applies to general-purpose calculating machines.

Even more complex media are basically large groups of related techniques, combined together in institutional form. The construct of television or radio as broadcasting, for instance, requires that we conceive of the production and consumption of broadcast material in certain ways. On the production and distribution end, a broadcast medium requires a massive infrastructure of institutions, people, and technologies, all of which undertake routine, repetitive action. Broadcasting is techné on a massive scale: from the skills and cultivated instincts of the engineers at the station; to the ways in which cables, switches, and satellites direct signals; to the ways in which these technologies implement corporate or national policies. On the consumption end, people employ countless techniques of listening to experience "radio," as we know it, and the same can be said for spectatorship and television. Publishing, public speaking, or recording all invoke related but different sets of techniques, relations, and institutions.

So communication as technology and communication as technique share the same root: communication as techné. I have suggested an analytical approach that sees both on a continuum. But conceiving of communication as techné also runs counter to at least one major habit of communication historians, which I call the "add technology and stir" model of communication history. Technology has not fared well in our histories of communication. The tale usually told is that before the invention of writing, communication happened as speech, inside the subject's mind and out through the subject's breath. It was ephemeral, transitory, and even magical. This "primacy of speech" thesis suggests, as did Plato in the *Phaedrus* (1961), that writing is the first true technology of communication. Indeed, a parade of communication historians have likened all other communication technologies to writing. In the primacy of speech model, we "add technology and stir" to speech to get other kinds of communication. Along with this model comes a series of laments about the alienation of modern life, the loss of community, and the decline of intersubjective recognition as humans use tools more and more to communicate with one another.

The problem here is both political and descriptive. The "add technology and stir" model is a political problem because it leads communication scholars to invoke a bizarre nostalgia, where the stark inequalities and everyday struggles for survival that characterized life in previous centuries disappears. It is not that our world today is perfect—far from it! If you are not upper-class, male, heterosexual (in many cases), able-bodied, and a member of the dominant ethnic and religious group in your region, your life chances—and the choices of what to do with your life—would have been severely diminished in any historical period prior to our own. So we should be wary of any theory or history of communication that asks us to look back to earlier periods for examples of more just, equitable, or harmonious societies.

There are additional good descriptive grounds for a model of communication with techné as its driving metaphor. Techné is at the very historical core of what it means to communicate, and, contrary to the "add technology and stir" model of communication history, techné is, in some senses, historically *prior to* the advent of human communication. If one is looking for that special something that separated our evolutionary ancestors from other animals, it would have to be humans' peculiar combination of language and tool use. Indeed, archaeologists have found evidence of painting, sculpture, and musical instruments that go "all the way back" to the origins of the human race. The earliest known sculptures, for instance, are over 35,000 years old, but archaeologists have speculated that sculpture itself goes back at least 70,000 years. If these hypotheses are correct, they trouble the model of communication that claims humans once lived in a world of communication to which technology was added. The dimensions of craft, tool, and "practical art" were there from the very beginning.

Indeed, Lewis Mumford has argued for a sense of language as techné as well. Mumford writes that there is a "vital connection between *all* physical movement and speech" (1966, p. 86, emphasis in original). Speech is one technique of the body among many. But for Mumford, spoken language also is intimately related to tool use through the process of standardization, because they followed the same historical pattern. Once satisfactory forms of tools or words were reached, there is little evidence, he says, for "wanton variation" in their form. In this way, language and tool use are part of a shared human history of techné. Communication requires both language and technology—and *both* are forms of techné.[2]

It would be unfair at this point to take the pragmatist escape from essences and say that the question of what communication *is* should be replaced with what communication *does*. But communication as a practical art—as doing—should be a central concern for us. To put it another way, communication is a philosophical and political problem, because it is a practical art through which people make, break, or maintain their worlds. We should conceive of communication as techné because the most important parts of communication are precisely the unthought second natures of technique and technology. Communication as techné highlights the two most important aspects of communication today: the widespread use of technology in conjunction with other forms of interaction and the simultaneously social and habitual forms of interaction that make up modern life. If one goal of communication scholarship is to find and describe ways to live ethically and well in large-scale and diverse societies, communication as techné may be our best path there.

Notes

1. Bourdieu's comments quoted here appear in discussions of his concept of *habitus*, which is somewhat beyond the scope of this essay. See Sterne (2003) for a longer discussion of Bourdieu and technique.

2. Students of Mumford may argue that this reading goes against the grain of his project in *Myth of the Machine*, which aims to dethrone a historical narrative of technological progress with "modern" (1960s era) technology at its apex. Perhaps, but my goal is not to celebrate modern technology, but rather to identify the shared roots of language, technique, and technology in the concept of techné.

Additional Readings

Aristotle. (1962). *Nicomachean ethics* (M. Ostwald, Trans.). Indianapolis, IN: Bobbs-Merrill.

Bourdieu, P. (1990). *The logic of practice* (R. Nice, Trans.). Stanford, CA: Stanford University Press.

Foucault, M. (1991). Questions of method (C. Gordon, Trans.). In G. Burchell, C. Gordon, & P. Miller (Eds.), *The Foucault effect: Studies in governmentality* (pp. 73–86). Chicago: University of Chicago Press.

Latour, B. (1988). Mixing humans and nonhumans together: The sociology of a door-closer. *Social Problems, 35*(1), 298–310.
Mumford, L. (1966). *The myth of the machine: Technics and human development* (Vol. 1). New York: Harcourt, Brace and World.

References

Aristotle. (1962). *Nicomachean ethics* (M. Ostwald, Trans.). Indianapolis, IN: Bobbs-Merrill.
Bourdieu, P. (1981). Men and machines. In K. Knorr-Cetina & A. V. Cicourel (Eds.), *Advances in social theory and methodology: Toward an integration of micro- and macro-sociologies* (pp. 304–317). Boston: Routledge and Kegan Paul.
Bourdieu, P. (1990). *The logic of practice* (R. Nice, Trans.). Stanford, CA: Stanford University Press.
Chomsky, N. (2004). *Language and politics* (2nd expanded ed.). Oakland, CA: AK Press.
Deleuze, G. (1988). *Foucault* (S. Hand, Trans.). Minneapolis: University of Minnesota Press.
Foucault, M. (1977). *Discipline and punish: The birth of the prison* (A. Sheridan, Trans.). New York: Vintage Books.
Foucault, M. (1991). Questions of method (C. Gordon, Trans.). In G. Burchell, C. Gordon, & P. Miller (Eds.), *The Foucault effect: Studies in governmentality* (pp. 73–86). Chicago: University of Chicago Press.
Goffman, E. (1963). *Stigma: Notes on the management of spoiled identity.* Englewood Cliffs, NJ: Prentice-Hall.
Heidegger, M. (1977). *The question concerning technology and other essays* (W. Lovitt, Trans.). New York: Harper and Row.
Latour, B. (1988). Mixing humans and nonhumans together: The sociology of a door-closer. *Social Problems, 35*(1), 298–310.
Mumford, L. (1966). *The myth of the machine: Technics and human development* (Vol. 1). New York: Harcourt, Brace and World.
Parry, R. (1993). Episteme and techne. In E. N. Zalta (Ed.), *The Stanford encyclopedia of philosophy.* Available online at http://plato.stanford.edu/archives/sum2003/entries/episteme-techne
Plato (1961). Phaedrus (R. Hackforth, Trans.). In E. Hamilton & H. Cairns (Eds.), *The collected dialogues of Plato* (pp. 475–525). Princeton, NJ: Princeton University Press.
Sapir, E. (1949). *Selected writings of Edward Sapir in language, culture and personality.* Berkeley: University of California Press.
Sterne, J. (2003). Bourdieu, technique and technology. *Cultural Studies, 17*(3/4), 367–389.
Whorf, B. L. (1956). *Language, thought and reality: Selected writings of Benjamin Lee Whorf.* Cambridge: MIT Press.

PART III

Contextualizing

12

Communication as Dialogue

Leslie A. Baxter

I n arguing for a conception of communication as dialogue, I could draw upon any of several theorists in the emerging area of dialogue studies (Anderson, Baxter, & Cissna, 2004). Instead, however, I am relying on the dialogism theory of Russian social philosopher Mikhail Bakhtin, whose works span more than a half-century beginning in 1919 (primary translated works of relevance to communication scholars include Bakhtin, 1981, 1984a, 1984b, 1986, 1990; Voloshinov, 1973). For the past decade and a half, my colleagues and I, informed by Bakhtin's dialogism, have been actively pursuing a dialogic theory of communication in the context of friendship, romantic relationships, and familial relationships (for a recent review, see Baxter, 2004). I will not present the details of that theory here but instead will address more broadly the significance of a dialogic conceptualization of communication.

For Bakhtin (1984a), the essence of dialogue is the simultaneous differentiation from, yet fusion with, another. Parties form a unity in conversation but only through maintaining two distinct voices. Because all language use is riddled with multiple voices (to be understood more generally as discourses, ideologies, perspectives, or themes), meaning-making in general can be understood as the interplay of those voices. For Bakhtin (1981, p. 272), this interplay is "a contradiction-riddled, tension-filled unity of two embattled tendencies," the centripetal (i.e., unity) and the centrifugal (i.e., difference). Contrasted against the multivocality of dialogue is the single-voicedness of monologue, and Bakhtin's life work can be understood as a critique of the monologization of the human experience that he perceived in the dominant linguistic, literary, philosophical, and political theories of his time. He was critical of efforts to reduce the unfinalizable, open, and multivocal process of meaning-making in determinate, closed, totalizing ways.

Three interrelated implications of communication as dialogue will be examined in this essay. First, I will address the significance of locating difference at the intellectual center of communication. Second, I will examine the value of creation in communication as dialogue. Third, I will address the merits of the dialogic move away from cognitively centered approaches to communication.

Locating Difference at the Center

Diversity is the ubiquitous condition of humanity, yet communication scholars partition it off, view it negatively, or ignore it completely. Like other intellectual traditions in which dialogue features prominently, Bakhtin's dialogism opens up space for communication scholars to conceive of difference in new ways. Difference is, of course, already featured prominently in the cluster of subfields in which "culture" is positioned as a key component in the study of face-to-face communication: cross-cultural communication, intercultural communication, and cultural communication. Although these subfields study culture differently, as a set they function as a marked contrast: to mark a subfield as one focused on cultural differences is to imply unmarked contrasts—that is, subfields where cultural difference is absent (e.g., the fields of interpersonal communication, organizational communication, small group communication, and so forth). At the assumptive level, then, the implication is that encounters based on (cultural) difference occupy a subset of communicative encounters rather than the whole. Difference is thus partitioned off for consideration in a particular kind of encounter.

By contrast, a dialogic perspective argues that difference (of all kinds) is basic to the human experience. All of communication, not just a subset of communicative encounters, is in the play of difference. Three qualities of language use make all communication dialogic. First, words are not originary with the speaker but are laced with the interplay of meaning-traces from prior conversations and from prior utterances within the same conversation. "Every utterance," Bakhtin (1986, p. 91) tells us, "must be regarded primarily as a response to preceding utterances . . . . Each utterance refutes, affirms, supplements, and relies on the others, presupposes them to be known, and somehow takes them into account." A range of other voices produces this quality of intertextuality in the utterance—cultural premises that are taken for granted or made explicit, the multiple meanings of words that circulate in the communal dictionary of language use, traces from past conversations of the speaker, traces from prior conversations between the participant-interlocutors, and traces from prior utterances in the same conversational encounter.

But words are not only in play with what Bakhtin calls "already spoken's"; they are in play, as well, with anticipated responses of the other, the second quality of language use that makes communication inherently dialogic:

> The word in living conversation is directly, blatantly, oriented toward a future answer-word; it provokes an answer, anticipates it and structures itself in the answer's direction. Forming itself in an atmosphere of the already spoken, the word is at the same time determined by that which has not yet been said but which is needed and in fact anticipated by the answering word. Such is the situation in any living dialogue. (Bakhtin, 1981, p. 280)

Utterances respond to anticipated reactions—a quality Bakhtin (1986, p. 95) called addressivity. The anticipated other can be fellow participant-interlocutors or what Bakhtin called the superaddressee—an "indefinite, unconcretized other" (1986, p. 95).

Third, and last, language use is also highly situated (or chronotoped, in Bakhtin's terms). Words are uttered at a particular cultural epoch by interlocutors who occupy particular social locations (Bakhtin, 1981). Individual utterances are also embedded in larger streams of enacted coherence—speech genres (Bakhtin, 1986). This "authentic environment of an utterance" (Bakhtin, 1981, p. 272) brings additional voices to bear—the systems of meaning, ideologies, and themes that are associated with cultural and social memberships and the communicative rules that accompany various talk genres. When taken together, these three qualities of language use provide the "dialogic overtones" (Bakhtin, 1986, p. 92) of utterances, and meaning emerges from the interplay of the various voice-traces.

A second partitioning off of difference is found in the literature on interpersonal conflict. In this scholarly domain, difference is reduced to incompatibility (Roloff & Soule, 2002, p. 518) and is equated with conflict—niggling ruptures of the consensual social order framed as challenges or problems to be managed or resolved through appropriate conflict management practices. Consider this classic definition by Deutsch (1973): "Conflict exists whenever incompatible activities occur . . . . An action that is incompatible with another action prevents, obstructs, interferes, injures or in some way makes the latter less likely or less effective" (p. 73). As this definition reveals, when difference is reduced to incompatibility and conflict, there is limited room to contemplate its positive potential.

From a dialogic perspective, difference is the key to growth, change, and vitality. When friends, romantic partners, and spouses have been asked by researchers to reflect on the role of difference in their lives, they are able to articulate a rather substantial list of positively valenced functions of difference, including facilitating individual growth, facilitating individual autonomy in the relationship, symbolizing that the relationship is richly textured and strong, providing a source of stimulation and change in the relationship, and enhancing communicative effectiveness through complementarity (Baxter & West, 2003; Wood, Dendy, Dordek, Germany, & Varallo, 1994). However, these positive functions are not theorized when difference can only be understood within the limiting framework of interpersonal conflict.

To be sure, the difference of dialogue is rife with tensionality. Dialogic interplay is the struggle of competing, often contradictory, voices. As Bakhtin (1981) has noted, "The word, directed toward its object, enters a dialogically agitated and tension-filled environment of alien words, value judgments and accents, weaves in and out of complex interrelationships, merges with some, recoils from others, intersects with yet a third group" (p. 276). Contrary to popular stereotype, dialogue is not a sappy, "group hug" sort of affair! In a communication-as-dialogue approach, however, tensionality is not a problem to be managed or regulated, unlike the view found in the interpersonal conflict literature. Further, although some tensionality can surface person-against-person, more typically it is the play of discursive themes with and against one another.

At least the literature on interpersonal conflict features difference prominently, even if it is conceptualized negatively. More typically, difference has been ignored in favor of the monologue of similarity. Among scholars of interpersonal communication, similarity has a long history. Few phenomena have received the research attention devoted to similarity, particularly its role in interpersonal attraction and relationship formation and its role in social influence. However, from a dialogic perspective, similarity positions communication as a profoundly reproductive enterprise: How are self and other reproduced in one another? Reproduction closes off the generative, or productive, capacity of difference. As Bakhtin has indicated, "What do I gain by having the other fuse with me? He will know and see but what I know and see, he will but repeat within himself the tragic dimension of my life. Let him rather stay on the outside vantage point, and he can thus enrich essentially the event of my life" (as quoted in Todorov, 1984, p. 108). A generative approach to difference segues to the second implication I will examine: the centrality of creation in a dialogic conception of communication.

Communication as Creation

The second advantage of a dialogic conception of communication is to open up an alternative vision of what communication does. The traditional, and still dominant, view of communication is variously referred to as a transmission, representational, or informational model of communication (Craig, 1999). This traditional conception positions communication as a conduit through which a variety of antecedent psychological and sociological factors are merely played out. From the traditional view, communication functions to express the self's attitudes and beliefs, to transmit those to others so that the self can be understood, and to influence others' attitudes, beliefs, and actions so that they are conformable to those of the self. In short, communication is conceptualized as an instrumental activity of replication.

By contrast, a dialogic perspective empowers communication to create, or construct, the social world, including self, other, and the relationship between them. A conduit is situated in a social world already accepted as given, whereas a generative view asks how communication constructs that social world. As Bakhtin (1986, pp. 118–119) has expressed, "An utterance is never just a reflection or an expression of something already existing outside it that is given and final. It always creates something that never existed before, something absolutely new and unrepeatable." Of course, several other constitutive conceptions of communication share the dialogic focus on creation (see Craig, 1999, for a discussion). The unique contribution of a dialogic view is an articulation of the generative mechanism for the meaning-making process: the interplay of different, often opposing, voices.

The power of communication to create is best illustrated in Bakhtin's (1990) discussion of how self is created through interaction with a different other. "The very capacity to have consciousness is based on otherness," Bakhtin (p. 18) argued. Interlocutors always have a unique excess of seeing with respect to one another, which Bakhtin described thusly:

> At each given moment, regardless of the position and the proximity to me of this other human being whom I am contemplating, I shall always see and know something that he, from his place outside and over against me, cannot see himself: parts of his body that are inaccessible to his own gaze . . . , the world behind his back, and a whole series of objects and relations, which in any of our mutual relations are accessible to me but not to him. (p. 23)

Selves, then, are created by persons sharing their unique excesses of seeing with one another. But excesses of seeing are themselves fluid through interaction with another. One important implication of this creation process is that the self is fluid and dynamic, always changing and growing dependent on the other with whom it comes in contact and the unfolding of conversation.

Just as self is forged through interplay with a different other, so all of meaning-making is created from the play of different voices. From a dialogic perspective, the emphasis shifts from transmission to creation, from representation of already-mades to the making of meaning. To be sure, in individualistic U.S. society, we have vocabularies, communicative habits, and taken-for-granted cultural premises that refer to various internal mental states and objectified things and events in the world "out there." We talk as if the self is a preformed container of dispositions, feelings, and memories; and we talk as if the world consists of objects, things, events, and processes that are separate from, yet potentially controlled by, us. These vocabularies, habits, and premises are essential discursive devices through which we organize and anchor the indeterminate, continuous flow of social experience. But they are constructions nonetheless. Different speech communities have different assumptions, habits, and vocabularies about self and the world, and those are constructions as well.

The shift from transmission to creation holds the potential to reposition communication studies in the intellectual landscape. As a conduit, communication is positioned as the handmaid of other masters—including psychological desires and beliefs, social institutions, and social memberships. It is these other masters that have determinative value in shaping outcomes for individuals, groups, and societies. However, when we adopt a constitutive view, desires and beliefs, institutions, and group identities are the result of, not the cause of, communication. Within the traditional framework of transmission, communication efficacy is judged against the standard of fidelity: was the "real state of affairs" represented accurately? Within a dialogic framework of creation, communication efficacy is judged by the quality of its creations: what social realities are constructed and what alternative possibilities for creation have been ignored?

Given the dialogic focus on the emergent construction of self, it comes as no surprise that a conception of communication as a cognitive enterprise of autonomous individuals is challenged from a communication-as-dialogue perspective.

From Individual Cognition to the Social "Between"

The Enlightenment gave birth to many modernist ideas, perhaps the most influential of which is a view of the individual as "a coherent, integrated, singular entity whose clear-cut boundaries define its limits and separate it from other similarly bounded entities" (Sampson, 1993, p. 17). As noted above, this individual-as-monologue is transformed if we undertake a conceptual move to the individual-as-dialogue. But the individual-as-monologue has such a powerful grip on our study and understanding of communication that it is worth more detailed examination in its own right. The individual-as-monologue has resulted in the overpsychologizing of communication studies (Cronen, 1998). Let me be clear: I am not engaging in psychology bashing; psychology provides a strong disciplinary mooring for many interesting and important questions. As communication scholars, however, we ought to be interested first and foremost in understanding communication rather than the individual mind. However, as I peruse the intellectual landscape of interpersonal communication in particular, I see a project centered in social psychology, where the individual unit of analysis reigns supreme with its emphasis on individual difference variables and cognitive processes. I am not mounting the oft-made critique that communication scholars study self-reports on communication rather than communication practices per se (although such a critique is certainly warranted and supportive of my claim that the individual mind occupies the center of interpersonal communication). I am instead mounting a more basic critique: our view of communication centers on the individual mind. A dialogic view moves the center from individual mind to the "between"—the joint communicative practices of interlocutors.

The individual mind seeps into communication scholarship in many ways. In general, however, meaning-making is located in the individual mind; individuals make sense of one another's communicative messages and react to those based on their prior states of mind (e.g., their cognitive expectations, mental models, and feeling states). The motivations and goals of the individual usher in cognitive plans, which are assembled strategically to culminate in the production of linguistic and nonverbal actions. Thus, whether processing another's messages or producing one's own messages, the individual mind is positioned as the driver of the communication engine.

From a dialogic perspective, by contrast, the conception of mind as an "internal sovereign territory" (Bakhtin, 1984a, p. 311) is itself a social construction. To the extent that dialogic scholars are interested in the individual mind, their focus is that of understanding how psychological and mental states are discursively constructed (e.g., Sampson, 1993; Shotter, 1993). As Bakhtin (writing as Voloshinov, 1973) has stated it, "It is not experience that organizes expression, but the other way around—expression organizes experience. Expression is what first gives experience its form and specificity, or direction" (p. 85).

Because meaning-making is emergent—creative and unfinalizable—there is limited utility from a dialogic perspective in emphasizing individual goals and plans, for they inevitably will be aborted even if they existed prior to an interaction. Truer to the spirit of dialogism, however, is a focus on how goals are themselves jointly constructed during interaction (for an interesting empirical example, see Hopper & Drummond, 1990).

A dialogic perspective moves from the individual mind to the interaction between interlocutors. However, as noted above, utterances are intertextual. An analysis of meaning-making of necessity must consider the multiple, often opposing, voices that circulate with and against one another in uttered talk, including but not limited to the embodied voices of the participant-interlocutors.

In this essay, I have advanced three arguments that have been important in bringing me to a conception of communication as dialogue. The interplay of differences is at the heart of meaning-making. This interplay constructs the social world, rather than transmitting information about an already-given world. Meaning-making is accomplished in multivocal utterances between interlocutors, rather than in the minds and actions of sovereign individuals.

Additional Readings

Anderson, R., Baxter, L. A., & Cissna, K. C. (Eds.). (2004). *Dialogue: Theorizing difference in communication studies*. Thousand Oaks, CA: Sage.

Baxter, L. A. (2004). Distinguished scholar article: Relationships as dialogues. *Personal Relationships, 11,* 1–22.

Baxter, L. A. (in press). Mikhail Bakhtin and the philosophy of dialogism. In P. Arneson (Ed.), *Perspectives on philosophy of communication*. West Lafayette, IN: Purdue University Press.

Holquist, M. (2002). *Dialogism* (2nd ed.). New York: Routledge.

Sampson, E. E. (1993). *Celebrating the other: A dialogic account of human nature*. San Francisco: Westview.

References

Anderson, R., Baxter, L. A., & Cissna, K. C. (Eds.). (2004). *Dialogue: Theorizing difference in communication studies*. Thousand Oaks, CA: Sage.

Bakhtin, M. M. (1981). *The dialogic imagination: Four essays by M. M. Bakhtin* (M. Holquist, Ed.; C. Emerson & M. Holquist, Trans.). Austin: University of Texas Press.

Bakhtin, M. M. (1984a). *Problems of Dostoevsky's poetics* (C. Emerson, Ed. & Trans.). Minneapolis: University of Minnesota Press.

Bakhtin, M. M. (1984b). *Rabelais and his world* (H. Iswolsky, Trans.). Bloomington: Indiana University Press.

Bakhtin, M. M. (1986). *Speech genres and other late essays* (C. Emerson & M. Holquist, Eds.; V. McGee, Trans.). Austin: University of Texas Press.

Bakhtin, M. M. (1990). *Art and answerability: Early philosophical essays by M. M. Bakhtin* (M. Holquist & V. Liapunov, Eds.; V. Liapunov & K. Brostrom, Trans.). Austin: University of Texas Press.

Baxter, L. A. (2004). Distinguished scholar article: Relationships as dialogues. *Personal Relationships, 11*, 1–22.

Baxter, L. A., & West, L. (2003). Couple perceptions of their similarities and differences: A dialectical analysis. *Journal of Social and Personal Relationships, 20*, 491–514.

Craig, R. T. (1999). Communication theory as a field. *Communication Theory, 9*, 119–161.

Cronen, V. E. (1998). Communication theory for the twenty-first century: Cleaning up the wreckage of the psychology project. In J. S. Trent (Ed.), *Communication: Views from the helm for the 21st century* (pp. 18–38). Boston: Allyn & Bacon.

Deutsch, M. (1973). *The resolution of conflict: Constructive and destructive processes*. New Haven, CT: Yale University Press.

Hopper, R. L., & Drummond, K. (1990). Emergent goals at a relational turning point: The case of Gordon and Denise. *Journal of Language and Social Psychology, 9*, 39–66.

Roloff, M. E., & Soule, K. P. (2002). Interpersonal conflict: A review. In M. L. Knapp & J. A. Daly (Eds.), *Handbook of interpersonal communication* (3rd ed., pp. 475–528). Thousand Oaks, CA: Sage.

Sampson, E. E. (1993). *Celebrating the other: A dialogic account of human nature*. San Francisco: Westview.

Shotter, J. (1993). *Cultural politics of everyday life*. Toronto, Canada: University of Toronto Press.

Todorov, T. (1984). *Mikhail Bakhtin: The dialogical principle* (W. Godzich, Trans.). Minneapolis: University of Minnesota Press.

Voloshinov, V. N. (1973). *Marxism and the philosophy of language* (L. Matejks & I. R. Titunik, Trans.). Cambridge, MA: Harvard University Press.

Wood, J. T., Dendy, L. L., Dordek, E., Germany, M., & Varallo, S. M. (1994). Dialectic of difference: A thematic analysis of intimates' meanings for differences. In K. Carter & M. Prisnell (Eds.), *Interpretive approaches to interpersonal communication* (pp. 115–136). New York: SUNY Press.

13

Communication as Autoethnography

Arthur P. Bochner and Carolyn S. Ellis

Setting: Wrap-around deck of a white pine log cabin recently built on a 3,400-foot, western-facing ridge of Cowee Mountain in rural North Carolina.

Characters:

Art, a 6-foot, bearded, graying, 58-year-old professor

Carolyn, a 5-foot 5-inch, blondish, 53-year-old sociologist and communication professor

Jim, a local neighbor, who teaches Art and Carolyn the values and ways of mountain culture

Buddha, a 6-month-old, 8-pound, mostly white, rat terrier; energetic, spirited, and playful, much tougher and more domineering than she looks

Sunya, an 8-year-old, 60-pound, tricolor Australian Shepherd; guardian of the family, sweet and gentle, shy though protective of her herd

Scene: Art and Carolyn stare at the clouds moving in over the mountain as they eat breakfast cereal with blackberries they picked the night before. They drink strong, but mostly decaffeinated, coffee. At a loss without a *New York Times* to read over breakfast, their conversation turns to work.

Art: I have an idea about how to do that article Greg Shepherd wrote to us about.

Carolyn: The one for the book on communication theory? [Art nods.] Tell me.

Art: Greg, Jeff, and Ted want each author to take a different stance on communication theory.

Carolyn: And ours is communication as autoethnography, right?

Art: [Nods.] It would be a lot simpler to talk about autoethnography as communication.

Carolyn: That's true. The autoethnographer is first and foremost a communicator and a storyteller. Instead of talking *about* communication, autoethnography shows people in the process of using communication to achieve an understanding of their lives and their circumstances.

Art: And the circumstances usually are ones in which they have to make choices that are difficult. Autoethnography depicts people struggling to overcome adversity—you know, going through bad times. In life, we often have to make choices in difficult and uncertain situations. At these times, we feel the tug of obligation and responsibility. Autoethnographies show people in the process of figuring out what to do, how to live, and the meaning of their struggles. That's why I consider autoethnography an ethical practice. People want to do the right thing, the sensible and helpful thing.

Carolyn: That suggests a good question to ask about communication theory. How does it help people get through bad times? There is a caregiving function to communication as autoethnography. That's why some writers refer to autoethnographic stories as gifts. They can nourish you on occasions when you need something other than food to keep you going.

Art: I like how you put it in *Final Negotiations*[1]—personal stories offer readers companionship when they desperately need it. Maybe not *now*, but everyone's time surely will come.

Carolyn: I'm glad you remembered that. Maybe we can use it in our chapter.

Art: We'd better get writing. Greg, Jeff, and Ted want something from us pretty soon. [Art and Carolyn put their empty cereal bowls on the floor. Buddha jumps off Carolyn's lap, and she and Sunya lap up the remaining milk.]

Carolyn: Let's get back to the question of how communication can be understood as autoethnographic. It may confuse readers if we put too much emphasis on how autoethnography is communicative.

Art: True enough. I just wanted to make the point that too much of communication theory is not communicative. It doesn't invite readers into a conversation; it isn't accessible to ordinary people who haven't mastered the jargon; it is *about* communication but it does not *show* or *enact* communication as a living, breathing, active process.

Carolyn: Yes. I understand what you're saying—that autoethnography is dyadic, not monadic. It does not seek to be received by the other as much as it seeks to be *with* the other. But for this book, our topic is how communication is autoethnographic.

Art: Sorry I got carried away again. I wasn't trying to change the subject, though I guess it looked that way. Okay, then, let's take up the issue of communication as autoethnography. I think a good place to start is with the section on defining autoethnography that you wrote for our chapter that was published in *The Handbook of Qualitative Research.*[2] Do you remember how you said it there?

Carolyn: I emphasized the connection in autoethnography between the personal and the cultural. Is that what you mean?

Art: That's a good place to start because we want to emphasize how communication itself is usually an expression of both the personal *and* the cultural. The next step would be to define autoethnography.

Carolyn: Well, if you take apart the term, *auto-ethno-graphy,* you get *auto* meaning *self; ethno* meaning *culture*(s) or *people*(s); and *graphy* meaning a *representation, description,* or *showing.*

Art: And if you look at communicative acts as expressions of self and culture, it becomes clear that communication has an autoethnographic dimension. As R. D. Laing[3] suggested in *Self and Others,* our communicative acts always embody projections of the self, however unconscious they may be.

Carolyn: And, they are expressions of culture as well. Culture is both outside and inside us. Critical ethnographers like to say that culture is a complex circuit of production and mediation. Thus it becomes impossible to say where self ends and culture begins.

Art: Or where culture ends and self begins.

Carolyn: So it's not at all difficult to see how communication can be considered autoethnography. All of our communicative acts are expressions or representations of the meeting place of self and culture, of what is inside us and can be made visible to outsiders, and what originates outside us yet eventually circulates within us.

Art: In the world of communication, the distinction between the personal and the cultural becomes blurred. Most of our communicative acts express the personal and the cultural, the particular and the general, the unique and the universal. When we act and talk, we express both our subjectivity and our cultural socialization. . . . [Just then Jim, a neighbor, drives up in his red Toyota pickup. Carolyn and Art go out to greet him.]

Jim: Want some beans and squash from our garden?

Carolyn: [Her eyes widen and hands reach out.] Sure. Hey, thanks.

Art: Thanks. [Art follows Carolyn's lead and watches the southern ritual of gift giving and receiving take place.]

Jim: We've got more than we can eat. And Joy [his wife] has already put up over one hundred cans of beans. We're happy to share.

Carolyn: Green beans are my favorite. I used to love them fresh out of the garden when I was growing up in Virginia. We'll have a good dinner tonight.

Jim: A little fatback and they'll be just right.

Carolyn: You're not kidding. Can I help you pick tomorrow?

Jim: No need, but if you want, come on down. [Jim drives off, waving, and Carolyn and Art return to the deck.]

Carolyn: Where were we before Jim drove up?

Art: We were just about ready to tackle the heart of autoethnography. Once we understand that communication embodies both the personal and the cultural, then we legitimate the need to show how individuals use communication personally to cope with difficult moments in their lives. This brings up the intricate connections among experiences, meanings, and language. So much of life—each person's life—is a quest or struggle to make sense of experience, grasp what personal experiences mean, and express those meanings to one's self as well as to others. Writers, such as Marcel[4], may be right to point out that one's life is essentially ungraspable, but as humans we seem compelled to make sense of our lives, to grasp the ungraspable.

Carolyn: That's a poetic way of expressing it.

Art: I'm not a poet but I do think of autoethnography as poetic insofar as it represents how we use communication to attach meanings and values to experience, to bring experiences to language and to life.

Carolyn: I like that a lot. We breathe life into our experiences by telling autoethnographic stories that give meaning to them. [She pauses in apparent deep thought, then continues.] Does this focus set us apart from the mainstream of communication theory?

Art: Certainly our goals are different. In mainstream communication theory, emphasis is on the scientific dimensions of communication, such as the ways we use communication to reduce uncertainty and to make everyday interactions more routine and predictable. But when we move to the realm of human meanings, we're not looking at communicating people as scientists. We're looking at them as poets and storytellers. The experiences that concern us usually are those beyond the clutch of cause and effect.

Carolyn: Greg, Jeff, and Ted suggested that authors stipulate a metaphor through which they understand communication. Ours would be communication as poetic. Meanings aren't given; we have to make meaning or draw meaning from experiences—that's the poetic dimension of experience.

Art: Mark Freeman[5] says that experiences have "untold potentials of meaning." In a sense, meanings are always unsettled and revisable. When we go through epiphanies or crises in our lives, we can find ourselves in chaos because we don't know where we are heading, we don't know the plot, and we don't have a story of how things will turn out.

Carolyn: At those moments, we become especially aware of the poetic quality of experience. We feel a need to understand what's happening to us, to gain clarity, to be able to reveal and articulate.

Art: They are also the moments we become aware of the inadequacy of language. Yet language is all we have. It's our only means of satisfying our drive for continuity.

Carolyn: And this need for a sense of continuity makes us aware of time. I think time is one of the least understand and most important qualities associated with language, experience, and communication. The difficulties of fitting language to experience bring out the temporal demands of narration. You called your narrative about the crisis of meaning you felt after your father's death "It's about time . . . ".[6] Weren't you trying to show how autoethnographic storytelling synthesizes the three orders of time? How past, present, and future merge?

Art: My goal was to show how we remake the past in the present in order to move life forward. We do this through communicative acts of self-creation. I wanted to show the dialectic in autoethnography between the life and the story across time. I like how Adrienne Rich[7] put it, "The story of our lives becomes our lives." Of course, I was demonstrating how important this whole process is when one feels as if life is falling apart. How does one make it come together again through personal narrative?

Carolyn: I hadn't thought of this before, but the challenge offered by the drive toward coherence makes each of us a theorist. You can say that experience doesn't speak, that meanings don't inhere in experiences, and that we have to find words that give sense to or make sense of our experience. But the danger is that you end up implying a larger gulf between experience and narrative than actually exists. In the world of everyday life, experience and narrative are inextricably connected. We're continually working through, digging beneath the surface of experiences, mulling them over.

Art: You mean theorizing them.

Carolyn: [Nods.] The autoethnographer's story theorizes personal experience. And that theorizing is both personal and cultural.

Art: What does that mean?

Carolyn: It means that one's personal experiences extend to a larger social and cultural context. We all draw our meanings to some extent from the cultural context in which we are embedded.

Art: So what you're saying is that culture circulates through all of us, right?

Carolyn: Yes. [Pause.] But more than that. Culture makes certain meanings available or accessible to us, for example, through music, television, or film, which shape the meanings we attach to love, romance, intimacy, and sexuality.

Art: In this sense, personal meanings reflect the canonical stories that circulate in one's society.

Carolyn: Yes, and a lot of the meanings and values we think we choose ourselves are really chosen for us, not by us.

Art: Though not all of our meanings are determined by culture. People's stories often deviate from the canonical.

Carolyn: [Nods.] In the process of working through one's experiences, one also moves inward, to the place of the vulnerable, subjective, emotional self, a self who is moved by but also may resist or move away from conventional, cultural meanings.

Art: Culture is not completely deterministic of our meanings. Is that what you mean?

Carolyn: That's it. Humans have a dazzling capacity to reform or reframe the meaning of their actions. We do not blindly succumb to all of our culture's meanings or stories. A lot of autoethnography shows people struggling to resist or revise meanings that are not of their own making. [Carolyn notices Art drifting off in thought.] What are you thinking?

Art: [Nods.] I was just thinking about your use of the term *theorizing*. If we buy into this use of theory, then we breach the traditional distinction between theories and stories. Sense-making involves turning experiences into stories that theorize experience. The auto-ethnographer theorizes experience as a storyteller. The story is a theory.

Carolyn: Isn't that what we mean when we say a story has a plot?

Art: Yes, of course. There has to be a moral to the story.

Carolyn: That's one of the things I find most difficult about teaching autoethnography.

Art: Say more.

Carolyn: Students mistake experience for story. They write an account that takes the form of a chronicle—this happened, then this happened, then this. They don't understand that they have to search for the story in their experience. They simply report the details of what happened to them. They don't realize that they need to be inquiring, digging, mucking around in the details in order to produce something more than a chronicle—some drama, insight, or a fresh discovery.

Art: Such as a larger social pattern.

Carolyn: Sometimes that will be the outcome, but critics of autoethnography miss the point when they complain that a story is not useful unless it reveals universal patterns.

Art: They want to hearken back to the positivist, empiricist model of knowledge production. They don't grasp how telling stories functions as an act of caring, of generosity, witnessing, becoming . . .

Carolyn: Or making experience available for others to witness, encounter, and engage.

Art: I like how Arthur Frank[8] puts it, that "the truth of stories is not only what *was* experienced, but equally what *becomes* experience in the telling and its reception."

Carolyn: That reminds me of when we first started our collaborations and we emphasized the goal of creating an experience of the experience. The goal was to lift the reader into the experience. When I work with students, I tell them I want their stories to feel immediate.

Art: Usually I want the reader or listener to identify or empathize with the storyteller, which is similar to what we want when we tell stories to our friends in everyday life.

Carolyn: Yes, which brings us back to our earlier discussion about connections between the writer and the reader. A well-told story helps others see and *feel* the truth in the story. The readers or listeners go through an experience of their own by virtue of witnessing the story, as if the events were happening to them.

Art: Feel the truth. That's a wonderful way of expressing narrative truth. A lot of theorists talk about knowing or discovering the truth. Is *feeling the truth* the same thing?

Carolyn: Maybe truth isn't the right word. Language fails us again! I mean it doesn't make a lot of sense to talk about true or false experiences. An experience might *feel* good or *feel* bad. But there's really no such thing as a false experience.

Art: So autoethnographies aren't about knowledge, at least not propositional knowledge. Michael Jackson's[9] distinction is useful here. He says "we need to replace our craving to know how to know with a desire to know how to live," which we talked about in the beginning of this conversation.

Carolyn: I like that. In autoethnography, we see people enacting the process of learning how to live, struggling to make sense of their lives and their losses, healing their wounds, trying to move on from and survive the unnerving blows of fate to which all of us are vulnerable.

Art: And that's the function of much of interpersonal communication—to create meaning, to heal wounds, to recover from loss, to make sense of our lives. Thus we've come full circle back to communication as autoethnography.

Carolyn: Now I think it would work to circle the conversation back to the issue of communication as autoethnography. This would be a good place to give a brief synopsis of our perspective.

Art: The way I understand it, this book is about multiple perspectives and standpoints. Our standpoint is communication as autoethnography. The metaphor we emphasize is communication, and life itself, as poetic because the struggle to find language that is adequate to experience makes poets (and autoethnographers) of all of us. I think most of our readers will understand that, don't you?

Carolyn: I think so. I like the contrast between humans as scientists and humans as poets. This should give students something to think and talk about. All of us suffer loss sooner or later, and our capacity to make sense of and to work through pain is the foundation for rebuilding a life that has been shattered by loss.

Art: Your reference to pain and loss is interesting. We don't usually equate knowledge and research with pain and suffering.

Carolyn: Good researchers often use the source of pain in their lives as a starting point for their work. Besides, being an intellectual doesn't make you immune from pain.

Art: [Laughs.] Or emotion. I certainly have learned that in my life.

Carolyn: Me, too! But, too often, intellectuals turn themselves into talking heads cut off from everything below the shoulders, don't they? Emotions seem to frighten them. They're against feeling, against what is personal.

Art: Of course I agree, though I think we have to be careful about how we generalize about intellectuals. It's probably enough to say that autoethnography privileges the heart, the emotions, and the moral center of lived experience.

Carolyn: Good point. Ruth Behar[10] says research that doesn't break your heart isn't worth doing. And that's something everyone needs to think about. Is what I'm doing worthwhile? Does it help anyone?

Art: At my age, I worry a lot about how meaningful the work I do can be. The canonical orientation to communication theory emphasizes controlling and predicting. But Michael Jackson's point about knowing how to live underscores the importance of caring and empathy. There is no good reason to prefer controlling to caring. Instead of constantly asking, how is that true, Jackson thinks we should ask, how is it useful?

Carolyn: Again we come back to the whole issue of connection between storytellers and story listeners or readers. One of the main uses of autoethnography is to allow another person's world of experience to inspire reflection on your own. The best autoethnographies have this inspirational quality. You recontextualize what you already know about your own life in light of your encounter with someone else's life or culture.

Art: Maybe another thing that scares people about autoethnography is the kinds of experiences we ask people to reflect on. Often we focus attention on experiences that normally are shrouded in secrecy—events people are afraid or ashamed to tell about such as illness, family trauma, incest, domestic abuse, abortion, and addiction.

Carolyn: It's not just that autoethnographies depict the suffering and hurt associated with stigmatized identities, but it's also because the good stories, the really good ones, grab us by the collar and demand that we listen and that we feel. Dorothy Allison[11] says you should take your readers by the throat, break their hearts, and heal them again.

Art: Readers can't just sit back and be spectators. They are thrust into scenes that invite them to feel, care, and desire.

Carolyn: Some writers refer to these stories as close to the bone. Laurie Stone[12] says they are a source of erotic knowledge. They arouse our senses and desires and help us breach divisions between the head and the heart.

Art: Knowledge as caring, as coping, as empathic, and now as erotic. This certainly changes the aims of communication theory from what I was taught and what I taught my students for many years.

Carolyn: The times they are a-changin'. Class, race, ethnicity, disability, sexual orientation—a lot of these issues were bypassed in traditional communication theory. But if the study of communication is to have an ethical center, we can't avoid these topics. It would be dangerous and wrong to go on imagining that people don't live, feel, and suffer under conditions of inequality that make certain experiences almost unspeakable. Our ethical mandate as communication theorists and teachers is to find ways to talk about, care about, and empower suffering people.

Art: At the very least, communication theory should help us devictimize and destigmatize people and experiences on the margins by providing opportunities to bear witness to autoethnographic stories and other narratives that function as a source of empowerment and a form of resistance to the domination and authority of canonical stories.

Carolyn: That's asking for a lot of change in how we look at communication theory, but I'm all for it. Now I'm ready for a hike and the dogs are ready, too. [Carolyn laces her hiking shoes, and the dogs bounce up and down on cue.] But I almost forgot—you said you had an idea about how to do the article for Greg and his coeditors. What was your idea?

Art: [Chuckling.] Ah, guess we never got to that, did we? I thought we'd just turn on a tape recorder and have a conversation like we did in "Talking Over Ethnography."[13]

Carolyn: [Smiling and kissing Buddha who climbs up her chest, Carolyn reveals a tape-recorder that has been running throughout their conversation.] You must be kidding. A conversation, not an essay? That'll never work!

Notes

1. Ellis, C. (1995). *Final negotiations: A story of love, loss, and chronic illness.* Philadelphia: Temple University Press.

2. Ellis, C., & Bochner, A. (2000). Autoethnography, personal narrative, reflexivity: Researcher as subject. In N. Denzin & Y. Lincoln (Eds.), *Handbook of qualitative research* (2nd ed., pp. 733–768). Thousand Oaks, CA: Sage.

3. Laing, R. D. (1971). *Self and others.* New York: Penguin Books.

4. Marcel, G. (1950). *The mystery of being: Vol. 1. Reflection and mystery.* Chicago: Henry Regnery.

5. Freeman, M. (1998). Experience, narrative, and the relationship between them. *Narrative Inquiry, 8,* 455–466.

6. Bochner, A. (1997). It's about time: Narrative and the divided self. *Qualitative Inquiry, 3,* 418–438.

7. Rich, A. (1978). *On lies, secrets, and silence: Selected prose 1966–1978.* New York: Norton.

8. Frank, A. (1997). *The wounded storyteller: Body, illness, and ethics.* Chicago: University of Chicago Press.

9. Jackson, M. (1995). *At home in the world.* Durham, NC: Duke University Press.

10. Behar, R. (1996). The *vulnerable observer: Anthropology that breaks your heart.* Boston: Beacon Press.

11. Allison, D. (1995). *Two or three things I know for sure.* New York: Penguin.

12. Stone, L. (1997). Introduction: Recalled to life. In L. Stone (Ed.), *Close to the bone: Memoirs of hurt, rage, and desire* (pp. xi–xxvii). New York: Grove Press.

13. Bochner, A., & Ellis, C. (1996). Talking over ethnography. In C. Ellis & A. Bochner (Eds.), *Composing ethnography: Alternative forms of qualitative writing* (pp. 13–45). Walnut Creek, CA: AltaMira.

Additional Readings

Behar, R. (1996). *The vulnerable observer: Anthropology that breaks your heart.* Boston: Beacon Press.

Bochner, A. (2001). Narrative's virtues. *Qualitative Inquiry, 7,* 131–157.

Ellis, C. (2004). *The ethnographic I: A methodological novel about autoethnography.* Walnut Creek, CA: AltaMira.

Ellis, C., & Bochner, A. (2000). Autoethnography, personal narrative, reflexivity: Researcher as subject. In N. Denzin & Y. Lincoln (Eds.), *Handbook of qualitative research* (2nd ed., pp. 733–768). Thousand Oaks, CA: Sage.

Goodall, H. L. (2000). *Writing the new ethnography.* Walnut Creek, CA: AltaMira.

14

Communication as Storytelling

Eric E. Peterson and Kristin M. Langellier

L et us begin with a brief story.[1]

The title of this essay reminds me of the first writing assignment I received in a communication theory course taught by Richard Lanigan. The assignment asked for a theoretical explanation for one of eight metaphors: language is speech, speech is language, language is communication, communication is language, communication is speech, speech is communication, consciousness is communication, or communication is consciousness. At the time, I was a student of performance with little background in communication studies. I was confounded by this initiation into communication theory. The more I worked on the assignment, the more perplexing it became. I could recognize individual words: nouns that named foundational concepts and the verb is that asserted a relationship of inclusion. While I could make sense out of individual metaphors, they no longer seemed so sensible when considered in combination. Instead of eight metaphors, I discovered four reversible pairs of relations, and potential tautologies, with no explicit standards for selecting one direction rather than another. Should I choose language is speech or speech is language? Furthermore, by combining alternate metaphors, I could create a proposition that had the appearance of a theoretical explanation— for example, language is speech is communication is consciousness—but, again, no criteria for selecting particular elements and ordering them in a meaningful series. Worse and worse. What was I to do?

In order to participate in storytelling, even in this fragment of a story, storytellers and audiences draw upon and mobilize a variety of discursive resources and conventions. They take these resources and conventions from within a particular social and material context in order to turn back upon the world and communicate about it. Participants draw upon their knowledge of the English language and of how stories work, they draw upon feelings of confusion with classroom writing assignments, they make or take time to read the story and reflect on it, they imagine and recall similar experiences. Such participation in storytelling is common, mundane, ordinary.

In approaching storytelling as a mundane and common experience, we take a perspective that runs counter to more traditional views of storytelling as a heightened, aesthetic, or parasitic form of communication that is set off from ordinary communication and daily life. These traditional views define storytelling as a specialized subset of a larger range of communication acts. Nor do we follow more contemporary views that would define storytelling as a paradigm or art set in opposition to social science or positivism. In this essay, we argue that storytelling is not derivative of everyday communication nor is it opposed to it; instead, what we think of as "ordinary" communication draws upon and emerges from the human capability for storytelling. Storytelling is the human capacity for making something (a story) out of the practice of communication (listening and telling). Storytelling, to use the classical Greek concepts, combines *poeisis* and *praxis*. In short, as the title of the essay suggests, we argue for communication as storytelling.

The argument for communication as storytelling incorporates semiotic and phenomenological research on storytelling (Langellier & Peterson, 2004), communication (Lanigan, 1992, 2000), and especially Roman Jakobson's (1960, 1971, 1976) contributions to communication theory. These researchers theorize communication from a tradition of human sciences that rigorously interrogates the conscious experience of communication as embodied and practiced. Jakobson is a key figure in this tradition because of his distinction between information and communication theory as it relates to poetics. In his critique of approaches to poetics, Jakobson rejects the supposed separation of "casual" forms of everyday communication from the "noncasual" forms of communication found in poetry. The aesthetic, purposeful, and stylized features of communication are not limited to poetry or storytelling, but can be found in all forms of communication. Jakobson (1976) writes that "every verbal act in a certain sense stylizes and transforms the event it depicts. How it does so is determined by its slant, its emotional content, the audience it is addressed to, the preliminary 'censorship' it undergoes, the supply of ready-made patterns it draws from" (p. 170). The simile advocated here—communication as storytelling—suggests the pervasive ambiguity which stylizes communication (in the listening and telling) and transforms it (into a story).

One of Jakobson's goals is to explicate the mutability and autonomy of the poetic function in communication. He locates the poetic as one of six functions based in six corresponding elements or constitutive factors of communication. In theory construction terms, his description of elements and functions specifies the necessary and sufficient conditions for human communication.[2] Hence, the description of elements and functions should not be reduced to parts of a model as is often the case in information theory–based depictions of communication. Instead, Jakobson focuses on how communication is given in consciousness (eidetic) as the conduct of embodied discourse (empirical) and not merely as decontextualized and disembodied data.

Jakobson (1960) describes the six elements as follows:

> The ADDRESSER sends a MESSAGE to the ADDRESSEE. To be operative the message requires a CONTEXT referred to ("referent" in another, somewhat ambiguous, nomenclature), seizable by the addressee, and either verbal or capable of being verbalized; a CODE fully, or at least partially, common to the addresser and addressee (or in other words, to the encoder and decoder of the message); and finally, a CONTACT, a physical channel and psychological connection between the addresser and addressee, enabling both of them to enter and stay in communication. (p. 353, emphasis in original)

While each element can be differentiated from the others, Jakobson (1976) argues that the orientation toward the message—the poetic function—"necessarily transforms the other elements and determines with them the nature of the whole" (p. 174). As a way of developing the significance of the poetic in Jakobson's theory of communication, we describe each of these six elements and their corresponding functions.

With the opening sentence of this essay, "Let us begin with a brief story," we are already caught up in discourse that establishes a storyteller and an audience for a story. The focus on the storyteller or addresser emphasizes the *emotive* function of communication. The "I" emerges from and is positioned by the discourse as the person who tells the story. The storyteller encodes or expresses a story by taking the experience of a writing assignment and putting it into words with a particular slant, or emotional content. The "I" of the present act of storytelling recalls the assignment received by the past "I" of the communication classroom. The discourse expresses the storyteller's varying attitudes and emotional orientations through the selection of words throughout the story: the "I" in the story is confounded by the assignment, then more perplexed after working on it. In terms of narrative movement, the storyteller shifts from embodying the act of remembering ("this essay reminds me"), to reporting ("at the time") and commenting ("I could recognize"), and then to performing ("Worse and worse") that perplexity. The question, "What was I to do?" succinctly captures these overlapping emotions by combining temporal markers from the past ("What *was* I to do?"), present (the interrogative form of questioning), and future ("What was I *to do?*").

For the audience, the addressee in communication, the focus of discourse is one of decoding, or the *conative* function. The opening sentence, "Let us begin with a brief story," is vocative; that is, it calls to or indicates an audience. Such a beginning does not ask a question but commands someone to "listen!" or "follow along!" The audience listens to the storyteller's utterances in order to understand the story. The reader follows along by combining words into sentences, and sentences into a perceived story. Of course, the storyteller is also an audience to her or his storytelling—as Jakobson notes in his comment about the preliminary "censorship" the verbal act undergoes. The storyteller hesitates over the selection of words, phrases, and meanings that will take the story closer to where it needs to go. Correspondingly, the audience can take up the orientation of the storyteller by anticipating what will happen next, by supplying the word, phrase, or meaning called for by the storyteller's hesitation, or by contributing another story. The storyteller is capable of being an audience and vice versa.

Just as the initial sentence expresses a storyteller and calls forth an audience, it also announces a context or something to which it refers. The story is *about* something; communication performs a *referential* function. In this case, the act of storytelling has multiple referents. It refers to the experience of a writing assignment that the storyteller recalls. But, layered on top of that reference to a past event is the contemporaneous reference to the title of the essay and the context of other "communication as . . ." essays. The current situation stands in relationship to the past situation in some way, as suggested by the phrase "reminds me of." The nature of this reference can be that of an icon, index, or symbol (Lanigan, 2000). The relationship of current to past situations may be that of an icon where the series of metaphors in the earlier writing assignment displays a structural similarity to the series of similes inscribed as essay titles in this volume. The relationship may be that of an index, where both the series of metaphors and the series of similes are contiguous with or point to the study of communication theory. And, as is often the case in storytelling, the relationship between the two situations may be that of a symbol where the meaning is not immediately apparent and where storytellers and audience combine to discover the nature of the relationship. The referential function is emphasized in the expectation that storytelling must be relevant in some way, even if that relevance is yet to be revealed or discovered. Stories are expected to be about something, to have a point worth telling.

These three functions—emotive, conative, and referential—emerge from the collaborative efforts by which audiences and storytellers work together in storytelling. These collaborative efforts constitute the element of physical and psychological contact, the *phatic* function of communication. Storytelling is participatory, and participants perform the work of establishing, maintaining, prolonging, modifying, and discontinuing the interaction. This phatic function can be seen in the myriad ways that embodied participants speak and listen or write and read with each other, but also it is evident when audiences talk about how a story "touched" or "moved" them. In order for a reader to make it this far in the essay requires both physical engagement (the work of focusing eyes and moving hands, reading words and sentences, turning pages, and so on) and an intentional connection (following the story where it goes, consciousness of what is going on). Storytelling is the site of interpersonal and intrapersonal contact.

The contact by which storytellers and audiences participate does not proceed by happenstance or accident. Storytelling is made possible by the operation of a code, what Jakobson calls the "metalinguistic" function of communication. Both audiences and storytellers draw upon their knowledge of and familiarity with language in order to perform storytelling. This metalinguistic function is emphasized within the story when the storyteller identifies particular words as nouns and verbs, and their combination as metaphors, tautologies, and explanations. In a similar way, these comments about the story as composed of actions by the narrator also realize the metalinguistic function. In addition to language, audiences and storytellers draw upon what Jakobson calls "the supply of ready made forms"—the conventions of narrative construction and storytelling performance. "Let us begin" is a ritualistic opening; the story can be identified as one instance of a particular kind or genre of stories about school; the way the story is told can be identified as employing particular kinds of performance techniques and conventions. Is this a "triumph over adversity" story and is the narrator emphasizing the difficulty of the assignment to increase empathy and audience identification?

The final element, the orientation toward the message for its own sake, yields the *poetic* function in communication. The message, according to Jakobson, is a complex structure of word selection and combination. In the story, the narrator describes how a relatively simple message—the assignment to choose three simple words—becomes an increasingly complex text the more the narrator considers it. The selection of words having to do with communication and their combination in a sentence takes on added significance because of the repetition and variation of that simple three-word combination. The assignment creates a puzzle or challenge for the student by emphasizing the poetic function, which, as Jakobson (1960) more elegantly puts it, "projects the principle of equivalence from the axis of selection into the axis of combination" (p. 358). The student's selection or choice of *language, speech, communication,* or *consciousness* is equalized with any other selection in the sequence of phrases. Furthermore, because any noun can replace any other noun and any phrase can replace any other phrase, the specific combination of words and phrases the narrator makes in response will be taken by the professor as meaningful. In the context of a classroom assignment, or the referential function, whatever choice the narrator makes will be taken as revelatory: that is, the response paper will be taken as a message about what the student understands of communication theory and evaluated for a grade.

What is important for the classroom assignment, and for the poetic function in general, is not the repetition of the same message as a reply to the instructor but the formation that results from the student's transformation of the axis of selection and the axis of combination. When teachers say, "don't just parrot back my words to me," they express the importance of the productive aspects of the poetic function. In other words, it is not enough to merely reproduce a message in order to communicate. The teacher here is looking for what the student makes of class readings and discussions, for understanding and knowledge, and not merely the reconstitution of information. Communication is productive—it makes something—as well as reproductive—it does something. As Maurice Merleau-Ponty (1964) notes, the productivity of communication is hazardous because it "introduces us to unfamiliar perspectives instead of confirming us in our own" (p. 77).

In a parallel way, the story of the classroom assignment and the essay on communication as storytelling are transformations of each other. Gregory Bateson (1979) captures the complexity of the poetic function when he defines story as "a little knot or complex of that species of connectedness which we call *relevance*" (p. 13). Think of the story and the event it relates—or the story and the essay that analyzes it—as two sides of a long, narrow strip of paper. What storytelling does is to take one end of that strip of paper and rotate it 180 degrees and connect it to the other end. Storytelling, like a Möbius strip, transforms a two-sided surface into a one-sided surface, a knot or complex, through the "connectedness," or relevance, which rotates a two-dimensional object through three dimensions. Storytelling draws the audience and storyteller, and the order of experience and the order of analysis, into connection by transforming one into the other and vice versa.

Jakobson emphasizes the poetic function and the ambiguity of the message—that "knot," or complex, formed by the transformations of selection and combination, repetition and variation. He writes that "the double-sensed message finds correspondence in a split addresser, in a split addressee, and besides in a split reference" (1960, p. 371). The doubled message of telling a story and the story of the telling finds correspondence in a split between the "I" of the storyteller and the "I" in the story, between an implied "you" in the story and the "you" that is a reader of this volume, and between storytelling as true and storytelling as fictive. Jakobson's "split" and Bateson's "knot" are not accidental outcomes, artistic embellishments, or an aesthetic subgenre of communication. The Möbius strip of conscious experience is not unique to storytelling but stems from communicative practice in general.

We embed this argument for communication as storytelling within the telling of a story in order to make a further point about the practice of theory construction itself: attempts to circumscribe communication theoretically are also performances of storytelling. That is, communication theories attempt to put communication "on stage" so as to see it for itself. In this sense, then, this essay and the other essays in this volume are performative gestures which attempt to communicate—to tell stories—about communication and are therefore themselves communicative and so on ad infinitum. Lacoue-Labarthe (1989) calls this performative gesture the "trick of the abyss." Like the attempt to follow a line on a Möbius strip to its conclusion, theorizing about communication is never complete. The "subject," Lacoue-Labarthe (1989) remarks, "never *coincides* with *itself*" (p. 136). Moreover, he continues,

> this is precisely the reason why theorization, for the one who writes, is not only inevitable but absolutely *necessary*. It is at bottom always impossible not to convert the enunciator into a speaker, the speaker into an actor (a character, a figure, ultimately, a pure "voice")—and the sayable into the visible or the audible. It is even impossible, because this conversion is never sufficient or truly successful, not to strive to accomplish one more theoretical turn—to use the trick of the abyss. (pp. 137–138)

The ever shifting combinations of all six functions in communication—emotive, conative, referential, phatic, metalinguistic, and poetic—underscore that communication is productive, or *poeisis* (Lanigan, 1992, p. 212). Communication is as much a question of performance or making something—whether we are making small talk, making the best of a bad situation, or making love—as it is a question of conduct, or doing something (*praxis*). Communication as storytelling emphasizes the combinatory sense of communication as both making and doing, as both *poeisis* and *praxis*.

By way of conclusion, let us return to the brief story with which we began.

At the end of the second week of classes, and after much agonizing, I turned in my short paper. I would like to say that I discovered some clever and insightful way to respond to what seemed an intractable puzzle. Failing that,

I would be happy to report that my response was competent, adept, or even satisfactory. It wasn't. I was unable to make much of the metaphor, much less achieve the theoretical explanation called for by the assignment. I was unhappy when I submitted my essay and no less unhappy when it was returned to me with a barely passing grade. I had treated the terms of the metaphor as if they were static entities, as if I could find in a dictionary definition an understanding of what it means to use language, to speak and listen, to communicate, to experience consciousness. My response was incoherent and illogical because I tried to eliminate and exclude the ambiguities of communication rather than to explore them. As I look back at that essay, I can see the irony of my efforts to exclude what needed to be included. While storytelling makes it possible to revisit the class, the danger of this return and rejoinder is that it is all too easy to take the position of a more enlightened observer outside the story I—and we—perform. If there is a moral to the story, it is that the title of this essay does not define communication in isolation but invites it through participation: communication as storytelling.

As Jakobson (1976) comments, "a short anecdote is in order here" (p. 166).

Notes

1. The use of *we* and *us* in the essay refers to both authors, while the use of *I* and *me* in the story refers to Eric Peterson.
2. For a technical description of terms from Roman Jakobson, see Lanigan (1992, pp. 229–236).

Additional Readings

Blum-Kulka, S. (1997). *Dinner talk: Cultural patterns of sociability and socialization in family discourse.* Mahwah, NJ: Lawrence Erlbaum.

Mishler, E. G. (1999). *Storylines: Craftartists' narratives of identity.* Cambridge, MA: Harvard University Press.

Ochs, E., & Capps, L. (2001). *Living narrative: Creating lives in everyday storytelling.* Cambridge, MA: Harvard University Press.

Pollock, D. (1999). *Telling bodies, performing birth: Everyday narratives of childbirth.* New York: Columbia University Press.

Smith, S., & Watson, J. (1996). *Getting a life: Everyday uses of autobiography.* Minneapolis: University of Minnesota Press.

References

Bateson, G. (1979). *Mind and nature: A necessary unity.* New York: E. P. Dutton.

Jakobson, R. (1960). Closing statement: Linguistics and poetics. In T. A. Sebeok (Ed.), *Style in language* (pp. 350–377). Cambridge: MIT Press.

Jakobson, R. (1971). Linguistics and communication theory. In R. Jakobson (Ed.), *Selected writings II: Word and language* (pp. 570–579). The Hague: Mouton.

Jakobson, R. (1976). What is poetry? In L. Matejka & I. R. Titunik (Eds.), *Semiotics of art: Prague School contributions* (pp. 164–175). Cambridge: MIT Press.

Lacoue-Labarthe, P. (1989). *Typography: Mimesis, philosophy, politics* (C. Fynsk, Ed.). Cambridge, MA: Harvard University Press.

Langellier, K. M., & Peterson, E. E. (2004). *Storytelling in daily life: Performing narrative.* Philadelphia: Temple University Press.

Lanigan, R. L. (1992). *The human science of communicology: A phenomenology of discourse in Foucault and Merleau-Ponty.* Pittsburgh, PA: Duquesne University Press.

Lanigan, R. L. (2000). The self in semiotic phenomenology: Consciousness as the conjunction of perception and expression in the science of communicology. *American Journal of Semiotics, 15–16,* 91–111.

Merleau-Ponty, M. (1964). Indirect language and the voices of silence. In R. McCleary (Trans.), *Signs* (pp. 39–83). Evanston, IL: Northwestern University Press.

15

Communication as Complex Organizing

James R. Taylor

M ark Twain is reputed to have said, "Everyone talks about the weather but no one does anything about it." I feel somewhat the same way about organization: Everyone talks about organization but no one seems to know for sure what it is. One strategy is to resort to analogy (Morgan, 1986): An organization is like a machine, or an organism, or a brain, or a system, or a prison. But, although each of these metaphors captures some aspect of organization, none of them really gets to the heart of the matter.

Communication scholars are as responsible as anyone else for the confusion. Ruth Smith (1993) built a dissertation around her analysis of how organizational communication researchers had conceptualized the communication-organization link since its inception as a field in the 1960s. She found that about 70% of the time they thought of communication as something occurring *in* or *within* an organization. This usage accords onto-logical precedence to organization: something existing before, and indepen-dently of, communication. This begs the question, Smith pointed out, of how organization got to *be* organization to begin with. Others—fewer—were prepared to think of communication as a product of organization: its cul-ture, for example. How organization came to exist in the first place is, how-ever, still left unanswered. A few—very few, in fact—went so far as to claim that organization is a product of, or perhaps equivalent to, communication.

That is a more promising line of inquiry, and a rationale for the "interpretive" school of organizational communication (Putnam & Pacanowsky, 1983).

I count myself as a member of this latter school, but in this chapter I will argue that interpretivism, and more generally constructivist theories, need to take into account the substantial as well as the symbolic, or sensemaking, dimension of communication. I will claim that (a) organizing is endemic to communication in all of its manifestations, local and global, but that (b) the "how" of organizing in what Weick (1985) called "tight" organizational contexts is different from that which binds people together into an organizational unit in "looser" organizational association networks. The difference is in the role played by the medium, or substantial basis, of conversational exchange: text.

Organization Is Endemic to Communication: The Contribution of Speech Act Theory

Organization is already present, I propose, in the elementary kernel of communication that consists of one person conversing with one other person about something. To delimit our search for the origins of organization is this manner means, however, also restricting our choice of a theory of communication. We will, for example, be obliged to eliminate from consideration what has often been adopted as the basis of communication studies, information theory (messaging, diffusion, transmission of information). The weakness of information theory from the perspective of organizing is not in what it explains, transmission of data (which it does well), but in what it does *not* explain, the organizing role of communication. It, like the "communication in the container of organization" metaphor described by Smith (1993), assumes an established sender-receiver relationship to start with—and thus assumes, by implication, that organization already exists.

An alternative model such as speech act theory (SAT) is predicated on a different assumption, that language-in-use is where organizing occurs. Both information theory and speech act models assume that communication is interactive, and involves one person talking (or messaging) and one person listening (or receiving). Where the schools differ is not so much in how they punctuate the flow but in what they then read into the units they have selected for attention. SAT focuses our attention on a facet of communication that the information theorists gloss over, namely that when you speak you are also acting. You are influencing, deliberately or not, other people to believe and to act in certain ways, and, to the extent that you succeed, you will have changed the world:

acted on it. It may be a social world you are acting on (and in) but there will be consequences that are felt in the real, material world as well. Wittgenstein (1958), for example, employed the homely example of a builder and an assistant. The builder calls out the word "pillar," and the assistant hands him a pillar (both having learned what *pillar* means and how to use the word).

It is this idea that is at the heart of Wittgenstein's concept of a language game. Language is an instrument people use to get on with, and influence, the world they live in. The summative practices of people using language to communicate come to constitute a form of life. Language is not just about people transmitting knowledge to each other as information (the *epistemic* modality of speech). It is also about acting on the world and taking responsibility for the action (the *deontic* modality of speech). It is also how social relationships are both initiated and expressed (what Katambwe, 2004, terms the *taxemic* modality of discourse: taxemic because it "taxes" members or, in other words, situates them with respect to categories that imply membership rights and duties). Language is a resource that people exploit to accomplish real actions in a mixed material and social world (it is, in other words, an *authoritative* as opposed to an *allocative* resource, to borrow Giddens' 1984 distinction). But it is also how they simultaneously establish their own sociality.

Conversation: The "Site" of Organizing?

SAT has sometimes almost seemed to merge with formal linguistics (Katz, 1980; Sadock, 1974), and this highlights its pervasive emphasis on the individual speaker's action, as opposed to the conversational dynamic. It has, as a result, drawn the fire of the empirically oriented field of conversation analysis because of SAT's foreshortening of the dynamic and highly interactive character of sensemaking in face-to-face contexts. Once we place the act of speech in its context of an ongoing conversation, we have to recognize that the capacity to act, using language, is not so much a privilege of the single actor as it is a feature, and outcome, of the back-and-forth interaction within which knowledge and a mutual understanding about the responsibility to act (duty) of each participant are being either explicitly or implicitly negotiated.

This is the kind of organizational context that Weick (1985) had in mind when he introduced the idea of a "segmented" organization. All organizations are decentralized, not monolithic, at the level of practice, he argued. When the segments are "small and stable" (a maximum of "ten strong pairwise relationships") communication occurs as a conversation (pp. 116–117).

Such minisocieties are not unstructured. As Watzlawick, Beavin, and Jackson (1967) pointed out, the cumulative effect of any sustained sequence of communication is to produce a relationship. The relationship may be that of equal partners ("symmetrical"), or unequal partners ("complementary"), or a mixture of the two. Either way, without ever necessarily being explicit about it, people who continue to interact with each other in some common context are in the process of establishing a hierarchy. To cite Haley (1976, pp. 100–101): "If there is any generalization that applies to men and other animals, it is that all creatures capable of learning are compelled to organize. To be organized means to follow patterned, redundant ways of behaving and to exist in a hierarchy."

Summary and Critique

Even in spontaneous interpersonal interaction, people are both acting (a social world) and creating the conditions for acting (the material world). They are making sense of the world they are in and jointly working out the terms of a coordinated response to it to generate, if they are successful, a single collective unit of action: a team. They are establishing the basis of a rule-governed minisociety of at least two (rules in the sense of tendencies to act in established patterns): a kind of "behavioral constitution" (MacKenzie, 1978). They negotiate a division of labor and, in the process, establish a more or less stable hierarchy.

There it is: coordinated action, distribution of labor, established organizational constitution, goal-oriented activity, specialization of function. We have, it would seem, shown the genesis of organization in communication—not only what it is, but how it came to be. Mission accomplished?

Well, no, not quite.

What I have been explaining might work for smallish communities, where everyone knows each other, and the interaction is regular and sustained: what Weick called "tightly coupled." How to get from these microuniverses with everyone communicating in the same time-space continuum to the more loosely coupled conglomerations that dominate the socioscape of early twenty-first century global enterprise and government is not immediately evident. We confront a problem of scaling up. I propose to do so in a way that retains the insights from SAT while adding a new conception, drawing on a different literature—that which is concerned with narrative theory, currently a central theme of the literature on organization (Alvesson & Karreman, 2000; Boje, Oswick, & Ford, 2004; Fairhurst & Putnam, 2004; Grant, Keenoy, & Oswick, 1998; Putnam & Cooren, 2004; Putnam & Fairhurst, 2001; Westwood & Linstead, 2001). The emphasis will now be on the role of text, not just as medium, but as one of the agents that we have to take into account when we scale up from local to global.

Thinking About Texts in a Different Way

When people use speech and writing to interact with others, they do so by generating strings of language. Halliday and Hasan (1985, p. 10) call these strings "texts." They explain their reasoning this way:

> What do we mean by text? We can define text, in the simplest way perhaps, by saying it is language that is functional. By functional, we simply mean language that is doing some job in some context, as opposed to isolated words or sentences that I might put on the blackboard.

Text, they go on, whether it is realized orally or graphically, is both product and process. It is *product* because it is the trace our interaction leaves behind itself as it unfolds: an artifactual record. Text is *process* because it is "an interactive event, a social exchange of meanings" (p. 11). My colleagues and I (Taylor, Cooren, Giroux, & Robichaud, 1996; Taylor & Van Every, 2000) have dubbed these the dimensions of, respectively, text and conversation, but the terminology is not crucial. The idea that we use texts as the building blocks of conversation is. Even in face-to-face conversation, we expect our texts to be acting for us, as *agents* that convey our beliefs, attitudes, and intentions to others. In more extended networks, the text-as-agent mediation becomes more salient, and a good deal more important to take into account.

Conversation and text are mutually enabling. There would be no conversation without text, and no text without conversation (in Halliday and Hasan's definition, in any case). But the mutuality is richer than may at first be evident. The grounds for this assertion are laid out by both Giddens (1984) and Weick (1995). According to Giddens, social practices are inherently reflexive. Reflexivity implies "the monitored character of the ongoing flow of social life" (p. 3). Acts, he writes, "are constituted only by a *discursive* moment of attention to the *durée* of lived-through experience" (p. 3, emphasis added to *discursive*). Conversation is, after all, "a lived-through experience." It flows in time, has *durée*. But the speech that enables the conversation is not an act, if we credit Giddens, until it is reflexively interpreted *as* an act: taken out of its immediately experienced time/space situation, and universalized. *Textualized*, in other words.

Bruner (1991), in his discussion of narrative, makes a similar point. "Particularity," he writes, "achieves its emblematic status by its embeddedness in a story that is in some sense generic" (p. 7). "A narrative," on the other hand, "cannot be realized save through particular embodiment." Our experience as individuals is singular, unique; categories of meaning, however, are universal, generic. Monitoring of one's experience is thus an ongoing reading of the particular by interpreting it in the categories of the general: using language as a basis for how to make sense of things—turning conversation into text and vice versa. Halliday and Hasan's process/product dichotomy is thus essential, not incidental.

Karl Weick (1995) is even more explicit:

> People can know what they are doing only after they have done it. . . . Experience as we know it exists in the form of distinct events. But the only way we get this impression is by stepping outside the stream of experience and directing attention to it. (pp. 24–25)

He calls this retrospective interpretation of events "sensemaking." Sensemaking, of course, is realized as texts, overtly expressed or still immanent in the cognitions of organizational members.

Text, then, is not just a resource for constructing a conversation but how we recursively, reflexively, and retrospectively discover the meaning of our communicative experience for ourselves: literally *make* sense of it, using language. We do this, Bruner (1991) observes, not so much by interpolating cause-effect relationships as the source of events, as by attributing reasons, motives: "*interpreting* why a character acted as he or she did" (p. 7, emphasis in the original). As he says, "some measure of *agency* is always present in narrative" (p. 7, my emphasis).

Scaling Up From Tightly to Loosely Coupled Organization

Now consider the role of text, thus understood, in the more extended networks than the tightly coupled groupings of the segmented organization. In small communities where interpersonal relationships are supported by frequent interaction and a shared agenda of activity, the source of the explicitly verbalized texts that people employ to construct their conversation is known. People can trace their origin to the context of previous conversations. There is a shared background knowledge grounded in a common experience. And the texts constituting each person's speech acts are accompanied by a rich accompanying "given-off" (Goffman, 1959) spectrum of nonverbal signs. Other people's texts seem relatively comprehensible, hermeneutically speaking.

In communication *between* these local communities of practice and cognition, the origin of the texts linking the communities is veiled and the nonverbal information is no longer available. The background understandings that make ordinary conversation so flexible are attenuated. People are obliged to focus on the text itself and its properties—properties that are grounded in narrative logic (Weick, 1995).

Consider some of those properties (Taylor & Van Every, 2000):

1. Narrative establishes what is important to pay attention to, motivated by a "precipitating event" (Bruner, 1991), or disturbance, and thus sets an agenda.

2. Narrative establishes a protagonist and an antagonist (Greimas, 1987): a competitor, perhaps within the organization itself.

3. Narrative establishes who is entitled to initiate a response to the disturbance: frequently that person who can claim to be most knowledgeable about it.

4. Narrative establishes not only those who are responsible for acting, but also their readiness to undertake the performance: their motivation and their qualification.

5. Narrative establishes a network of helpers who can be called on in undertaking action, including both people and technology.

6. And finally, narrative establishes how the performers will be rewarded, and who is entitled to sanction their performance.

In small, coherent communities of practice, none of this needs, normally, to be explicitly enunciated. Who is most knowledgeable about what, who is responsible for initiating and carrying through certain aspects of work, and how sanctions work is part of background knowledge. There is a kind of tacit "sub-text" that governs collective behavior (Katambwe & Taylor, in press).

In large, loosely joined networks of a segmented society composed of many distinct communities of practice, unanimity can no longer be taken for granted. The text has to be made explicit if there is to be a sufficient level of unity of purpose. Toward this end, narrative is a potent motivator of human action and a powerful tool for the production of a sense of community. It establishes not just reasons for action, but also the identities of people (their qualifications, and their rights and obligations), *including that of the organization itself.*

Texts, however, have to be authored. And they must be made operative in the conversations of the organization if they are to exert authority. The authoring and legitimating of an organization's texts, wherever it occurs and whoever participates in it, are what we refer to as a "meta-conversation" (Robichaud, Giroux, & Taylor, 2004). It is where power resides. As Giddens (1984) observed, interpretation of events, the exercise of power, and the establishment of legitimate authority constitute a single phenomenon.

An organization-in-the-large is thus a complex mix of segmented—potentially fragmented—local conversations that are loosely joined by an ongoing meta-conversation out of which the identity of the organization and its network of agents emerges.

That is why organizations are complex. As the ultimate actor in the network that constitutes the organization, the organization-as-actor had to have been authored. Its intentions, attitudes, motives, and reasons had to have been constructed, recursively, reflexively, and retrospectively, in the conversations that make up its network and in the wider conversation of society as a whole. But that collective sensemaking is not singular, and it may be—normally is—characterized by conflicting views and contrasting perspectives (Taylor, 2004). Controversy is endemic to any complex organization. There is an irreducibly polemical edge to all sensemaking grounded in narrativity. Agency implies *anti*agency (Greimas, 1987). Coorientation implies opposition. The result is complexity. Unfinished business. Issues still on the table to be resolved later. Ambiguity.

Conclusion

What, then, *is* an organization? As Flores (1981) pointed out, an organization is a *network,* composed of the transactions of all its members. But it is also an *actor,* entitled—legally entitled, in our society—to enter into contracts, sue and be sued, lobby and be lobbied, and take over and be taken over. How can an organization be *both* a network (a dispersed collection of multiple agencies, reasons, motives) and a unitary actor (a single agency, reason, motive)? Isn't that a paradox (Taylor & Robichaud, 2004)?

Of course it's a paradox. Organizations, incorporating a collective will, can only act through emissaries: agents. And *every* member of the organization is, by definition, an agent of the organization. On the other hand, those same members have been constituted *as* agents because they represent the organization, as its emissaries. They thereby constitute, in its daily manifestations, the organization. The logic is circular. The logic of paradox.

We need to see human communication as always occurring on two levels. On one level, there is the usual conversation situated by its anchoring in concrete circumstances of time and place. On the other level, there is the *meta*conversation, out of which the identity of the organization to which people belong must be constructed. This latter metaconversation is often a contentious affair, characterized by parties and movements, by intrigue and the making of deals. Even if the latent conflicts, grounded in differing communities of practice and sensemaking, were to be suppressed, the disagreements would not have vanished; they would simply have been marginalized (Stacey, 2000).

I have been addressing issues of organizational communication because that is where my interests lie. But on a deeper level, I believe *all* communication is organizational. We are all members of society, and we all bear the responsibility for constructing the social framework of a society that not only encompasses, but invades, the everyday interpersonal and community activities in which our ordinary life takes place. We are all, in the end, citizens. Nowadays, society is most visibly exemplified by huge corporations and massive government agencies. We are as responsible for *their* behavior as they seem to be preoccupied with *ours*. We, too, are implicated in, and responsible for, the metaconversation. We are all agents: not just acting as individuals, empowered because we are members of a powerful society, but also as authors of that society and its understandings, choices, and actions.

Additional Readings

Cooren, F. (2004). Textual agency: How texts do things in organizational settings. *Organization, 11*(3), 373–393.

Robichaud, D., Giroux, H., & Taylor, J. R. (2004). The meta-conversation: The recursive property of language as the key to organizing. *Academy of Management Review, 29*(4), 1–18. [Special issue on language and organization, edited by D. Boje, C. Oswick, & J. Ford]

Taylor, J. R., Cooren, F., Giroux, N., & Robichaud, D. (1996). The communicational basis of organization: Between the conversation and the text. *Communication Theory, 6*(1), 1–39.

Taylor, J. R., & Robichaud, D. (2004, May). Finding the organization in the communication: Discourse as action and sensemaking. *Organization, 11*(3), 395–413.

Weick, K. E. (1985). Sources of order in underorganized systems: Themes in recent organizational theory. In Y. S. Lincoln (Ed.), *Organizational theory and inquiry: The paradigm revolution* (pp. 106–136). Beverly Hills, CA: Sage.

References

Alvesson, M., & Karreman, D. (2000). Taking the linguistic turn in organizational research: Challenges, responses and consequences. *Journal of Applied Behavioral Science, 36*, 136–158.

Boje, D. M., Oswick, C., & Ford, J. D. (2004). Language and organization: The doing of discourse. *Academy of Management Review, 29*(4), 571–577.

Bruner, J. (1991). The narrative construction of reality. *Critical Inquiry, 18*, 1–21.

Fairhurst, G. T., & Putnam, L. (2004). Organizations as discursive constructions. *Communication Theory, 14*(1), 5–26.

Flores, C. F. L. (1981). *Management and communication in the office of the future.* Unpublished doctoral dissertation, University of California, Berkeley.

Giddens, A. (1984). *The constitution of society.* Berkeley: University of California Press.

Goffman, E. (1959). *The presentation of self in everyday life.* New York: Doubleday.

Grant, D., Keenoy, T., & Oswick, C. (1998). *Discourse and organization.* Thousand Oaks, CA: Sage.

Greimas, A. J. (1987). *On meaning: Selected writings in semiotic theory* (P. J. Perron & F. H. Collins, Trans.). Minneapolis: University of Minnesota Press.

Haley, J. (1976). *Problem-solving therapy.* New York: Harper.

Halliday, M. A. K., & Hasan, R. (1985). *Language, context, and text: Aspects of language in a social-semiotic perspective.* Oxford, UK: Oxford University Press.

Katambwe, J. M. (2004). *La nature du lien organisationnel: Une étude de cas selon une approche discursive* [The nature of the organizational link: A case study using a discursive approach]. Unpublished doctoral dissertation, Université de Montréal, Montreal, Canada.

Katambwe, J. M., & Taylor, J. R. (in press). Modes of organizational integration. In F. Cooren, J. R. Taylor, & E. J. Van Every (Eds.), *Communication as organizing: Empirical inquiries into the dynamic of text and conversation.* Mahwah, NJ: Lawrence Erlbaum.

Katz, J. J. (1980). *Propositional structure and illocutionary force: A study of the contribution of sentence meaning to speech acts.* Cambridge, MA: Harvard University Press.

MacKenzie, K. D. (1978). *Organizational structures.* Arlington Heights, IL: AHM.

Morgan, G. (1986). *Images of organization.* Newbury Park, CA: Sage.

Putnam, L. L., & Cooren, F. (Eds.). (2004). Special issue on text and agency: Constitutive elements of organizations. *Organization, 11*(3).

Putnam, L. L., & Fairhurst, G. T. (2001). Discourse analysis in organizations. In F. M. Jablin & L. L. Putnam (Eds.), *The new handbook of organizational communication: Advances in theory, research and methods* (pp. 78–136). Thousand Oaks, CA: Sage.

Putnam, L. L., & Pacanowsky, M. E. (Eds.). (1983). *Communication and organization: An interpretive approach.* Newbury Park, CA: Sage.

Robichaud, D., Giroux, H., & Taylor, J. R. (2004). The meta-conversation: The recursive property of language as the key to organizing. *Academy of Management Review, 29*(4), 1–18.

Sadock, J. M. (1974). *Toward a linguistic theory of speech acts.* New York: Academic Press.

Smith, R. C. (1993, May). *Images of organizational communication: Root-metaphors of the organization-communication relation.* Paper presented at the annual conference of the International Communication Association, Washington, DC.

Stacey, R. D. (2000). *Strategic management and organizational dynamics: The challenge of complexity*. London: Pearson Education.

Taylor, J. R. (2004). Dialogue as the search for sustainable organizational communication. In R. Anderson, L. Baxter, & K. Cissna (Eds.), *Dialogue* (pp. 125–140). Thousand Oaks, CA: Sage.

Taylor, J. R., Cooren, F., Giroux, N., & Robichaud, D. (1996). The communicational basis of organization: Between the conversation and the text. *Communication Theory, 6*(1), 1–39.

Taylor, J. R., & Robichaud, D. (2004, May). Finding the organization in the communication: Discourse as action and sensemaking. *Organization, 11*(3), 395–413.

Taylor, J. R., & Van Every, E. J. (2000). *The emergent organization: Communication as its site and surface*. Mahwah, NJ: Lawrence Erlbaum.

Watzlawick, P., Beavin, J. H., & Jackson, D. D. (1967). *The pragmatics of communication: A study of interactional patterns, pathologies and paradoxes*. New York: W. W. Norton.

Weick, K. E. (1985). Sources of order in underorganized systems: Themes in recent organizational theory. In Y. S. Lincoln (Ed.), *Organizational theory and inquiry: The paradigm revolution* (pp. 106–136). Beverly Hills, CA: Sage.

Weick, K. E. (1995). *Sensemaking in organizations*. Thousand Oaks, CA: Sage.

Westwood, R., & Linstead, S. (Eds.). (2001). *The language of organization*. London: Sage.

Wittgenstein, L. (1958). *Philosophical investigations* (3rd ed., G. E. M. Anscombe, Trans.). New York: Macmillan.

16

Communication as Structuring

David R. Seibold and Karen Kroman Myers

S ocial institutions, including groups and organizations, are organized around members' interactional processes and practices: disseminating information, allocating resources, accomplishing tasks, making choices, managing disagreements, and the like. As Poole, Seibold, and McPhee (1996) note, "the key to understanding (these) practices is through analysis of the *structures* that underlie them" (p. 117; emphasis added). In turn, we contend, the key to understanding the relationship between system practices and social structures that enable and constrain them is through analysis of members' *structuring interactions* that create and recreate the structures. More fundamentally, we propose that communication is inherently and importantly a structuring activity: system members' appropriation of the underlying structures that enable system performance is accomplished through structuring interaction, and the structures themselves are social products produced (and reproduced) in structuring interaction.

We develop this stance on communication in three sections of this essay. First, we offer a brief review of relevant tenets of structuration theory (cf. Giddens, 1984), which underlies our approach to structuring interaction. Second, we discuss how structuring interaction occurs—that is, how structures are appropriated, reproduced, and transformed through system members' communication practices. In particular, we examine members' microlevel moves to appropriate structures, more global patterns of members' use of structures, and modalities of structuration (Poole et al., 1996). Throughout our discussion, we provide relevant examples of communication as structuring interaction from studies of group and organizational communication. Third, we close by summarizing the advantages of conceptualizing communication as structuring.

Structure and Structuration

Our use of the term *structure* stems from a distinction British social theorist Anthony Giddens (1979, 1984) draws between system and structure. *Systems* are social entities, such as groups and organizations, engaged in interactional practices that result in observable patterns of relationships, such as hierarchies, decision-making routines, newcomer assimilation procedures, and appraisal/advancement rituals. They are "reproduced relations between actors or collectives, organized as regular social practices" (Giddens, 1984, p. 25). Banks and Riley (1993) describe systems as "the patterning of social relations across stretches of time and space" (p. 173).

Structures are the rules and resources that members use to create and maintain the system we witness. As "recipes" for acting (Giddens, 1984), rules and resources enable and constrain members' behaviors. *Rules* are tacitly known general procedures guiding them on how to function appropriately and competently. *Resources* include members' capabilities to command authoritative resources (social conditions and other persons) and allocatable resources (material entities). For example, new organizational members may find it normative to behave in ways that accord special status to older, more skilled, and/or more experienced coworkers, producing an informal hierarchy (Myers & Oetzel, 2003). Indeed, the norm (a rule-like standard of conduct) may be so strong that even supervisors' selection of members higher on this "pecking order" for choice assignments—and allocation of material resources to support them—further creates the informal organizational hierarchy (and simultaneously reinforces their own place as supervisors in the formal hierarchy). Systems have patterns, such as these hierarchies, because of members' structuring processes surrounding rules and resources. Indeed, as Poole et al. (1996) underscore, "the observable system is of interest and can influence structures, but the structure is what does the real work" (p. 117).

The dynamic and recursive relationship between system and structure is captured in Giddens' (1984) concept of *structuration,* or the process by which systems are produced and reproduced through members' use of rules and resources. Poole et al. (1996) explicate this process and the key aspects of it:

> Not only is the system produced and reproduced through structuration, but the structures themselves are, too. Structures are dualities: they are both the medium and the outcome of action. They are the medium of action because

members draw on structures to interact. They are its outcome because rules and resources exist only by virtue of being used in a practice. Whenever the structure is employed, the activity reproduces it by invoking and confirming it as a meaningful basis for action. (p. 117)

The structures that enable and constrain system behaviors are continually being produced and reproduced as a result of interaction. For example, organizational members' interactions produce a system of interacting with leaders based on their rules (structures) for following those leaders. These "rules" of engagement, forms of knowledge that mediate interaction, become known to other organizational members and have institutional ramifications. It is in this sense that there is a *duality of structure* (Giddens, 1984): "the structural properties of social systems are both the medium and outcome of practices they recursively organize" (p. 26). System and structure are not independent, but enable and constrain each other in interactants' behaviors.

As patterns of interaction are repeated across time and space, institutional/social relationships are formed and reinforced as recognized features of group/organizational/community/social life. This recognition is apparent to most agents, and occasions *social integration,* "the reciprocity of practices among persons in face-to-face contexts of interaction" (Banks & Riley, 1993, p. 176). So, although individuals are knowledgeable agents, they are also subject to "situated practices" that work to resist complete autonomy. Instead, individuals exercise personal agency mindful of, but not necessarily adhering to, established rules and resources.

Finally, human social activity is recursively reflexive as individuals monitor their communication, actions, and the outcomes. We communicate with some level of knowledgeability and, in fact, recursiveness assumes a level of knowledgeability and reflexivity (Giddens, 1984). This reflexivity can cause individuals to modify goals, plans, and future action (Poole, Seibold, & McPhee, 1985). In addition, humans are capable of rationalizing actions, but their purposes do not always match their actions. Social interactions are complex blends of both intentional and unintentional consequences (Giddens, 1979). Structures change as a result of intended and unintended consequences, and these patterns of intended and unintended consequences produce institutionalized practices (Giddens, 1984).

Communication and Structuring Interaction

Before examining the structuring nature of communication and how structures figure in interaction, it is important to highlight the centrality of communication in organizing and organization. As individuals communicate, they produce and reproduce relationships with others. Part of developing relationships involves positioning—individuals are enabled to locate themselves in connection to others through interaction (Van Langenhove & Harre, 1995). As Giddens (1984) observes, social interaction is built on positioning of individuals in time-space relative to others. The social interaction enabling positioning is also the very essence of organizing that constitutes organizations. Through interaction, individuals create and modify the rules, or structures, underlying their relationships.

Boden (1994) observes that interactants are doing more than just keeping their turns straight, they also are "working through an account." As coworkers talk, for example, they are not only discussing the topic at hand but contributing to their definition of the structures of their relationship in a hierarchy that is recognized and affirmed in the dialogue. And the "lamination" of conversations (Boden, 1994), or the interlacing of numerous localized conversation episodes into a pattern, cumulates to the organization as a whole.

We can now turn to the structuring nature of communication. Interaction is the nexus of structuration in what, we have seen in previous paragraphs, are communicatively constituted organizations. And as discussed at the introduction, social entities produce, and consequently reproduce, their unique structures in streams of ongoing interactions. But how does structuring interaction occur? How are structures appropriated, reproduced, and transformed through system members' communication practices? Following Poole and DeSanctis's (1992) analysis of three system "levels" at which structuration can be studied (microlevel acts, global patterns within a system, and the societal layer across systems), Poole et al. (1996, pp. 133–137) identify three mechanisms central to structuring interactions: (a) members' microlevel moves to appropriate structures, (b) patterns of members' use of structures, and (c) modalities of structuration. We treat each in turn.

First, structuring interactions can occur in discrete as well as in conjoined "moves" that interactants—acting individually and in tandem with others—make in order to appropriate structures. In studying group argument, Seibold and Meyers (Meyers & Seibold, 1990; Seibold & Meyers, 2004) and their colleagues have utilized a scheme developed by Canary and others (Canary, 1989; Canary, Ratledge, & Seibold, 1982; Meyers & Brashers, 1995; Meyers, Seibold, & Brashers, 1991; Seibold, McPhee, Poole, Tanita, & Canary, 1981) that attempts to capture such moves. Group members appropriate underlying structures invoking canons of logic (Toulmin, 1969) through advancing *potential arguables* (assertions and propositions), *reason-using arguables* (elaborations and responses), and *reason-giving arguables* (amplifications and justifications). They also use moves that draw upon conventions surrounding disagreement and disagreement repair in conversations

(Jacobs & Jackson, 1980), including *promptors* (objections and challenges) and *reinforcers* (agreement acts). And they enact *delimitor* moves (frames as well as acts that forestall refutation by securing common ground or removing possible obstacles) that are consistent with structures producing and reproducing convergence (Perelman & Olbrechts-Tyteca, 1969). Canary, Brossman, and Seibold (1987) found that these acts were conjoined to produce identifiable argument structures (simple, compound, convergent, and eroded arguments) that, in turn, were used as structuring moves for advancing and resisting decision choices. Finally, these microlevel structuring moves need not be produced by individuals alone. Seibold et al. (1981) as well as Brashers and Meyers (1989) found evidence for joint structuring and the collaborative production of argument structures by subgroups of system members, a practice they termed "tag-team argument."

Second, structuring can be seen in broader *patterns of interaction* in social systems. For example, Heller (1992) investigated how groups supported by decision-support technology appropriated features of the GDSS into their practices across multiple meetings. Utilizing Billingsley's (1990) global-level scheme for coding appropriation-related interaction, Heller found that groups with prior experience interacting together demonstrated greater use of not only selected features of the technology but of other process structures than offered by the technology, the moderator, or other resources available to them.

Barley's (1986) study of radiologists and radiological technologists also is illustrative of the structuring apparent in broader communication patterns across an entire process or set of processes. Radiologists entered the new CT scanning laboratory assuming, normatively, that they were in positions of superiority relative to the technologists due to their extensive medical educations and backgrounds (resources). After dealing with the technologists, new rule-related relationships were negotiated. Interaction revealed the technologists' valuable resources, including their superior ability to operate the CT scanners. When the radiologists realized that they were dependent on the technologists' specialized skill set, new roles were negotiated giving the technologists more autonomy in performing their duties. Emerging patterns of communication between the radiologists and the technologists worked to change structures of the radiology departments.

Similarly, Browning and Beyer (1998) provide a compelling example of system-level patterns of structuring interactions in their study of the SEMATECH consortium. The researchers found that increased voluntary communication altered organizing by increasing trust and cooperation among members. They did not initially perceive themselves to be interdependent, but through interaction provoked by crises, structures of communication changed, and this changed the structures of their social system.

Third, structuring can be found in the three *modalities of structuration*, in which structures are simultaneously manifested. As Giddens (1979, pp. 129–130) proposes, structures can simultaneously serve as norms guiding action, as facilities enabling the exercise of power, and as interpretive schemes. Lewis and Seibold's (1993) analysis of employees' communication surrounding a new work arrangement in their food processing plant reveals the structuring nature of interactions vis-à-vis the interrelationships among modalities and their transformation in interaction. In the context of members' interactions concerning how to cope with the innovation, different work groups interpreted management's vision for the new "line technician" position quite differently and their varying interpretations affected how they "modified" the innovation. But the resulting differences in how they produced the program carried power-related implications insofar as some forms of the innovation were more effective than others—thus increasing their power bases with other work groups, with management, and with external consultants who had designed the (modified) program. At the same time, this had normative implications for all the groups, as the degree of modification required to be successful (but still acceptable to management) served as a legitimation structure in the groups' communication about how to structure themselves around the new position. Other analyses of groups' uses of collaborative technologies (DeSanctis & Poole, 1994), teachers' contract negotiations (Keough & Lake, 1993), and temporal variations in work groups (Ballard & Seibold, 2003) offer examples of how structuring interaction operates across several modalities.

Advantages of Communication-as-Structuring Stance

Conceiving of communication as structuring interaction makes communication central to social action. It is axiomatic that social entities such as groups and organizations cannot exist without communication. Viewing communication as structuring illuminates *how* communication is central to the creation and transformation of social systems. Relatedly, communication structuring occurs at three levels (micro, global, and societal; Poole et al., 1996) in this view, so individual communication scholars must cast their theoretical and research nets more broadly than they usually do.

Another advantage of conceptualizing communication as structuring is that it reframes what appear to be 'fixed' institutions more dynamically and locates them in the structuring interactions of their members. Consistent with the structuration theory (Giddens, 1984) footings of our stance, the groups and organizations that seem so stable and static are instead continuously fluctuating. Members' structuring interactions are continually producing and reproducing the structures that opaquely enable and constrain the systems we observe. Hence, communication scholars' challenge is to probe how the recursive production/reproduction process inherent in all structuring interaction fosters relative permanence for some periods of time and change at others.

For example, communities of practice (COP) are groups of individuals who "share a concern, a set of problems, or a passion about a topic, who deepen their knowledge and expertise in this area by interaction on an ongoing basis" (Wenger, McDermott, & Snyder, 2002, p. 4). In a COP, members' structuring interaction serves to negotiate meanings of action and practices, and to define qualities of the COP, member practices, and their reactions to outside influence (Wenger, 1998). Locales of participation and reification serve to construct meaningful group identity and social practices. Foundational to the COP construct is the notion that practices constitute structures through mutual engagement, shared repertoire, and joint enterprise, which, in turn, structure future social practices in the COP. This premise undergirding the COP perspective is similar to the duality of structure conception at the core of structuration theory, and pushes scholars to study how the recursivity of production and reproduction also oscillates between occasions for changes and reconfirmation of ongoing practices in COPs.

Third, viewing communication as structuring problematizes, for both theorists and practitioners, how structuring interaction *occurs*. We have surveyed a number of studies of structuring including argument structures, procedural structures appropriated from GDSS technologies, performance hierarchies among work groups undergoing restructuring, voluntary standards in a semiconductor industry consortium, social order in a radiology department, and temporal structures contributing to differences in work groups performing the same tasks. We have drawn on Poole et al.'s (1996) trifold mechanisms of structuring interactions—members' microlevel moves to appropriate structures, patterns of members' use of structures, and modalities of structuration—and we have noted a number of schemes in the studies above for conceiving and investigating structuring moves, broader patterns of appropriation, and structuration modalities. Is this a theoretically and empirically satisfactory view, and are other mechanisms for understanding how structuring interaction occurs superior?

Finally, taking the stance that communication is structuring at root also invites analysis of how interaction *mediates* other significant structures. In the study of processes central to groups and organizations (e.g., decision making, assimilation, and identification, among many others), exogenous factors often are privileged as "independent" (read *causal*) forces: task type, member characteristics, cognitions, technological support, and so forth. An important implication of the communication-as-structuring stance is that these influences are mediated in members' structuring interactions. Specifically, what appear to be external factors can be seen as structures that interactants produce communicatively and then appropriate in ways that channel or challenge action. On the communication-as-structuring view, differences across social entities such as groups and organizations can be understood as how each entity produces its own forms of the external variables and responds to them, rather than as differences supposedly inherent to the exogenous variables. Hence, communication scholars might profitably (re)structure their research practices to find the communicative construction of what may appear to be noncommunication influences on the processes of interest.

Additional Readings

Browning, L., & Beyer, J. (1998). The structuring of shared voluntary standards in the U.S. semiconductor industry: Communicating to reach agreement. *Communication Monographs, 65,* 220–243.

Keough, C., & Lake, R. (1993). Values as structuring processes of contract negotiations. In C. Conrad (Ed.), *The ethical nexus* (pp. 171–191). Norwood, NJ: Ablex.

Lemus, D. R., Seibold, D. R., Flanagin, A. J., & Metzger, M. J. (2004). Argument and decision making in computer-mediated groups. *Journal of Communication, 54*(2), 302–320.

Poole, M. S. (1994). The structuring of organizational climates. In L. Thayer & G. Barnett (Eds.), *Organization-communication IV* (pp. 74–113). Norwood, NJ: Ablex.

Poole, M. S., Seibold, D. R., & McPhee, R. D. (1996). The structuration of group decisions. In R. Y. Hirokawa & M. S. Poole (Eds.), *Communication and group decision-making* (2nd ed., pp. 114–146). Thousand Oaks, CA: Sage.

References

Ballard, D. L., & Seibold, D. R. (2003). Communicating and organizing in time: A meso-level model of organizational temporality. *Management Communication Quarterly, 16,* 380–415.

Banks, S. P., & Riley, P. (1993). Structuration theory as an ontology for communication theory. In S. A. Deetz (Ed.), *Communication yearbook 16* (pp. 167–196). Newbury Park, CA: Sage.

Barley, S. (1986). Technology as an occasion for structuring: Evidence from observations of CT scanners and the social order of radiology departments. *Administrative Science Quarterly, 31,* 78–108.

Billingsley, J. M. (1990, June). *Studying the use of technological resources: Development and test of an interaction coding instrument.* Paper presented at the annual meeting of the International Communication Association, Dublin, Ireland.

Boden, D. (1994). *The business of talk: Organizations in action.* Cambridge, UK: Polity Press.

Brashers, D. E., & Meyers, R. A. (1989). Tag-team argument and group decision-making: A preliminary investigation. In B. Gronbeck (Ed.), *Spheres of argument: Proceedings of the sixth SCA/AFA conference on argumentation* (pp. 542–550). Annandale, VA: Speech Communication Association.

Browning, L., & Beyer, J. (1998). The structuring of shared voluntary standards in the U.S. semiconductor industry: Communicating to reach agreement. *Communication Monographs, 65,* 220–243.

Canary, D. J. (1989). *Manual for coding conversational argument.* Unpublished manuscript, Pennsylvania State University.

Canary, D. J., Brossman, B. G., & Seibold, D. R. (1987). Argument structures in decision-making groups. *Southern Speech Communication Journal, 53,* 18–37.

Canary, D. J., Ratledge, N. T., & Seibold, D. R. (1982, November). *Argument and group decision-making: Development of a coding scheme.* Paper presented at the annual meeting of the Speech Communication Association, Louisville, KY.

DeSanctis, G., & Poole, M. S. (1994). Capturing the complexity in advanced technology use: Adaptive structuration theory. *Organization Science, 5,* 121–147.

Giddens, A. (1979). *Central problems in social theory: Action, structure, and contradiction in social analysis.* Berkeley: University of California Press.

Giddens, A. (1984). *The constitution of society: Outline of the theory of structuration.* Berkeley: University of California Press.

Heller, M. A. (1992). *Group decision support use: A contextual contingencies approach and the role of group history in understanding GDSS effects.* Unpublished master's thesis, University of California, Santa Barbara.

Jacobs, S., & Jackson, S. (1980). Structure of conversational argument: Pragmatic bases for the enthymeme. *Quarterly Journal of Speech, 66,* 251–265.

Keough, C., & Lake, R. (1993). Values as structuring processes of contract negotiations. In C. Conrad (Ed.), *The ethical nexus* (pp. 171–191). Norwood, NJ: Ablex.

Lewis, L. K., & Seibold, D. R. (1993). Innovation modification during intraorganizational adoption. *Academy of Management Review, 18,* 322–354.

Meyers, R. A., & Brashers, D. E. (1995). Multi-stage versus single-stage coding of small group argument: A preliminary comparative assessment. In S. Jackson (Ed.), *Argumentation and values: Proceedings of the ninth SCA/AFA conference on argumentation* (pp. 93–100). Annandale, VA: Speech Communication Association.

Meyers, R. A., & Seibold, D. R. (1990). Perspectives on group argument: A critical review of Persuasive Arguments Theory and an alternative structurational view. In J. Anderson (Ed.), *Communication yearbook 13* (pp. 268–302). Newbury Park, CA: Sage.

Meyers, R. A., Seibold, D. R., & Brashers, D. E. (1991). Argument in initial group decision-making discussions: Refinement of a coding scheme and a descriptive quantitative analysis. *Western Journal of Speech Communication, 55,* 47–68.

Myers, K., & Oetzel, J. (2003). Exploring the dimensions of organizational assimilation: Creating and validating a measure. *Communication Quarterly, 51,* 438–457.

Perelman, C. H., & Olbrechts-Tyteca, L. (1969). *The new rhetoric: A treatise on argumentation* (J. Wilkinson & P. Weaver, Trans.). South Bend, IN: University of Notre Dame Press.

Poole, M. S., & DeSanctis, G. (1992). Microlevel structuration in computer-supported group decision-making. *Human Communication Research, 19,* 5–49.

Poole, M. S., Seibold, D. R., & McPhee, R. D. (1985). Group decision-making as a structurational process. *Quarterly Journal of Speech, 71,* 74–102.

Poole, M. S., Seibold, D. R., & McPhee, R. D. (1996). The structuration of group decisions. In R. Y. Hirokawa & M. S. Poole (Eds.), *Communication and group decision-making* (2nd ed., pp. 114–146). Thousand Oaks, CA: Sage.

Seibold, D. R., McPhee, R. D., Poole, M. S., Tanita, N. E., & Canary, D. J. (1981). Argument, group influence, and decision outcomes. In G. Ziegelmuller & J. Rhodes (Eds.), *Dimensions of argument: Proceedings of the second SCA/AFA conference on argumentation* (pp. 663–692). Annandale, VA: Speech Communication Association.

Seibold, D. R., & Meyers, R. A. (2004, November). *Group argument: Review of a structurational research program.* Paper presented at the annual meeting of the National Communication Association, Chicago, IL.

Toulmin, S. E. (1969). *The uses of argument.* Cambridge, UK: Cambridge University Press.

Van Langenhove, L., & Harre, R. (1995). Cultural stereotypes and positioning theory. *Journal for the Theory of Social Behavior, 24,* 359–372.

Wenger, E. (1998). *Communities of practice: Learning, meaning and identity.* Cambridge, UK: Cambridge University Press.

Wenger, E., McDermott, R., & Snyder, W. M. (2002). *Cultivating communities of practice: A guide to managing knowledge.* Boston: Harvard Business School Press.

PART IV

Politicizing

17

Communication as Political Participation

Todd Kelshaw

As you read the words *political participation,* maybe you envision protesters or ralliers carrying signs and chanting, community-meeting members deliberating over coffee, poll workers signing in voters, or other decidedly "civic" behaviors. Perhaps, as well, you assign the phrase some kind of value, distinguishing it from terms like *political apathy* and *disenfranchisement.* Likely you think of political participation as some kind of potentially empowering democratic activity set within a particular sphere, which overlaps with "public" but diverges from "private." In other words, you may view political participation as one kind of contextualized communication that sometimes you do and sometimes—that is, most of the time—you don't do. Certainly, this conception is useful because it allows us to embody civil society in special kinds of talk that observably affect public policymaking: deliberation, debate, dialogue, rhetoric, heresthetic, and so on. However, my goal here is to inflate this bounded conception of political participation and, centrally, to assert that, in essence, *all* communication is consequential involvement in political relationships, processes, and structures.

Really? Surely there must be private or insulated communicative moments that are somehow apolitical, like when I read my daughter a bedtime story, share a joke with a coworker, or honk my car horn "hello" (or "Get out of my way!" for that matter) at a neighbor, right? In this essay's reconception of politics, my answer is no. There are some big stop-offs along the way to this "no": First, communication is relational and participatory. Second, relationships are negotiations of values based in stake and power. Third, such negotiations occur in both private (interpersonal) and public (societal) contexts, which are inextricably braided. My final point is that it is within this inextricability that politics—as I define it—occurs. In other words, my major idea is that the mundane interaction of day-to-day life is just as political (if not as obviously and conscientiously) as any extraordinary public act, at least in the sense that both have consequences beyond their seemingly discrete spheres.

Communication Is Relational and Participatory

The assertion that communication is relational is, in contemporary thought anyhow, somewhat of the "duh" variety. It seems that concern for communication's relational nature is increasingly what defines today's communication discipline over and against fields like psychology, linguistics, and political science. As Roberts and Bavelas (1996) trace them, dominant assumptions about where meaning resides have shifted in recent decades from *in words,* to *in words and their context,* to *in the speaker's intention,* and, finally, to *in between interlocutors.* The "in between" is entirely a relational notion that characterizes communication as an interactive process rather than as a merely active thing.

Stanley Deetz's (1994) commentary on the future of the discipline—written when a relational conception was still more of a "huh?" than a "duh" for many—asserts the new approach's importance by fleshing out implications of the shift from an expressive to a constitutive take. The former sees communication as a means of information dissemination and control. In so doing, it ignores complex psychological, sociological, and economic undercurrents of heterogeneous societies while supporting the "reality" of dominant ideological traditions and the social groups that benefit from them. The new paradigm, though, aims to understand codeterminative dimensions of meaning-making, in which subtle ideological struggles and contradictory realities constantly play out. Whereas I momentarily defer discussion of these dynamics (which are at the heart of my definition of politics), I point out the general idea that relational conceptions of communication highlight the playing-out of complex and subtle dialectical tensions.[1] More specifically, I draw on Deetz's idea that paying attention to such dynamics may help us better reflect and respond as we engage with others, thereby contributing to a world made more by collaborative management of contradictions than by domination and consent.

There is an important and rudimentary condition of our relational bonds with others: our participation. The by-now trite way of putting this is that we cannot *not* communicate. We participate in the words that we speak and write, and in our intended and unintended nonverbal behaviors. In doing so, we weave ourselves into social fabrics. Everything we do is inherently communicative, which means that our behaviors arise from and contribute to our experiential worlds. This applies to the student at the back of the room who lowers her eyes, the citizen who refuses (or does not bother) to vote, and the boyfriend who hangs up the phone to avoid a quarrel. All are active—rather, interactive—instances of participation, which have consequences despite any desire one might have for invisibility and insulation. We not only participate regardless of our intentions, but regardless of our levels of awareness. It is impossible to reflect consciously on our nonstop interaction and its role in our world-making, but we cannot deny that our meanings do *mean* things to us, at all times. That we *do* coinhabit worlds that make sense to us means that we are, in fact, always participating somehow.

This infinitude and continuity of our participation concerns our various social realities' unfolding natures. "In understanding, we are drawn into an event of truth and arrive, as it were, too late, if we want to know what we are supposed to believe," Gadamer beautifully observed (1995, p. 490). Communicated meaning is at once a noun and a verb—both product and process—that is real only in its ever pending consequences. In addition to being ever unfolding, relational participation is always *with*. So relating is somewhat of a democratic enterprise (in a particular sense) in that all participants have at least some control and some lack of control over what happens among them. Regardless of social disparities among participants, no one ever has total communicative control—not the dictator, the professor, the parent, the op-ed editor, nor the boss. There are too many converging dynamics within the spaces between us.

Relationships Are Negotiations of Values, Marked by Stake and Power

That no one ever has total control over a relationship does not suggest that a relationship is ever devoid of questions about control. Relationships manifest dynamically imbalanced forces and are thus ever changing. This idea applies to relationships ranging from those with formal status differences (e.g., manager/laborer, teacher/student, sergeant/private, parent/child, and landlord/tenant) to those that we might swear up and down are equal partnerships (e.g., some friendships and romances) and simple power-free neutralities (e.g., anonymous and zero-history relationships among, say, fellow bus passengers). Along the continuum, though, our ideals and expectations of control—its causes, presence, functions, and outcomes—tend to differ.

With relatively formal, hierarchical relationships, we are more likely to perceive a kind of stable imbalance, insofar as we presume inequities to be hardwired as obvious power currencies (like the promotion that your boss dangles before you). The status quo in such relationships, we think, only breaks down in dramatic, revolutionary fashion, as when you tell your boss to "take this job and shove it, I ain't workin' here no more" (Coe, 1978). On the other end of the continuum—in informal, nonhierarchical relationships—we are likely *not* to notice systemic inequities. This is because their currencies are less recognizable and the dynamics are more subtle and fluid. In these informal, nonhierarchical relationships, we are likely to think of power "problems"—slights, fights, and the like—as anomalous, discrete, maybe even sweep-it-under-the-rug events. Regardless of our assumptions and ideals about various kinds of relationships and their stabilities and visible currencies, though, *all* relationships experience the playing-out of shifting and multilayered power disparities—the ebbs, flows, flip-flops, and perpetual inequities of which are the drivers of meaning-making. Relational dynamics just vary in their levels of tumultuousness, subtlety, and calculation.

How is this so? Why is force an inescapable factor in relationships, even those we believe are founded on pacifistic, egalitarian ideals? If we view meaning as made within our interactions, then it follows that interactions are dynamic, creative processes. The creativity of relating cannot happen by means of stasis, which would result, impossibly, in the death of meaning. If you and I were perfect replicas and if there were no one else on Earth to interfere with us, we would neither disagree nor change (nor need to communicate, for that matter), and we would live together in perfect peace (not to be confused with harmony, which requires aligned difference; ours would be unison). Given the preposterousness of this scenario and the Earth's abundance of diverse people and peoples, such stasis is not feasible. We are a varied lot, and our heterogeneity is both reflected and made in our distinct languages and voices. This polyphony is sometimes harmonic but more often dissonant—and the composition itself is ever detuned within our relationships' pushes and pulls. Our only constant is our mutual yet imbalanced and fluctuating forcefulness.

So, what is being pushed-and-pulled over? Information? Factual knowledge? Hardly, since we have nothing quite that brute in our fluidly unstable worlds. What we instead tussle over are the unfixed premises of our beings as people: values. Everything we understand is, in measures, good, bad, right, wrong, beautiful, ugly, funny, somber, important, trivial. . . . These understandings not only *accompany* our senses of everything we know, they *are* our senses of everything we know, and they guide us moment by moment. Since everything we know is relationally made, relationships may be defined in this way: as negotiations of values that gird personal and social ethical frameworks and—in effect—make us who we are in light of others.

We place great stake in these negotiations because everything we have is in the balance (well, *im*balance). If communication is relational, then "I" is contingent on how others respond to me and how I respond to them. To maintain my identity, then, *I value having my values valued by others whom*

I value. So do you, of course, so when you and I interact, we engage in moral confrontations, however imperceptibly at times. The intricate and shifting web of these confrontations among innumerable diverse people is called humanity.

Humanity, it follows, is an organic network of persuasive power in which staked values are continually inscribed, enforced, and transformed. In every interaction, we illuminate and confront certain moral preferences. Do we protect them? Propagate them? Relinquish them? No matter what, we do not have full control, because many other superseding values concurrently play out within our complex and changing ethical systems. This multilayered interplay of values is where personal and relational instability and change happens. (A mundane and very simple example: I hate sushi. You love sushi. I love doing things with you more than I hate sushi. So I grow to love sushi, at least when I eat it with you.) Our means of tinkering with values, then, are values themselves, which spiral in on themselves concentrically. Note that the persuasive power in which we stake our values is *itself* a manifestation of values, having currency only if our resources are things that we imbue with fear, want, need, or whatever. So communication is a process of persuasive evaluation *and* evaluative persuasion that continually spirals—and sometimes tumbles—in on itself.

Value Negotiations on Local and Societal Levels Are Intertwined

The large point thus far is that communication is inevitably persuasive, even if our levels of reflection, intentionality, and assertiveness vary. It is through these persuasive transactions that we build and rebuild our humanistic worlds, which are appropriately understood as fluid and complex systems of power-laden relationships. Now I address these systems, defining them as interweavings of local and societal discourses.

In local settings, we interact with varying qualities. To borrow from Stewart and Logan's (1998) conception, these variations may be laid out on a continuum. On one end, we fulfill social roles for each other in generic contexts, enacting and reacting to acceptably decorous scripts (e.g., "Paper or plastic, ma'am?" or "Get up to your room, young man, and don't come down till you've thought about what you've done!"). Moving along the continuum, we communicate in ways that affiliate and differentiate us according to our senses of often-overlapping cultural memberships (e.g., the Grateful Dead sticker you see on that Mercedes' bumper, or the two female students who sit next to each other in an otherwise all-male class). The other end of the continuum finds us interacting not in measurable and scripted social roles, but as unique persons capable of reflecting and responding in dialogic ways. As we move fluidly through these varied modes, we enact and reproduce different ethical versions of ourselves. Many of these moral structures exist simultaneously, and typically overlap and even contradict.

We also participate nonlocally, engaging in group- and mass-discourses in relatively "public" contexts. These discourses generally affiliate and coordinate us within more-or-less cohesive yet permeable organizations and cultural bodies, creating and recreating overlapping structures and social orders. They do this by enabling the interplay of stabilizing and destabilizing social movements, which ensures that larger social formations—like big-scale versions of interpersonal relationships—are always in flux. In an age of ever-expanding technologies and media, our mass discourses defy regional, temporal, and cultural confines, plugging us into more-complicated arrays of relationships and understandings. In these arrays, we encounter and contribute to multiple overlapping ethical frameworks.

"It is always the case," notes Anthony Giddens (1984), "that the day-to-day activity of social actors draws upon and reproduces structural features of wider social systems," which are "not necessarily unified collectives" (p. 24). To speak of interpersonal, societal, private, and public communicative moments in the same breath is to invoke what Giddens calls a braided "copresence" that is manifested in "fluctuating lines between enclosure and display" (p. xxvi). However convenient it may be to tease apart interpersonal and collective communicative processes and structures (as I have done in the prior two paragraphs), doing so risks the trappings of a dualist approach: missed opportunities to recognize the subtle, complicated, and organic qualities of the interplay. In seeing relational life as interwoven—at once private and public, local and global, and immediate and timeless—I hope to do away with simplistic dissociations of free will (agency) and determinism (functionalism), while celebrating the fact that we do have, well, *some* personal control. But our potentials to conscientiously affect our worlds are limited—ironically by structural constraints of our own comaking.

Communication as Political Participation

Politics, in my definition, lives in those innumerable interstices and intersections of interpersonal and societal relating. It is not a discrete sphere within a so-called public realm, occasionally bumping into other spheres such as economics and law.[2] Nor is its chief (or only) function to develop and execute public policy. Instead, politics is our universal condition. It is brought to life when we interact, confront others' ethics and our own, and forge senses of each other and ourselves in relation to broader social groups. In making sense of these things together, we bring them into existence. The tensions that play out in this amorphous web have enormous (mostly unintended) consequences, from the qualities of our friendships to the invasiveness of our laws. It is this ongoing tensional process that galvanizes us all as coparticipants within a shared political state of being.

When I watch CNN's *Crossfire,* for example, I understand why we are reluctant to think of politics in this way. I also get a hint as to why political apathy and cynicism so miserably pervade American society (Ansolabehere & Iyengar, 1995; Cappella & Jamieson, 1997). Even when political matters gain our attention, they tend to do so in ways that abstract themselves from our everyday experiences on the job, in the home, at the bowling alley, or wherever our "real" lives take us. We talk *about* politics, but not, we think, *within* it. Politics bores us, entertains us, angers us, affiliates and divides us . . . but always from a distance and with implicit permission to simply turn it off. It is something mostly done by other people (politicians) in other places ("inside the Beltway") and tends to be, by definition, ugly, mean-spirited, and backhanded. (The appropriated term *office politics* exemplifies this sense.) The potentially definitive *Crossfire* version of politics is *The Jerry Springer Show* dressed up in white collars (and bow ties). We see that how people with ideological differences relate to each other is no different than how people with marital differences do when performing for a live studio audience: with divisive simplifications, personal insults, yelling, and worse. And just as violent videogames purportedly relieve our pent-up angst rather than train us to enact it in real life, our ability to abstract those politicos on *Crossfire* (as with those "trailer-trash hicks" on *The Jerry Springer Show*) as objects of spectacle seems to vaccinate us from obligation to participate ourselves.

This *Crossfire*-ization of politics, though, is merely a symptom of a more systemic problem. What underlies and precipitates this symptom are the notions that participation and obligation pertain only to democratically leaning societies like the United States and, more troubling, that political participation is something we may choose to do. This essay's biggest point is that we—meaning *all of us*—are *always* participants in encompassing political relationships, processes, and structures, *all of which* exceed formal jurisdictions. This is true, by default, of our constant communicative involvement with others, regardless of whether our immediate government is dictatorial (in which we believe we are not allowed to be political), republican (in which we celebrate our choice whether to exercise certain political rights, even in light of Sean "P. Diddy" Combs's famous 2004 directive to "vote or die"), or anything else. Being political is not a prohibited thing, a choice, or an obligation; it is a condition. The root question is not whether we choose or have the power to behave politically, but whether we recognize the political consequences of our minute-to-minute interactions.

As I have claimed throughout this essay, our personal value systems are reconstructed in these minute-to-minute interactions, and they bleed into and out of larger societal value systems. This complicated intereffluence is what I call "politics" because it is where *unum* and *pluribus* confront and absorb one another, then seep forth again, transformed.[3] In my conception, the private and the public are not distinct spheres, either detached or overlapping. They are one and the same. So as I read my daughter a bedtime story, share a joke with an office colleague, or honk my car horn at a neighbor, the best thing I can do is reflect on how we are affecting each other and what values are transpiring between us. Once I have done that, I am a bit better poised to reflect on how such value constructs are not "mine" by possession or right, but how they are "ours." I may notice that as we continue to engage with others in our complex worlds, the "ours" transcends my local dyadic settings and interacts with innumerable other "ours" in that great boundless public of intersecting ethical collectives.

A final point: My call is not derision of those (myself included) who work hard to promote explicit forms of civic engagement. Whereas I assert here that quintessentially "civic" discourses such as deliberation and dialogue are no more or less political than others, I do not intend to demean their real potentials for empowering common people and affecting public policy. Surely, citizens' direct involvement in policymaking is vital for any society, and utterly necessary for democracies. But I believe that we—as scholars, officeholders, reporters, laypeople, and whoever—tend to devote our attention to political tangibles like public opinion, grassroots movements, policy-making procedures, and campaign advertising effects largely because these are causal things that we are able to isolate and measure. Meanwhile, we neglect the ways in which all sorts of other invisible and untraceable discursive forces shape our societies and ourselves.

We ignore such forces for two chief reasons, I think. For one, these are fluid and complex things that defy our empirical methods. For another, the prioritization of simple causal factors in a supposedly delimited political sphere preserves our liberal-individualistic beliefs in freedom of choice and personal power. These commitments, in turn, preserve the potential for dominance and the perception of consent—the requisites of one's abilities for success in this increasingly globalized, free-market, and supposedly information-aged world of ours. To acknowledge that our political processes occur not just in our public, political spheres but within the universes of our relational webs, we fear, would be to acknowledge our partial lack of control and choice and, in so doing, to relinquish them completely.

Notes

1. See Baxter and Montgomery (1996) for an excellent articulation of a relational perspective.

2. This spherical conceptualization of politics is exemplified in this television news report: "As always, Wall Street has one eye on politics" (WCBS-TV, 2004).

3. Whereas the notion of *e pluribus unum* is a hallmark of republican democracies, the tension between individuals and their larger societies (and the global worlds beyond) is endemic to any social structure, from anarchies to dictatorships.

Additional Readings

Arendt, H. (1958). *The human condition.* Chicago: University of Chicago Press.
Dewey, J. (1954). *The public and its problems.* Athens, OH: Swallow Press.
Giddens, A. (1984). *The constitution of society: Outline of the theory of structuration.* Berkeley: University of California Press.
Shotter, J. (1993). *Conversational realities: Constructing life through language.* London: Sage.
Taylor, C. (1994). Interpretation and the sciences of man. In M. Martin & L. C. McIntyre (Eds.), *Readings in the philosophy of social science* (pp. 181–211). Cambridge: MIT Press.

References

Ansolabehere, S., & Iyengar, S. (1995). *Going negative: How political advertisements shrink and polarize the electorate.* New York: Free Press.
Baxter, L. A., & Montgomery, B. M. (1996). *Relating: Dialogues and dialectics.* New York: Guilford Press.
Cappella, J. N., & Jamieson, K. H. (1997). *Spiral of cynicism: The press and the public good.* New York: Oxford University Press.
Coe, D. A. (1978). Take this job and shove it [Recorded by J. Paycheck]. On *Take this job and shove it* [record]. Warner-Tamerlane.
Deetz, S. (1994). Future of the discipline: The challenges, the research, and the social contribution. In S. A. Deetz (Ed.), *Communication yearbook 17* (pp. 565–600). Thousand Oaks, CA: Sage.
Gadamer, H.-G. (1995). *Truth and method* (J. Weinsheimer & D. G. Marshall, Trans., Rev. ed.). New York: Continuum.
Giddens, A. (1984). *The constitution of society: Outline of the theory of structuration.* Berkeley: University of California Press.
Roberts, G. L., & Bavelas, J. B. (1996). The communicative dictionary: A collaborative theory of meaning. In J. Stewart (Ed.), *Beyond the symbol model: Reflections on the nature of language.* Albany: SUNY Press.
Stewart, J., & Logan, C. (1998). *Together: Communicating interpersonally* (5th ed.). Boston: McGraw-Hill.
WCBS-TV. (2004, June 28). *Live at five* [Television broadcast]. New York: CBS Broadcasting.

18

Communication as Deliberation

John Gastil

W e can best understand communication through the lens of deliberative democratic theory. When communication is not relevant to deliberation, it is frivolous or, more often, in no need of careful study. Communication for the sake of companionship, self-expression, or play is fine, even essential, but cultures have bonded, displayed, and thrived for millennia without careful study of (or even introspection on) such modes of talk. By contrast, much of human progress has centered on our ability to imagine a more deliberative society and work toward the establishment of increasingly deliberative institutions and cultural traditions.

In general terms, deliberation simply means to reflect carefully on a matter, weighing the strengths and weaknesses of alternative solutions to a problem. Deliberation aims to arrive at a decision or judgment based on not only facts and data but also values, emotions, and other less technical considerations. Thus, for a single, solitary individual, deliberation means careful thinking and analysis, a familiar process that all of us go through at different times.[1] Those scholars who speak of "intrapersonal communication"—the talk that goes on inside one's head—are familiar with this process. I prefer to call this

---

At the invitation of this volume's editors, I have written this essay in as forceful a style as possible. One might find it ironic that a deliberation scholar would write such a belligerent screed, but I would remind the reader that the deliberative ideal welcomes both satire and frank disagreement, all in the spirit of sifting out the truth (and having a good time doing so).

"thinking," rather than labeling it as a form of communication. When one carries out elaborate conversations in one's head, the most appropriate research perspective is that of the psychopharmacologist, not the communication scholar.

In any case, individual decisions are rarely, if ever, truly private ones. Even when a single person has the authority to make a choice, the deliberation that precedes a decision involves many other people and many forms of communication. More commonly, what people mean by deliberation is talking to make decisions together as a small group, an organization, or a nation. Whether the decision maker is a single person or a collective body, it is equally useful to think of the communication process as deliberation leading toward a decision.

In this brief essay, I will demonstrate the importance of deliberation in work and family, politics and public life, and our own search for the meaning of life. After revealing the ubiquity of deliberation, I'll narrowly avoid contradicting myself by arguing that we don't do it often enough. That which would seem common is, alas, most rare.

Deliberation in Everyday Life

If you own a small skateboard rental shop near the shore at Pacific Beach, well, you have it made. But seriously, imagine that you owned such a store and needed to decide whether to add in-line skates to your rental inventory. The decision is yours and yours alone, yet your deliberation on this decision will involve face-to-face conversations and online exchanges with friends, customers, beachgoers, and other shopkeepers. You might also do some reading to look at prices and learn the experiences of other renters. And you're likely to track relevant popular trends by drawing on what you've watched on television, heard on the radio, and seen at the movies and on the Internet. These different communication processes all mix together in your mind to yield a decision that is better understood as the culmination of a multichannel communicative process than as the result of a private, closed cognitive process.

Some workplaces, from equal-partner law firms to grocery cooperatives, involve collective, often face-to-face, deliberation among the members of a decision-making body.[2] Whether firing employees, renting a new facility, or purchasing new stock, these coworkers engage in a range of different communication activities, and all of these feed into a larger deliberative process oriented toward a final decision. Even in many hierarchical corporations or religious organizations, a board of directors or elders deliberates in a similar manner.

But there's more to life than work. Does deliberation have anything to do with how we live as individuals or in our families and close relationships? Again, when deliberation is generally understood as talk that is oriented toward making decisions through a reflective, analytic process of discovery and judgment, the most important aspects of our personal and family lives can be understood in deliberative terms.

Starting with a hard example, how about deciding where to live, which school to attend, what car to buy, or even whom to spend your time with? All are decisions, of course, as decision making is a ubiquitous feature of a free society. Happily, freedom is ascendant in the modern world, and the choices we make involve an ever expanding array of alternatives with incredibly complex sets of considerations.

Choice has become so pervasive, in fact, that some observers wonder whether it has become excessive, even burdensome.[3] Even if we sometimes reasonably avoid deliberation to make trivial decisions about what jeans to buy or which movie to see, we can't help but tend toward deliberating on the more important personal decisions we make.

Consider the example of marriage or choosing a life partner. This decision is, first of all, a joint one—even when the decision makers are parents setting up an arranged marriage. The parties deciding to join together may work through emotions, hopes, fears, sober financial considerations, and anything else you might imagine. Though the question may be asked on a Jumbotron screen in a sports arena and met with a quick and blushing yes, even then the move from engagement to marriage proceeds as a deliberative one, often involving complex negotiations about the wedding or the marriage itself. After all, many engagements end with separation, amicable or otherwise.

Once joined together as family, the deliberation continues, till death do they part. At this point, it is useful to illustrate the more subtle deliberative processes that take place in our lives. We engage in small struggles every day over how to conduct ourselves. Over time, these typically are resolved in favor of one view or another or some compromise in between.

For example, how should partners in a relationship speak to each other day-to-day? What forms of speech are loving versus cloying, playful versus mean? How often should one call one's partner on a cell phone? What topics are appropriate when strolling in a public park? Each of us answers these questions differently. When in a long-term relationship, partners often negotiate the answers to these questions, even if they never metacommunicate (i.e., talk explicitly about how to talk). Few couples broach these topics in a stereotypically deliberative way by, say, holding a "house meeting" with formal agendas and committee minutes. But most couples do work through these questions over the course of many years. The deliberation proceeds through small, seemingly offhand comments about each other's behavior, or unconnected observations about the way people on television or in movies address one another. Even unconsciously (though often, dare we say, deliberately), the partners talk through these issues and arrive at informal agreements or détentes.[4]

Deliberation, Politics, and the Meaning of Life

Deliberation characterizes not only the small, personal questions of our lives but also the largest, most profound decisions we must make together as publics. History has smiled on democracy, and the democratic ideal has spread quickly over the globe, at least when measured in geologic time. Most modern nations make their major decisions through an overlapping series of deliberative processes. Public assemblies, legislative committees, city councils, administrative bodies, judicial panels, and supreme courts all go through quasi-deliberative processes to draft, pass, judge, and execute laws.

Individual citizens also take part in a larger deliberative drama. From one perspective, the consumption of political news and entertainment, from the *New York Times* to *The Daily Show*, provides us with the information and viewpoints we need to arrive at our own private judgments about which candidates and policies to support. Political conversations add more to the mix of ideas and input, though they are often shaped by the same media content we've recently consumed.[5] ("Did you see *Oprah* yesterday? She had this woman on who . . .")

Taken together, these individual, mediated, and social deliberations add up to a process of public weighing and judgment, at least in theory.[6] In this way, citizens deliberate to decide who to vote for, so that they might deliberate on our behalf as our elected representatives. Or, when voting directly on initiatives, we deliberate through the media and informal interactions with fellow citizens to make laws ourselves, for better or for worse.

In the United States and a few other countries, citizens also deliberate as part of the criminal and civil justice system through the jury process. Complete strangers with no technical expertise listen to competing arguments and then retire to the jury room to deliberate. The research done to date suggests that over the course of the trial and in their private deliberation rooms, juries generally work through the relevant legal and evidentiary issues to arrive at verdicts quite similar to those that judges reach through their own deliberative process.[7]

If health care reform, foreign policy debates, and murder don't strike you as important (though they should), perhaps you could agree that there are other profound questions to answer during your brief existence on Earth. What, you might ask yourself, is the meaning of life? Is there a world beyond the flesh—a god or other supernatural force that transcends our lives?

Even a solitary seeker, such as the ones portrayed in such classic inspirational texts as *Siddhartha* or *Jonathan Livingston Seagull*, finds answers to these questions through contemplation inspired by social interaction. Encounters with sages, fellow seekers, and unreflective passersby provide the material necessary for further insight on a philosophical or spiritual journey. To turn about a philosophical truism, the unlived life is not worth examining. How could a person with no real social experience concoct a useful conception of human existence? The cliché of René Descartes sitting by the fireplace, sifting through his private musings, ignores the lifetime of conversations, social exchanges, and public activities that preceded his quiet nights by the hearth. Deliberation is the most apt metaphor for how we work through our most basic philosophical and moral questions.

A Deliberative Critique of How We Communicate

All of this is to say that we can think of much of our communication as part of a deliberative process. The preceding examples have shown the prevalence of deliberation in both obvious and obscure forms in our private, social, and public lives. But what I have really tried to show is how apt a metaphor deliberation is for how we *should* conduct ourselves. To an extent, deliberation is inevitable as we talk through our choices in life, but deliberation occurs by degrees. In this sense, deliberation might be even more apt as an *ideal* for much of our communication—a model by which to judge the way we actually make choices.

The ideal type of deliberation is commonly described as being democratic. A fully democratic process for public deliberation would involve rigorous analysis of problems and solutions, and it would require egalitarian discussion norms and an openness to dialogue when participants differed in fundamental ways, such as how to reason or even how to talk.[8]

If you would like an image, picture an idealized assembly of citizen-legislators working together to reach a decision in spite of their strong, principled disagreements. Or think of the best working group you've ever been on, collecting data, speaking frankly, sharing fears and hopes, encouraging the quieter members to speak up, and arriving at a final decision. These are ideal-types, and they can help us see the limitations of actual practice.

Returning to the workplace, consider how rarely an office deliberates on matters of grave importance. After all, the term *office politics* refers to petty power struggles and self-destructive infighting, not to the model of public deliberation. A workplace misses an opportunity for deliberation whenever a person is fired as a vendetta (instead of owing to proven incompetence), a marketing plan is adopted on the reputation of its author (rather than its merits), or a new set of procedures is adopted due to the whimsical judgment of a boss (in the absence of input from the staff). Even when an organization appears, on the surface, to undertake deliberation, critical meetings, memos, and musings may be nothing more than distractions from an autocratic decision by a manager or CEO who cares not for the thoughts of the rank-and-file membership. Though deliberation takes time, in examples such as these, the time spent deliberating more than pays for itself in higher morale and better decisions.

When we make decisions on our own behalf, we also often fail to deliberate when we should. Advertisers count on you uncritically absorbing mediated images, feelings, innuendos, and the like, slowly building loyalty toward brands and lifestyles. When you walk zombie-like into the coffee shop, muttering "Donuts . . . donuts," your choices have been reduced to automatic processes. If you think to yourself, "Sure, but that's not how I'd buy a car or a home," think again. The higher the stakes, the more companies invest in your miseducation. Sure, some advertising might really provide useful input into your deliberative process, but more often, the goal is to shift your preferences and build your appetite through guile. And it often works. After all, *Consumer Reports* has never jumped off the racks at the magazine stand.

The countless unconscious social decisions we make every day also fail to meet deliberative standards. More often than not, we uncritically accept the status quo rules for how to treat and view each other. Racist and sexist ideologies reinforce themselves through these daily oversights, even in the actions and thoughts of people who consciously oppose such views. By listening to the sexist gesture without comment, cringing as the stranger walks by, or correcting the dialect of a playmate, we make our argument (or silently assent to another's claim) for one particular way of living. Time and again, we let pass a moment where we could have made a modest contribution to a gradual cultural shift, a quiet revolution in how the sexes relate or how cultures comingle. The deliberative spirit asks us to engage, to share our views, and to reflect on our assumptions, and on those occasions when we do so, we feel alive, engaged, a part of the larger social drama.[9]

As a society, we also have many opportunities to make our public institutions more deliberative. Even the hallmark of deliberation, the American jury system, could benefit from reforms oriented toward making it more deliberative. Previous research has shown that these randomly selected groups of citizens are subject to pernicious gender, race, and class biases, such as the tendency to discount minority views and overvalue the perspectives of wealthier male jurors.[10] The deliberative perspective asks juries to be *more* deliberative by addressing biases such as these. This can be done with a reform as simple as adding a paragraph on group communication tendencies to the instructions juries hear before retiring to their chambers.

Elections could also be more deliberative. Politics in the United States is far from a model of deliberation. As is true almost everywhere else, political communication in the United States often consists of mudslinging, name-calling, empty stump speeches, misleading campaign mailings, deceptive television ads, and media coverage oriented toward the horse race more than the issues.[11]

There are ways, however, to make elections more deliberative. One proposal I have advanced is convening randomly selected, paid panels of citizens to evaluate candidates and ballot measures. The citizens would deliberate over a period of one week and write up reflections and recommendations that would appear in the official voting guide. This process would let other voters act on the insights of their peers' deliberations, and it could even orient the candidates themselves toward more deliberative platforms, lest they appear shallow or deceptive when evaluated by the citizen panels.[12] British Columbia, Canada, has done something similar by successfully convening a random sample of its citizens to draft a referendum on electoral reform.[13]

Aside from politics and structural reforms such as these, each of us has the opportunity to take part in ongoing conversations about the meaning of life and the purpose of human existence. We often think of these as personal questions, but in the modern context, I believe it's clearer than ever that these are questions we must explore together, even if we are unlikely to find the same answers.

Modern Islamic terrorism, for instance, relies on sharp cultural divisions between one set of believers and another. To the extent that all varieties of Muslims, Christians, Jews, atheists, and others can talk openly with one another about their convictions, we decrease the potential for misunderstanding, prejudice, and dehumanization. Theological deliberation does not eradicate terrorism, but the careful cultivation of the deliberative spirit undermines movements and ideologies that rely on ignorance, intolerance, and isolation.

Conclusion

In the end, the deliberative perspective is only one way of looking at communication. There are many other modes of talk that are useful, vital, and enjoyable. And there are other critical yardsticks by which we can measure our discourse. Nonetheless, deliberation aptly characterizes much of our communication, particularly the important decisions we must make as individuals and collectives, and it is equally valuable as a standard by which we can judge the ways we talk with each other.

Fortunately, it is likely that deliberation is a self-reinforcing process. The more often we deliberate together, the better we become at it, the more we come to expect it, the more often we expect it to work, and the more motivated we are to try it.[14] Scholars in political communication, political science, and public administration already have come to recognize the potential power of deliberation. Its reach could extend even farther if we came to recognize the prevalence of deliberation—and the value of deliberative critique—across all spheres of human experience.

Notes

1. John Dewey aptly described this process in his classic text, *How We Think* (1910). Dewey's work strongly influenced later writings on decision making, such as Dennis S. Gouran and Randy Y. Hirokawa's "Functional Theory and Communication in Decision-Making and Problem-Solving Groups: An Expanded View" (1996).

2. For a description of one such cooperative workplace, see my book *Democracy in Small Groups: Participation, Decision-Making, and Communication* (1993).

3. On the tyranny of choices in the modern world, see Barry Schwartz, *The Paradox of Choice: Why More Is Less* (2004).

4. Roger Fisher, famous as a coauthor of the bestselling *Getting to Yes*, saw how apt the negotiation metaphor was for relationships and cowrote with Scott Brown *Getting Together: Building Relationships as We Negotiate* (1989).

5. On how we talk about politics, see William Gamson, *Talking Politics* (1992).

6. On the mediated view of deliberation, see Benjamin Page, *Who Deliberates? Mass Media in Modern Democracy* (1996).

7. See Valerie P. Hans and Neil Vidmar, *Judging the Jury* (2001), and Hans' *Business on Trial: The Civil Jury and Corporate Responsibility* (2000).

8. This definition comes from Stephanie Burkhalter, John Gastil, and Todd Kelshaw's "The Self-Reinforcing Model of Public Deliberation" (2002).

9. Sociologist Anthony Giddens offers a comprehensive theory of society along these lines in *The Constitution of Society* (1984).

10. For a critique of juries and the promise of deliberation generally, see Lynn Sanders, "Against Deliberation" (1997), and Tali Mendelberg, "The Deliberative Citizen: Theory and Evidence" (2002).

11. On discourse in American politics, see Kathleen Hall Jamieson, *Dirty Politics: Deception, Distraction, and Democracy* (1992), and my review essay,

"Undemocratic Discourse: A Review of Theory and Research on Political Discourse" (1992). For a book on campaign communication from the perspective of those who practice it, read Judith S. Trent and Robert V. Friedenberg (editors), *Political Campaign Communication: Principles and Practices,* 4th edition (2000).

12. I propose citizen panels in *By Popular Demand: Revitalizing Representative Democracy Through Deliberative Elections* (2000). Early pioneers in deliberation include Ned Crosby and Jim Fishkin, both of whom have recently published books on how to make elections more deliberative. See Crosby's *Healthy Democracy: Empowering a Clear and Informed Voice of the People* (2003) and Fishkin's book, with Bruce Ackerman, *Deliberation Day* (2004).

13. For more on the Citizens Assembly, visit http://www.citizensassembly.bc.ca/ public

14. See the second half of the article by Burkhalter et al. (2002), *op cit.,* pages 411–418.

Additional Readings

Dewey, J. (1910). *How we think*. New York: Heath.

Gastil, J. (1993). *Democracy in small groups: Participation, decision-making, and communication*. Philadelphia: New Society.

Jamieson, K. H. (1992). *Dirty politics: Deception, distraction, and democracy*. Oxford, UK: Oxford University Press.

Page, B. (1996). *Who deliberates? Mass media in modern democracy*. Chicago: University of Chicago Press.

Sanders, L. (1997). Against deliberation. *Political Theory, 25,* 347–376.

References

Burkhalter, S., Gastil, J., & Kelshaw, T. (2002). The self-reinforcing model of public deliberation. *Communication Theory, 12,* 398–422.

Crosby, N. (2003). *Healthy democracy: Empowering a clear and informed voice of the people*. Edina, MN: Beaver's Pond.

Dewey, J. (1910). *How we think*. New York: Heath.

Fisher, R., & Brown, S. (1989). *Getting together: Building relationships as we negotiate*. New York: Penguin.

Fishkin, J., & Ackerman, B. (2004). *Deliberation day*. New Haven, CT: Yale University Press.

Gamson, W. (1992). *Talking politics*. Cambridge, UK: Cambridge University Press.

Gastil, J. (1992). Undemocratic discourse: A review of theory and research on political discourse. *Discourse & Society, 4,* 469–500.

Gastil, J. (1993). *Democracy in small groups: Participation, decision-making, and communication*. Philadelphia: New Society.

Gastil, J. (2000). *By popular demand: Revitalizing representative democracy through deliberative elections.* Berkeley: University of California Press.

Giddens, A. (1984). *The constitution of society.* Berkeley: University of California Press.

Gouran, D. S., & Hirokawa, R. Y. (1996). Functional theory and communication in decision-making and problem-solving groups: An expanded view. In R. Y. Hirokawa & M. S. Poole (Eds.), *Communication and group decision-making* (2nd ed., pp. 55–80). Beverly Hills, CA: Sage.

Hans, V. P. (2000). *Business on trial: The civil jury and corporate responsibility.* New Haven, CT: Yale University Press.

Hans, V. P., & Vidmar, N. (2001). *Judging the jury.* New York: Perseus.

Jamieson, K. H. (1992). *Dirty politics: Deception, distraction, and democracy.* New York: Oxford University Press.

Mendelberg, T. (2002). The deliberative citizen: Theory and evidence. *Political Decision Making, Deliberation and Participation, 6,* 151–193.

Page, B. (1996). *Who deliberates? Mass media in modern democracy.* Chicago: University of Chicago Press.

Sanders, L. (1997). Against deliberation. *Political Theory, 25,* 347–376.

Schwartz, B. (2004). *The paradox of choice: Why more is less.* New York: Ecco.

Trent, J. S., & Friedenberg, R. V. (Eds.). (2000). *Political campaign communication: Principles and practices* (4th ed.). New York: Praeger.

19

Communication as Diffusion

James W. Dearing

O nce, I gave a talk to faculty and students at the University of New Mexico. I was discussing research I'd done about entrepreneurial microbial ecologists and engineers, focusing on how they talked about new toxic waste–eating microbes and thermal extraction pumps for steaming pollutants out of the ground without digging up the soil. These technologies and processes hadn't yet spread, or diffused. I labeled this type of study "prediffusion." I then speculated about the commensurate importance of studying what goes on after diffusion—"postdiffusion." Bradford "J" Hall, an intercultural communication scholar, raised his hand.

"So is everything diffusion?" he asked.

I laughed nervously, for his was a good question that was difficult to answer. There's a lot to be said for narrowly defined paradigms of study. But some paradigms, some theories, defy and challenge the conceptual parameters with which we try to delimit them. They push here, prod there, and in fits and starts edge outward. The scholars who conduct the studies that cumulate in the paradigm keep speculating about new relationships and keep trying them out, often in different contexts.[1] For better or worse, that's the diffusion paradigm.

I know population ecologists, demographers, cultural anthropologists, and complexity scientists who would not laugh at Brad Hall's question, and instead answer, "Well, that's one way of looking at it." For the study of diffusion is a robust, well-aged, somewhat ungainly interdisciplinary body of scholarship, capable of subsuming big ideas. Kind of like—dare I write it?—the field of communication itself.

That's why thinking about communication as diffusion makes perfect sense.

To conceptualize communication as diffusion is quite efficient, for doing so is to focus on what really counts: the most important communications; the messages we interpret as both risky and rewarding; and the ideas that have real consequences, good and ill. For diffusion, whether concerned with purposive intent by some to spread an innovation to others, or whether focused on imitative behavior that constitutes real change by thousands or millions of people, is the study of meaningful and consequential ideas, the ideas that catch on and that wash over whole social systems of people, organizations, communities, and populations. Stated differently, although most of our communicative experience is devoid of much personal or social importance (like surfing the Internet, listening to music, watching television, or seeing others in a restaurant), diffusion is a way of focusing on the ideas in our lives with high personal and social relevance.

The Diffusion Paradigm

When Bob Dylan wrote "The Times They Are A-Changin'," he was describing diffusion.

When Amazon.com invested in a new inventory control system, it was adding to a product's diffusion.

When the Centers for Disease Control and Prevention promoted its obesity prevention guidelines, it was doing diffusion.

And when large-scale Colombian coffee farmers decided against planting low-yield, shade grown, high-quality, high-return coffee plants, they were limiting diffusion.

Diffusion is a social process by which an innovation is communicated over time among the members of a communication network or within a social sector. An *innovation* can be an idea, knowledge, a belief or social norm, a product or service, a technology or process, or even a culture, as long as it is perceived to be new. Innovations are communicated verbally, by one person telling another, and in many other ways such as magazine advertisements and via personal observation. Commonly, we first learn of innovations through impersonal mediated communication channels but only decide to adopt an innovation for ourselves later, after asking the opinion or observing the behavior of someone whom we know, trust, or consider to be expert. This latter point highlights the importance of studying how innovations are communicated from person to person, through the informal communication networks in which we are strongly and weakly tied, or in the social sectors within which we are structurally equivalent with others due to organizational or community position, similar training, employment, or interest.

Time is important in diffusion research, for we usually take time to adopt innovations when we think that they could be important to us. Different individuals take different amounts of time to adopt innovations. For some, only one or two people in their personal networks or "reference groups" are required to adopt before the focal individual then adopts; for others, nearly all others in their personal networks or reference groups must adopt before the focal individual finally converts. These differences are *thresholds* that vary person to person for any particular innovation.

Many highly effective, inexpensive, beneficial innovations have taken decades to diffuse into broad acceptance and use. Some demonstrably advantageous innovations never diffuse. And yes, we have many examples of innovations that have spread rapidly but are no better or are worse than those practices or products that they displaced. The low correlation between innovation quality and diffusion is what makes studying the diffusion of innovations intriguing.

Recent diffusion studies have traced and explained the spread of kindergartens across cultures throughout the world, the spread of schools-of-choice policies among most of the 50 states in the United States, the diffusion of smoking ordinances and laws throughout North America, and the adoption and institutionalization of public participation in community health planning. Diffusion scholars study the spread of rumors, strikes, and fast food. Using diffusion concepts, they explain the failed diffusion of condoms in Latin America as well as the rapid diffusion of ineffective drug use prevention programs in the United States.

Communication is central to diffusion at various points in time. Early on, potential adopters of new things want descriptive information about what a new thing is. Later, they seek feedback or examples from informal opinion leaders or role models about the evaluative worth of the new thing. Later still, people often doubt whether they made the right decision. They will seek out or attend to confirmatory messages that their decision was the right one.

Different people play different roles in the diffusion process, and at different points in time. Certain people, termed *innovators,* function to introduce ideas into communication networks or social sectors; *opinion leaders* evaluate and signal the appropriateness of the innovation for others to consider. When informal opinion leaders adopt an innovation, the communication network or social sector reaches a *critical mass* of adopters. Thereafter, system conversion is difficult to stop. Critical mass is not simply a matter of numbers. The right people (opinion leaders) have to adopt the innovation for others to follow. If opinion leaders ignore the new thing or develop a negative attitude toward it, diffusion will not occur. If people other than opinion leaders adopt, diffusion will be slow or partial, at best.

As you may have now guessed, rapid diffusion of an innovation is not a given. Typically, we watch and wait, passively allowing new things to pass us by. Most of us have a conservative bias regarding innovations. By and large, a conservative orientation toward the new serves us well. This tendency allows us to get on with our lives psychologically, by maintaining cognitive consistency, and socially, through engagement in routine behaviors.

Communication as Diffusion

To conceptualize communication as diffusion means to focus on change processes with consequential outcomes. For example, some people believe that more government regulation over corporations is necessary to safeguard public health. Others believe that government is big enough, that more bureaucracy means less efficiency. But for both beliefs, the question "how does government grow?" is relevant. Often, institutional expansion occurs through the diffusion of public issues. First, a social problem is identified by proponents or activists. Media attention follows. Issue opponents are sought out to counter issue proponents. If stories persist through the addition of new information, issue salience grows. Studies are commissioned, measures introduced, laws passed, and agencies directed to respond. Resources are allocated, staff hired, and services provided. The result of issue diffusion is the institutionalization of a response to a social problem. Such institutionalization rarely goes away (the same can be said for social problems). Theoretically, the process studied concerns change and the outcomes of that change.

Most of our communicative activity concerns stability, order, maintenance, and gradual revolutionary change (in the sense of going around and around). Redundancy—the replication of prior experience—is the primary function of feedback. Behavioral redundancy is a positive condition. Its predictability frees us to think of other things. But it can bore us, too.

Diffusion, on the other hand, is about creation, uncertainty, learning, destruction, and displacement. These unsettling conditions are the stuff of diffusion. When accumulated, diffusion processes result in social change through alteration of the parameters of our daily experience. This is a type of change demarcated by shocks or sudden disjunctures (in the sense of a step function during a linear progression).

Thus, to conceptualize communication as diffusion has the following consequences for theory and research about communication:

1. Thinking of communication as diffusion means that *scholarly attention should focus on communicative behavior that is personally and socially meaningful.* Only a small percentage of all the communication messages to which we attend so qualify.

2. Thinking of communication as diffusion means that *the communicative behavior we study should have demonstrable consequences.* Most of our daily communication experience is not very consequential.

3. Thinking of communication as diffusion means that *studying personal and social change, not continuity, should be the province of communication inquiry.*

4. Thinking of communication as diffusion means that *communication that is meaningful, consequential, and focused on change is processual.* Such communication takes time; thus, theory and research about communication must conceptualize and operationalize time.

5. Thinking of communication as diffusion means that *the messages we study should concern referents, objects, or events that are perceived as surprising, uncertain, and promising.* Newness begets attention, information seeking, discussion, and influence processes, and is thus fertile ground for study.

6. Thinking of communication as diffusion means that *influence as well as information is communicated to and among people.* Personal, social, and impersonal influence may each contribute to change.

7. Thinking of communication as diffusion means that *communication and influence are subject to the structural characteristics of communication networks and social sectors or systems.* Random samples of populations ignore such structures; purposive sampling allows us to make sure that the units studied are those with influence.

8. Lastly, thinking of communication as diffusion means that *degree and source of intentionality should take center stage.* Diffusion includes contagion (when neither sender nor receiver knows that influence is occurring), imitation (when only the receiver knows that she is copying someone), manipulation (when only the sender is aware of the influence attempt), and persuasion (when both sender and receiver are aware that the influence game is being played).

Diffusion researchers have focused on cases of persuasion and manipulation at the expense of studying contagion and imitation, though the latter social processes are perhaps more common and perhaps more successful in leading to diffusion. For, in thinking of communication as diffusion, it is possible and instructive to take the population perspective, that we do not so much adopt or reject innovations as *they select us*. This way of turning the diffusion paradigm on its head is the basis for the study of memetics, and hearkens all the way back to Gabriel Tarde, the French judge, lawyer, and philosopher who took note of the many fashions that took hold of the French citizenry 120 years ago. When communication is seen as diffusion, the population perspective of meme selection, adaptation, dominance, and replacement becomes quite intriguing, with obvious similarities to the garbage can model of organizational choice and of public policy decision making.

Note

1. Sincere apologies to the 14th-century philosopher and theologian William of Occam.

Additional Readings

Anderson, J. G., & Jay, S. J. (1985). The diffusion of medical technology: Social network analysis and policy research. *Sociological Quarterly, 26*(1), 49–64.

Castro, F. G., Elder, J., Coe, K., Tafoya-Barraza, L. M., Moratto, S., Campbell, N., et al. (1995). Mobilizing churches for health promotion in Latino communities: Companeros en la salud. *Journal of the National Cancer Institute Monographs, 18*, 127–135.

Dearing, J. W. (2004). Improving the state of health programming by using diffusion theory. *Journal of Health Communication, 9*, 1–16.

Rogers, E. M. (2003). *Diffusion of innovations* (5th ed.). New York: Free Press.

Valente, T. W. (1995). *Network models of the diffusion of innovations*. Cresskill, NJ: Hampton Press.

20

Communication as Social Influence

Frank Boster

To make the claim that communication can be viewed profitably by thinking of it as social influence requires clarifying the manner in which an important term and an important phrase are used, specifically the term *communication* and the phrase *social influence*. After completing these tasks, one can make an argument to render the claim plausible.

Scholars have generated numerous and diverse definitions of human communication (e.g., see Dance, 1970). Although comparing definitions highlights many points of disagreement, common themes do emerge. Notably, the proposition that human communication involves information exchange provides one commonality. These exchanges take place among persons sharing messages with one another, and messiness, as it does with so many facets of human behavior, characterizes the process. For instance, persons may not articulate well what they desire to convey, the meaning conveyed and the meaning intended may lack isomorphism, and even the most competent communicators may misinterpret well-articulated messages. Nevertheless, in the main, clarity sufficient to allow social intercourse to proceed smoothly results.

Social influence refers to a *change* in *belief, attitude,* or *behavior,* or some combination of these three factors, that occurs as a function of exposure to an external message or series of external messages. Change can connote several qualitatively different types of modification in beliefs, attitudes, or behavior. It can, for instance, suggest creation, as when a message extolling the virtues of hydroponically grown vegetables creates an attitude toward the topic among an audience never before exposed to the concept. Alternatively, change can imply reinforcement, as when a Sunday evening sermon in a fundamentalist Protestant church makes more or less certain the faith of members of the congregation. Change can also imply modified valence or state, as when a politician's speech convinces an audience member to vote for a candidate other than the one for whom the audience member had intended to vote, or changes the probabilities associated with this decision.

Scholars use the term *belief* to characterize the acceptance of a proposition of fact. Consequently, one can evaluate the veracity of beliefs, in principle, by comparing them with empirical evidence. For example, the proposition "the deceased was shot with a small-caliber pistol," serves as an example of a belief. Granted, this proposition lacks precision. Nevertheless, one might employ experts to set the range of what constitutes a small-caliber pistol, be more specific regarding the deceased, and clarify any additional points that require it. At the completion of this process, evidence could be examined and the proposition could be judged true or false or, perhaps, true within some range of probability.

The term *attitude*, on the other hand, connotes the manner in which persons evaluate concepts or objects. For instance, one might say that "vegetables are good" or "the Democratic Party is the best choice for a working class voter" or "classical music is beautiful." A critic might challenge such statements as being untrue in the sense of a speaker being duplicitous when asserting them. Or, a critic might claim that speakers of such statements lack self-insight. Nevertheless, challenges to the truth-value of such statements as empirical matters of fact are nonsensical. They do not make claims of fact, and empirical evidence cannot be generated to examine them. They reflect matters of liking, value, preference, or, generally, the evaluation of concepts or objects in a more or less favorable or unfavorable manner.

Behavior refers to action. Action presents observers with an undifferentiated stimulus stream. To make sense of behavior, one focuses on certain aspects, ignores others, and distorts yet others. Generally, communication scientists focus on certain dimensions of action, being led by substantive points of view, in order to promote sensemaking. Frequency is one such dimension. For example, mass communication scholars count the number of aggressive acts among television shows of various sorts and attempt to link these observations to subsequent aggressive behavior. Latency is another dimension. The difference in the time taken to understand the punch line of a joke may differ as a function of one's dogmatism, and scholars might employ such a measure to promote understanding of mental rigidity.

Strength of action is yet another important dimension. The amount of effort one exerts to convince others to conform might serve as an indicator of the depth of the influencing agent's conviction or reflect the agent's persistence.

These changes come about as a result of exposure to external messages. To be sure, messages may be generated internally (e.g., see Hunter, Levine, & Sayers, 1976), that is, they may be one's own thoughts, but they also may be generated externally. These external messages result from communicating with others, at times intentionally and at other times unintentionally. They are plentiful and may influence targets in many and diverse ways. You may awaken in the morning to a call from an electricity company representative threatening to cancel your power unless you pay your bill in the next 10 days. Omaha Steaks may then call with a tantalizing special offer on filets. Your spouse may ask you to mow the lawn, and when you refuse, may ask you (at least) to take out the garbage. As you find yourself complying with this request by carrying a heavy can to curbside, your neighbor may ask to borrow your lawn mower, a request to which you hastily accede after recalling your spouse's earlier request. On the way to work, you may hear 15 commercials and see billboards promoting visiting Hooter's, purchasing life insurance, attending a particular church, having a vasectomy at a local hospital, and ceasing to smoke.

When external messages are present in the environment but their targets' perceptual apparatus fails to process them, no communication occurs. These messages cannot impact beliefs, attitudes, or behavior. But, those external messages that are processed by some target's perceptual apparatus can be classified as instances of communication. To avoid variants of the awkward phrase "processed by one's perceptual apparatus," the term *exposure,* or a variant thereof, is employed. At times, a target may be exposed to and aware of an external message. In other instances, however, the target may be exposed (and affected) without awareness (e.g., Krosnick, Betz, Jussim, & Lynn, 1992; Olson & Fazio, 2001).

Diverse lines of scholarship converge on the notion that persons seek to make sense of their environment (Goffman, 1959; Miller & Steinberg, 1975; Weick, 1995). External messages make up a portion of those environments, and hence, people try to make sense of those messages to which they are exposed; that is, they generate internal messages to explain them. Indeed, when aware of external messages, they can be expected to have difficulty ignoring them (e.g., see Wegner, 1994).

Some of these messages make claims of fact; others make claims concerning how one should value objects, concepts, and the like. Yet others seek to motivate action. Regardless of their intended impact, they may also, or alternatively, have an effect on other constructs. For example, messages designed to affect beliefs may also affect attitudes. Or, messages designed to direct action may impact attitudes instead of action. External messages may have multiple effects, such as external messages that impact both beliefs and attitudes. Some of these effects may be direct and others may be mediated or moderated.

Given this background, *the thesis of this essay is that social influence is a result of all communication.* To make that argument, it is claimed initially that external messages always affect beliefs. Consequently, it is reasonable to say that all messages exert social influence. Because messages are units of information exchange, and information exchange is an essential element of communication, it is also reasonable to conclude that all communication results in social influence. Granted, one may be unable to recall the external messages to which one has been exposed. Granted, the effect of these messages may be miniscule, perhaps undetectable with available measuring instruments. The effect may not be as designed; it may be fleeting (e.g., see Kahneman, 2003). Nevertheless, the fact that an effect (or multiple effects) occurs remains.

The pivotal premise in this claim is that external messages always affect beliefs. Indeed, to the extent that this premise and the preceding definitions are embraced, the soundness of the conclusion follows. Reason to believe this premise is provided in a seminal line of research examining how external messages affect beliefs. Gilbert (1991) distinguished two views of cognition, the Cartesian and Spinozan positions. The former position posits that when exposed to a message, persons first comprehend it and then decide either to embrace it or reject it. The latter position posits that when exposed to a message, persons first comprehend it *and* accept it. Subsequently—and the elapsed period may be very short—they may reject it, but message rejection is a process that follows, and is subordinate to, message acceptance. The evidence presented by Gilbert, as well as more recent evidence, is consistent with Spinoza's, and not Descartes's, position. Comprehension coupled with acceptance is belief: the cognitive acceptance of a proposition of fact. This acceptance, however fleeting, may create a belief where none existed previously. It may modify or reinforce an existing belief. Nevertheless, this exchanged information changes beliefs in some manner. Therefore, any message to which one is exposed inevitably results in belief change.

Consider a mundane example reasonably far removed from what is generally thought of as a social influence situation. Suppose that in a conversation with a casual acquaintance, someone whose opinion of you is unknown to you, the acquaintance remarks, "Now that I have gotten to know you, I find you to be a very kind person." According to Spinoza's hypothesis and Gilbert's research, one must first comprehend, or make sense of, the statement, and in the process of so doing accept what is comprehended. Suppose further that one makes sense of the statement by accepting it quite literally, so that you now have a new belief; namely, that this person's impression of you is that you are kind. In rapid order, you then likely make additional attributions (or generate internal messages). If an acquaintance thinks you are kind, then that person probably thinks that you have other positive qualities. Moreover, because liking tends to be reciprocated (Berscheid & Walster, 1978), you find yourself evaluating the acquaintance more favorably. These beliefs and attitudes may or may not be short-lived. For instance, it is possible that in less than 5 seconds it may occur to you that you are being flattered in order to make you more susceptible to what you anticipate will be a subsequent request to write a letter of recommendation for the acquaintance. Alternatively, these effects may be long lasting and mark the start of a new friendship.

Logically, it is not required to show that external messages also necessarily affect both attitudes and behavior. The claim reduces to the proposition that external messages influence beliefs, attitudes, *or* behavior. Notwithstanding, it is profitable to consider the impact of external messages on attitudes and behavior.

Beliefs are inherent in the manner in which persons evaluate concepts or objects. Consequently, when external messages affect beliefs, they are likely to affect attitudes as well. For example, if registered voters in South Dakota express the attitude that term limits imposed on their governor are a good idea, a potential host of beliefs are implicated. One such voter might reason in the following manner:

Gubernatorial term limits will have the effect of increasing the number of new and innovating ideas in government. (Belief)

An increasing number of new and innovative ideas generated by elected officials will result in more government services at lower costs. (Belief)

More government services and lower taxes constitute improved government. (Attitude)

Improved government is a good idea. (Attitude)

Therefore, gubernatorial term limits are a good idea. (Attitude)

As this example indicates, what persons consider to be factual contributes to the evaluative conclusions they draw. It is plausible as well that how people evaluate affects the factual conclusions they draw (cf. Lazarus, 1982, 1984; Zajonc, 1980, 1984). Consequently, the impact of external messages on particular beliefs and attitudes may have far-reaching consequences for the cognitive structure of audience members.

Despite controversy, careful analyses of the predictors of action indicate that attitudes, when measured reliably and validly, are extremely strong predictors of behavior (Kim & Hunter, 1993). Certainly the history of persuasion research indicates that external messages frequently have strong effects on action, albeit often mediated by attitudes or behavioral intentions.

Nevertheless, the interplay among external messages, beliefs, attitudes, and behavior may be considerably more nuanced. For example, some compliance-gaining strategies may produce behavior change without any mediating change in attitude or behavioral intention (Cialdini, 2001). Moreover, as classic theory and research examining dissonance (Festinger & Carlsmith, 1959) and self-perception (Bem, 1970) processes have indicated, behavior change may causally precede, rather than follow, changes in attitude.

In sum, one can no more be unaffected by an external message than one can step into the same river twice. *Communication necessarily impacts beliefs.* Moreover, the effects of communication on attitudes and action are powerful and pervasive. Because it is profitable to think of and analyze communication in terms of its consequences, and because the most striking consequence of communication is social influence, it is of value to think of and analyze communication as social influence.

Additional Readings

Berlo, D. K. (1960). *The process of communication.* New York: Holt, Rinehart, & Winston.

Gilbert, D. T. (1991). How mental systems believe. *American Psychologist, 46,* 107–119.

Miller, G. R. (1967). A crucial problem in attitude research. *Quarterly Journal of Speech, 53,* 235–240.

Miller, G. R. (1968). Communication and persuasion research: Current problems and prospects. *Quarterly Journal of Speech, 54,* 268–276.

Miller, G. R., & Burgoon, M. (1973). *New techniques of persuasion.* New York: Harper & Row.

References

Bem, D. J. (1970). *Beliefs, attitudes, and human affairs.* Belmont, CA: Brooks/Cole.

Berscheid, E., & Walster, E. (1978). *Interpersonal attraction.* Reading, MA: Addison-Wesley.

Cialdini, R. B. (2001). *Influence: Science and practice* (4th ed.). Boston: Allyn & Bacon.

Dance, F. E. X. (1970). The "concept" of communication. *Journal of Communication, 20,* 201–210.

Festinger, L., & Carlsmith, J. M. (1959). Cognitive consequences of forced compliance. *Journal of Abnormal and Social Psychology, 58,* 203–210.

Gilbert, D. T. (1991). How mental systems believe. *American Psychologist, 46,* 107–119.

Goffman, E. (1959). *The presentation of self in everyday life.* New York: Doubleday.

Hunter, J. E., Levine, R. L., & Sayers, S. E. (1976). Attitude change in hierarchical belief systems and its relationship to persuasibility, dogmatism, and rigidity. *Human Communication Research, 3,* 3–28.

Kahneman, D. (2003). A perspective on judgment and choice: Mapping bounded rationality. *American Psychologist, 58,* 697–720.

Kim, M. S., & Hunter, J. E. (1993). Attitude-behavior relations: A meta-analysis of attitudinal relevance and topic. *Journal of Communication, 43,* 101–142.

Krosnick, J. A., Betz, A. L., Jussim, L. J., & Lynn, A. R. (1992). Subliminal conditioning of attitudes. *Personality and Social Psychology Bulletin, 18,* 152–162.

Lazarus, R. S. (1982). Thoughts on the relations between emotion and cognition. *American Psychologist, 37,* 1019–1024.

Lazarus, R. S. (1984). On the primacy of cognition. *American Psychologist, 39,* 124–129.

Miller, G. R., & Steinberg, M. (1975). *Between people: A new analysis of interpersonal communication.* Chicago: Science Research Associates.

Olson, M. A., & Fazio, R. H. (2001). Implicit attitude formation through classical conditioning. *Psychological Science, 12,* 413–417.

Wegner, D. M. (1994). *White bears and other unwanted thoughts: Suppression, obsession, and the psychology of mental control.* New York: Guilford.

Weick, K. E. (1995). *Sensemaking in organizations.* Thousand Oaks, CA: Sage.

Zajonc, R. B. (1980). Feeling and thinking: Preferences need no inferences. *American Psychologist, 35,* 151–175.

Zajonc, R. B. (1984). On the primacy of affect. *American Psychologist, 39,* 117–123.

21

Communication as Rational Argument

Robert C. Rowland

I f one imagines communication theory and democracy as the circles in a Venn diagram, the point of overlap is rational argument. Democracy is usually defined in terms of procedures and legal protections that allow the citizens in a society or an organization to either directly make decisions or choose representatives to make those decisions. What is not usually recognized is the crucial role that rational discourse plays in that process. It is through a process of rational give and take that the stakeholders in any organization assess the alternatives in front of them prior to casting a ballot. Absent that process of rational give and take, democracy cannot function because the people will have no basis on which to decide. In a broader sense, the rational give and take both empowers the individual to participate and provides a process of testing competing claims in what John Stewart Mill, writing in "On Liberty" (1963), called the free marketplace of ideas. In a very real sense, the procedures that define democratic decision making that are enshrined in the Constitution and Bill of Rights for the United States and in countless other documents for states, towns, universities, foundations, businesses, and so forth are primarily important because they create a process in which the people decide, but only after they have talked about the ideas first.

For nearly all of the time since the Greeks invented the liberal arts, the importance of rational discussion and debate has been widely accepted. The core function of higher education was not merely to train citizens in a subject matter, but to give them an understanding of what often was called "sweet reason" so that they could later master any subject. In particular, rhetorical and democratic theorists embraced rational argument as both a form of speech and a mode of life. From Aristotle to Madison and Mill, these theorists expressed a faith that over time, good arguments had a way of winning out over bad ones. Even those who doubted the workability of democracy embraced rational discourse. Plato's opposition to democracy and his view that rhetoric often led people to make irrational decisions can be seen as closely related. Today, the situation is quite different. Rational argument is viewed as merely one form of discourse and is not granted priority over other forms.

In this essay, I argue that a communication theory focused on rational argument is essential for democratic decision making at any level. In order to carry out that aim, I first will flesh out rational argument as a communication form and process. I will then explain the functions that rational argument fulfills in any democratic organization. I conclude by rejecting the objections that have been made to either the value or efficacy of rational argument as a core component in democratic decision making.

Rational Argument and Democracy

Rational argument is sometimes equated with specialized forms of reasoning in science or decried as a form of technical reason, practiced only by experts. While the specialized discourse of mathematicians and engineers is surely a kind of rational argument, the general form can be found everywhere that human beings back up what they say with evidence and reasoning. Rational argument is simply a kind of talk in which people support a claim by citing evidence that is linked by some type of reasoning to the claim. Evidence may take the form of examples, statistics, comparisons, authoritative statements, or more specialized forms of these general types. The reasoning linking this evidence to the conclusion will be either a general principle for interpreting evidence (such as the rule of thumb that an unbiased person with expertise is more likely to have a useful opinion than someone lacking those characteristics), a specialized principle for understanding evidence in a context (such as the rule of thumb that 300 is a good batting average), or an implied value principle (such as the rule of thumb that murder is wrong). With this very general description of form in mind, argument can be either very simple, as in a Socratic syllogism, or enormously complex, as in the findings of the 9/11 commission, in which literally hundreds of different bits of evidence are linked with a web of reasons to a variety of conclusions.

As a form of discourse, rational argument occurs any time people cite evidence and reasons for their claims. Surely, technical reasoning is a type of rational argument, but it is equally present in common activities, such as when a cook advises use of an ingredient or a technique based on his or her prior experience. A statement that the herb rosemary goes well with poultry and lamb is just as rational as a NASA technical report (perhaps more rational given NASA's recent track record). It is also important to note that the common view that rational argument and value-laden or emotional discourse are opposed is nonsense. One can argue about the nature of the good society or other value issues based on the value system accepted in the society. And as Aristotle observed long ago in the *Nicomachean Ethics* (1941a), emotions are often a rational response to a situation. It is both completely understandable and quite rational that Palestinians and Israelis respond to violence against them with anger.

While the importance of rational argument as a form of discourse has been recognized since Aristotle labeled it one of the three modes of proof, from the perspective of democratic decision making, the process in which rational arguments are produced and exchanged is still more important. The most common meaning of *argument* in our culture is a verbal fight, a form of bickering. Thus, commentators often decry the "argument" that they see in political talk shows or in other places in our culture. Deborah Tannen (1998) has written extensively on this point. From the perspective developed here, this view could not be more wrong. As a process, rational argument occurs as long as people make argumentative claims against each other. When they cease to make such claims, by engaging in name-calling, for example, they are no longer arguing. In this view, rational argument is the very antithesis of bickering; it requires the individual to listen to and respond to the other. It is for this reason that Wayne Brockriede (1972) famously compared arguers to lovers.

At this point, the relationship between rational argument and a democratic society is clear. Rational argument is both the vehicle through which citizens in the society express their views and the means of reconciling those views in making a decision. Of course, citizens often express views that are anything but rational. In an odd way, however, the very fact that so little public talk is fully rational points to the importance of rational argument in the process of democratic decision making. Theorists from Aristotle to Madison to Mill have argued that, in the long term, good arguments have a way of winning out over bad ones. Mill's free marketplace of ideas is built on this premise, as is Aristotle's comment that "things that are true and things that are just have a natural tendency to prevail over their opposites" (1941b, p. 1327). And the constitutional edifice that Madison more than any other individual created is based on this principle. Madison's faith in reason was evident when, on December 5, 1791, he wrote in the *National Gazette* of his hope that the nation could "erect of the whole, one paramount Empire of reason" (1999, p. 500). Writing in Federalist No. 41, he justified this vision by arguing that "a bad cause seldom fails to betray itself" (1999, p. 230). While differing on details, Madison, Mill, Aristotle, and other rhetorical and democratic theorists agree that, over time, good arguments will win out over bad ones because the ideas or policies supported by the good arguments will be more pragmatically useful than the ideas supported by the bad arguments. It is for this reason that democratic theorists have gone to such efforts to protect the right of free expression.

There is another function of rational argument in democracy that is of equal importance. The process of rational argument is, by its nature, empowering and person respecting. In the give and take of rational argument, it matters not a whit whether you are a billionaire or a poor kid from the Bronx; all that matters is what you have to say and how you back it up. A similar point can be made about rational argument in other contexts, such as an organization or the family. Rational argument is inherently person respecting because, in argument, all that matters is the evidence and reasoning that you cite, not race, religion, gender, and so forth.

In sum, a communication theory focused on rational argument is essential for fulfilling three great humanistic goals. First, a process based on rational argument is essential for empowering stakeholders in any organization to make democratic decisions. Second, rational argument is needed to test claims in order to make decisions that are both popular and in some sense sensible or pragmatically useful. Finally, rational argument recognizes and protects the authenticity of every person. As long as you are arguing with someone, you are taking his or her views seriously and responding to them. It is when one leaves the land of argument that cruel or violent actions can occur. In this way, decision making based on rational argument is the very opposite of violence or coercion.

The Assault on Rational Argument

Proponents of rational argument are fighting a two-front war. On the one hand, we are under assault from academics who deny that there is a case for privileging rational argument over other forms of communication and who, in some cases, go so far as to attack rational argument as a tool of elite domination. On the other hand, rational argument is also under assault from those who say that the world has changed and that Mill's free marketplace of ideas no longer functions adequately.

Three primary objections have been made to rational argument as a mode of communication and a key element in democratic decision making. First, some argue that in a postpositivist world, there is no reason to privilege argument over other forms. Second, argument has been attacked as a value-free form of technical reasoning. In this view, risk analysis is the very paradigm of rational argument, a form that often leads to terrible decisions, as in those that resulted in the Columbia and Challenger shuttle accidents. Finally, some argue that rational argument is a form used by the usually white and male elites to control society. In fact, all of these criticisms are based on the fundamental error of equating all forms of rational argument with the specialized forms of argument found in science.

The underlying justification for any theory of rational argument is quite simple. The general or specific principle of reasoning at the core of a given argument is justified when it has been found to be useful in dealing with some kind of epistemic issue. Viewed in this way, principles distinguishing good from bad arguments are not based on some arcane academic theory, but only on the fact that they have been found to be pragmatically useful over time. Complex scientific arguments and disputes over how much cilantro should be added to salsa are, in this way, based on the same principle. The ultimate test of any argument is whether it works to solve a problem facing the individual or group. General principles of argumentation theory, more specific principles guiding the use of argument in particular fields (such as the norms that govern reasoning in social science), and domain-specific principles (such as that a little bit of cilantro goes a long way) are all justified through the same process. Notably, the process of justification of rational argument is rational argument itself. This self-reflexivity is a hallmark of rational argument.

The criticism that argument is value neutral is, in a way, quite accurate. Rational argument is about practical principles that have been found useful in testing the epistemic value of claims. It says nothing about the underlying values of those claims. But this does not mean that rational argument lies behind the two shuttle accidents. Two points are relevant here. First, proponents of rational argument recognize that it is merely a tool for testing ideas and cannot substitute for basic principles of ethics. Second, the process of argument provides a good test against those who would manipulate decision makers, including the public, or place themselves in a position of dominance. NASA failed to recognize the dangerous conditions that ultimately resulted in the two shuttle accidents, not because of rational argument, but because they didn't apply principles of rational argument. The problem was not excessive reliance on argument but rather a failure to rigorously test ideas. Much the same argument could be made concerning the decision of the second Bush administration to invade Iraq.

Finally, it should be obvious that rational argument is merely a tool and has no relationship to gender roles or economic structures. For instance, an all-lesbian commune still would need rational argument in order to make the best decisions. And rational argument is, by its very nature, a tool that helps the oppressed more than the oppressor because the reflexive nature of rational argument applies to all equally.

Some years ago, I participated in a debate at the National Communication Association about whether rational argument could be justified as a method of decision making. In this valuable exchange, my opponents made a number of arguments about weaknesses in rational argument and ways in which it could be used to oppress people. Ironically, in using argument to attack argument, they revealed the fundamental value of the communicative form—it respects all people and is inherently self-reflexive.

The second front in the assault on argument comes from those who say that the contemporary public sphere proves that the idealistic vision of rational give and take at the core of the writings of Jefferson, Madison, and Mill is no longer applicable. In this view, the rise of a focus on celebrity and the enormous complexity of the world mean that the best arguments no longer will win out in free and open debate. The question, as Michael Ignatieff (2004, p. 14) wrote in a recent essay, is "whether the nation's rhetoric has degenerated into a ritual concealment of what the country has actually become." If so, then the aphorism often attributed to Lincoln that "you cannot fool all of the people all of the time" is no longer accurate.

To be sure, there is disquieting data on the status of public deliberation. Three developments are particularly troublesome. First, the rise of a celebrity culture in which people are famous for being famous certainly diminishes the quality of public talk. When I mention the name of an important senator from another state (say, Dick Lugar of Indiana), my undergraduate students are clueless, but they all are aware of the sexual antics of the latest star of a "reality" series. Second, public knowledge about the most important issues of the day is astonishingly low and sometimes quite inaccurate. The fact that a very significant portion of the American people continued to believe that Saddam Hussein had some involvement in the terrorist attacks of September 11, 2001 long after that view had been debunked is one sign of that problem. And on issues that receive less attention, the public is woefully ignorant. Third, there are many signs in our culture of the calcification of terministic screens. To take only one example, recent tell-all books on the Bush administration have revealed what the mainstream media has treated as a cavalier willingness to ignore the facts. Although, clearly, fact ignoring has been a strength of the administration, I think there is something else at work here. The terministic screen used by many conservatives has become so calcified that inconvenient facts are automatically discounted or ignored. Data indicating that tax cuts are producing deficits that are simply unsustainable is met with the response that Reagan proved deficits don't matter. The actuality that Reagan signed laws raising taxes several times after 1982, because his tax cuts also produced an unsustainable fiscal policy, is simply ignored. Precisely the same point undoubtedly could be made about the calcified worldviews of a group of committed socialists, 1960s liberals, Greens, and so forth, assuming that you could find a room small enough to hold such a group comfortably.

Although, as a citizen, I am appalled by the quality of public talk, as a rhetorician and a student of Aristotle, Madison, and Mill, I remain confident in the resilience of a democratic public sphere grounded in rational argument. In the long (but not always the short) run, being right is a powerful thing. And over time, strong argument has a way of overwhelming celebrity, terministic screens, and lack of attention. The power of rational argument is that it reveals error and finds solutions. I also suspect that every age has decried the quality of public deliberation and every age has been right. The reflexivity and pragmatic value of rational argument have a way of winning the public over in the long run. Consider the case of the two cooks who argue about making yeast bread. One says that really hot water will speed up the rising process; the other disagrees. No matter how strongly the first cook states his or her views, yeast will die if the water is too hot, and over time, even the most stubborn baker will accept that point.

Conclusion

Everyone knows the story of how it was only a small boy who had the innocence to point out that the emperor had no clothes. Consider what this story reveals about rational argument as a form of communication and also about a society that respects argument. Clearly, the child was a young, but still skillful, arguer. He ignored the comments of adults and let the facts guide what he saw. When the facts did not match what he had been told, he blurted out the truth. But the story also reveals something about a society that values argument. In many societies, anyone blurting out an unpleasant truth will be punished. Totalitarian societies of all kinds cannot stand skillful arguers. And that point applies to all human organization. The patriarchal father has to shout down a wife or daughter because he cannot argue with them.

Communication theorists should embrace rational argument because the rhetorical form is at the core of any society that recognizes the dignity of all human beings and empowers people to act. In a very real sense, democracy is a form of human activity in which people make decisions through rational argument.

Additional Readings

Brockriede, W. (1972). Arguers as lovers. *Philosophy and Rhetoric, 5*, 1–11.

Brockriede, W. (1975). Where is argument? *Journal of the American Forensic Association, 11*, 179–182.

Mill, J. S. (1963). *The six great humanistic essays.* New York: Washington Square.

O'Keefe, D. J. (1977). Two concepts of argument. *Journal of the American Forensic Association, 13*, 121–128.

Toulmin, S. E. (1958). *The uses of argument.* Cambridge, UK: Cambridge University Press.

References

Aristotle. (1941a). *Nicomachean ethics* (W. D. Ross, Trans.). In R. McKeon (Ed.), *The basic works of Aristotle.* New York: Random House.

Aristotle. (1941b). *Rhetoric* (W. Rhys Roberts, Trans.). In R. McKeon (Ed.), *The basic works of Aristotle.* New York: Random House.

Brockriede, W. (1972). Arguers as lovers. *Philosophy and Rhetoric, 5*, 1–11.

Ignatieff, M. (2004, June 27). *New York Times,* pp. 13–16.

Madison, J. (1999). *Writings.* New York: Library of America.

Mill, J. S. (1963). *The six great humanistic essays.* New York: Washington Square.

Tannen, D. (1998). *The argument culture: Moving from debate to dialogue.* New York: Random House.

22

Communication as Counterpublic

Daniel C. Brouwer

T he key communication dimensions of *counterpublic,* including the expression of opposition, the constitution of discursive spaces, and the participation in multiple publics, mark it as potentially exciting and beneficial to critical, interpretive, and rhetorical scholarship in the field of communication studies. Yet, licensed by the editors of this volume to extol the virtues of the concept of counterpublic, I begin instead with a qualification that exposes a limitation: Counterpublic is insufficient to capture or characterize all communication. It is not a global approach to understanding communication as are, for example, the concepts of *translation, impossibility, dialectic,* and *dissemination.* Instead, it is a conceptual lens through which to examine certain types of communication structures and practices or to examine communication structures and practices in a certain way. In many instances, counterpublic may be neither valuable nor appropriate as a conceptual lens. This is well and good, for I want to insist on the need to retain conceptual clarity and utility for counterpublic in contrast to other structures and practices of communication.

I wish to acknowledge the College of Public Programs for its support of this manuscript in the form of a Dean's Incentive Grant. Further, I express gratitude to Catherine Squires and Robert Asen for offering valuable criticism on a draft of this chapter and to participants in National Communication Association public sphere theory preconference seminars from 1998 to 2004 for their engagement with many of the issues and claims expressed in this chapter.

In this chapter, I will respond to the question, What does the concept of counterpublic offer or open up to communication scholarship? To do so, I survey scholarship in communication studies and allied fields that employs the concept of counterpublic, and I explicate what are, in my view, the most valuable aspects of counterpublic theory. Within the field of communication studies, rhetoricians have thus far been the scholars who have most vigorously taken up counterpublic theory; thus, my remarks will largely reflect the topics and vocabulary of rhetorical studies. Despite my focus and despite the relative neglect of counterpublic theory by other subdisciplines of communication studies, my hope is that by the end of this essay, I will have demonstrated (or at least suggested) the salience of the concept to other subdisciplines, particularly performance studies, media studies, critical/cultural studies, intercultural communication, and organizational communication. These subdisciplines typically share with counterpublic theory an interest in conflict and the presumption that communication structures and practices are politically charged and power-laden. Thus, these subdisciplines might facilitate the circulation of counterpublic within communication studies. To initiate my consideration of the utility of counterpublic theory to communication studies, I offer a brief history of the concept.

Emergences of Counterpublic(s)

Counterpublic first appeared in 1972 as *Gegenöffentlichkeit* in the German-language work of Oskar Negt and Alexander Kluge, *Öffentlichkeit und Erfahrung (Public Sphere and Experience)*. Negt and Kluge's work challenged Jürgen Habermas's (1962/1989) earlier account of the bourgeois public sphere; in it, they posit the proletarian public sphere as a counterpublic. Hansen (1972/1993, pp. xvi, xxxix) describes important elements of *Gegenöffentlichkeit/*counterpublic, including its emphasis on human experience; its dependence on perceptions of oppositionality; and its relational, provisional, and, thus, shifting constitution. Because *Public Sphere and Experience* was not translated into English until 1993, it is Rita Felski who initiated its appearance in English-language scholarship in 1989 in her book *Beyond Feminist Aesthetics*. Notably, Felski described the counterpublic constituted by feminist literature as "oppositional discursive space" that alters, even as it is shaped by, the ideological structures within which it emerged (p. 155). What Felski defines as counterpublic follows in important ways the claims made earlier by black literary critic Henry Louis Gates, Jr., in his discussion of "a simultaneous, but negated, parallel discursive (ontological, political) universe [that] exists within the larger white discursive universe" and that collides with the dominant semantic field of standard (white) English (1988, p. 49). The discursive universe that Gates describes is, of course, a black discursive universe characterized, in part, by rhetorical practices of "Signifyin(g)," or "black double-voicedness" (p. 51).[1]

Although there are several definitions of counterpublic (Nancy Fraser's [1990, p. 67] is perhaps most familiar[2]), most share these key features: *oppositionality, constitution of a discursive arena,* and a *dialectic of retreat from and engagement with other publics.* Oppositionality refers to a stance of resistance, rejection, or dissent. It is important to recognize that oppositionality is primarily perceptual; that is, counterpublics emerge when social actors perceive themselves to be excluded from or marginalized within mainstream or dominant publics and communicate about that marginality or exclusion. Communication about marginality or exclusion helps to constitute a discursive arena. It is important to clarify that *discursive* refers not just to *speech*—written or spoken language—but also to visual communication and bodily display. Further, the notion of discursive arena should be understood as a conceptual metaphor, often related to but never reducible to specific places. People who communicate oppositional stances may, in fact, meet together in physical spaces, but they may also create "imagined communities" (Anderson, 1991) through dispersed, asynchronous communication. Finally, counterpublic theorists emphasize a dialectic of inward and outward address. Those who constitute oppositional communication need to speak among themselves in moments of retreat, regrouping, reflection, or rejuvenation, in preparation for or anticipation of engagements with other publics. In this view, radical exclusions such as forced exile or chosen separatism, in which social actors cannot or do not address other publics, do not constitute counterpublicity.

Since 1989, scholarship about counterpublics has proliferated. In the field of communication studies, among the first to explore its conceptual utility were Margaret Zulick and Anne Laffoon, who in 1991 extended Nancy Fraser's remarks on enclaved publics in order to extol the generative, inventional functions of such publics (Zulick & Laffoon, 1991, p. 251).[3] Shortly after, Bonnie Dow (1992, p. 142) considered the concept of counterpublic, describing both the television show *Designing Women* and feminist scholarship generally as components of a feminist counterpublic sphere. Additional work done in the name of counterpublic theory includes a clarification of what constitutes the *counter* status of counterpublics, an exploration of the tension between withdrawn intellectual speculation and social change, and a resituation of counterpublic within a larger constellation of marginal publics

(Asen, 2000; Ramsey, 1998; Squires, 2002). Along these lines, contributors to a 2002 forum in the *Quarterly Journal of Speech* explored the significance of Michael Warner's remarks about publics and counterpublics to rhetorical studies (Deem, 2002; Greene, 2002; Wittenberg, 2002). Others have used the concept of counterpublic to illuminate the use of World Wide Web communities to facilitate political activism, participation in a nongovernmental organization by indigenous people of Bolivia, and disparate forms of breast cancer activism (McDorman, 2001; Pezzullo, 2003; Stephenson, 2002).

What explains the growing appeal of counterpublic? For rhetorical and other scholars prone to thinking in terms of agonistics, eristics, conflict, dissent, argument, controversy, or social movement, counterpublic's origins in oppositionality render it familiar and potentially productive. For scholars prone to examining marginality and identity, counterpublic's originary focus on the proletariat and its affirmation of experience further render it familiar and useful. In the remaining paragraphs, I attempt to explain the appeal of counterpublic in more detail by arguing that it advances rhetorical and communication theory in specific and productive ways.

The Generative Potential of Counterpublics

Counterpublic advances communication theory by *expanding our objects of inquiry beyond rational-critical norms of public deliberation.* This is not to deny the value of rational-critical norms of public deliberation: indeed, these norms can provide a stabilizing and efficient social apparatus, and they bear the potential for people who perceive themselves to be marginalized to witness the force of their better arguments winning the day. Still, these norms elide full consideration of the emotion, Eros, and *ludus* that motivate human communication, persuade, and more generally constitute a social realm. Studies of unruly, passionate, enfleshed, ironic, or other modes of counterpublicity underscore their significance to human communication. Additionally, the specification of "counterpublic" is an explicit recognition and warning that not all publicly significant speech occurs in officially sanctioned "public" forums, by official representatives of the public or the public good, or in dominant public idioms. The Barbie Liberation Organization's gender reassignment surgeries, performed by switching the voice chips of Teen Talk Barbie dolls and Talking Duke G.I. Joe action figures, underscore the value of impudent and clandestine tactics, for these surgeries politicized popular culture, parodied practices of gender socialization, and underlined the potential harm of such practices.

Counterpublic also advances communication theory by *forcing recognition that human actors participate in multiple publics.* Counterpublic was introduced as part of a larger theoretical argument about the multiplicity of spheres; as such, it should remind us of multiplicity each time it is deployed. In our manuscripts and presentations, qualifying phrases that clarify and delimit the scope of the study should at least nod to this multiplicity if not rigorously study it. Efforts to account for multiplicity have lead scholars to make distinctions between publics and counterpublics, active and passive publics (Chay-Nemeth, 2001), quasi- and counterpublics (Hoberman, 2002), emergent and established publics (Lowney, 2000), and counter and subaltern publics (Warner, 2002). Responding more rigorously to concern about the "frustrating vagueness" of counterpublic or the potentially anemic utility of a counterpublic concept spread too thin (Asen & Brouwer, 2001, p. 8; Squires, 2002, pp. 459–460), some have offered more elaborate typologies of publics: for example, circumscribed, co-opted, critical, circumventing publics (Chay-Nemeth, 2001, p. 129); and enclaved, satellite, and counterpublics (Squires, 2002).

It is important to note that the recognition of multiplicity promotes greater precision of description, understanding, and analysis of publics. That is, although counterpublics share the general characteristics that I outlined above, each is unique. Additionally, recognition of multiplicity also promotes studies that examine strategies and tactics of mediation, translation, and sense-making between publics. As an illustration, consider the career of the Tell It to ACT UP (TITA) forum. The weekly meetings of the New York chapter of the AIDS Coalition to Unleash Power (ACT UP) are famously contentious, heightened by the consensus-based decision-making process chosen by its members. Archival research indicates that as early as March 1990, members of ACT UP created TITA as a print-based forum for those unwilling or unable to speak at meetings and for those uncomfortable with the contentious dimensions of the meetings. Concerned about the use of the forum to circulate anonymous, *ad personam* attacks against ACT UP members, one member, Tony Davis, formally proposed that TITA refuse to publish anonymous contributions. Ultimately, TITA was deactivated, only to be reactivated in November 1993. What this controversy over TITA illustrates is that *within* the dissident organization of ACT UP, a counterpublic emerged. Defined by its quality as a discursive arena for the circulation of oppositional statements and arguments, TITA demonstrates the perceptual, relational, and protean status of counterpublics. Additionally, the emergence of TITA illustrates that liminal, in-between, and overlapping spaces of publics might be especially fertile spaces for the study and understanding of rhetorical practices.[4]

Third, and relatedly, *by positing a dialectic of inward and outward address*, counterpublic theory *foregrounds the status of relations between dominant and subordinate as one of mutual influence and the status of rhetorical structures and practices as contingent.* Theorists of counterpublics such as Rita Felski, Nancy Fraser, and Jane Mansbridge (1996) have emphasized this dialectic as a crucial component to understanding counterpublicity. This dialectic recognizes that although counterpublic activities may take the form of address among the like-minded, whether out in the open or in relative secrecy or obscurity, these activities occur with an understanding that oppositionality will be directed toward or constitute other, wider publics. Because counterpublic activities are directed toward or constitute other, wider publics, they evince relational dynamics between publics.

To explore this dialectic, one might examine a specific collective that generates counterpublic discourse, noting its activities in multiple settings and contexts.[5] Some of this discourse might be characterized as the "hidden transcripts" (Scott, 1990, p. 4) of debate and conflict—secretive, marginalized, or outlawed address, address that is different from more broadly disseminated or more broadly accessible address perhaps in terms of candor, propriety, or idiom. Examination of hidden transcripts in contexts of relative secrecy, such as the study of dissidents' private correspondences or the proceedings of restricted meetings, might expose the scholar to discussions about the risks of visibility, of engagement with disputants, and of the use of dominant idioms. In short, differences in the discourses deployed in different settings, including more explicit talk about strategies and tactics in contexts of self-address, remind us of the contingent nature of social advocacy and social change and the mutually inflecting relations between social groups. Emphasizing contingency and mutual influence, Doxtader (2001, pp. 61–62, 65) importantly announces that "*Counterpublic* is a verb," and he nominates "counterpublicity" as "rhetorical processes by which the grounds of agreement are cultivated from within expressions of agreement." Doxtader's introduction of counterpublicity as a companion term to counterpublic amplifies what he views as counterpublic theory's obligation to explain the forms of communication under its purview (pp. 60–61).

Fourth, counterpublic *requires recognition of resource disparities among social actors, a recognition that ought to be increasingly called for in communication studies.* If we take the view that counterpublics emerge from perceptions of oppositionality to dominant forces, then we should remain attentive to the ways in which both perceptual and actual disparities of resources inflect counterpublic activities and counterpublics' relations with other publics. In their typologies of publics, both Chay-Nemeth (2001) and Squires (2002) claim "resource dependency," or resource disparity, as one of the criteria that facilitates their distinctions: resource dependency refers to "the extent to which a public depends on other publics for access to funds, information, training, education, the mass media, and publicity for its cause" (Chay-Nemeth, p. 137), while resource disparities appear in the form of the quantity and quality of organizations (such as churches), media outlets (including print, radio, and popular music), and legal and political opportunities and protections (Squires, 2002). Beyond merely recognizing material (e.g., accumulated wealth, access to modes of production of goods) or cultural (e.g., adherence to dominant values, social authorization to speak) resource disparities, scholars link these disparities to rhetorical practices, explaining how various qualities and quantities of various resources delimit the available means of persuasion.[6]

Illustrative of resource disparities is self-abstraction. In his discussion of publics and counterpublics, Warner (1992, p. 382; 2002) has been especially helpful in exposing self-abstraction—the ability to render the particularities of one's body irrelevant to one's claims and an ability that historically has been a prerequisite for participation in the public sphere—as an "unequally available resource." Beyond mere recognition of resource disparities, scholars link these disparities to rhetorical practices, explaining how various qualities and quantities of various resources delimit the available means of persuasion. For example, returning to the example of self-abstraction, Warner suggests about counterpublics, "it might be that embodied sociability is too important to them; they might not be organized by the hierarchy of faculties that elevates rational-critical reflection as the self-image of humanity" (2002, p. 123). As such, counterpublic activities in which the flesh is made salient might evidence not an inability or lack of rhetorical skill but a deployment of a cultural resource, an indigenous mode of oppositional expression.

Finally, counterpublic advances communication theory by *functioning as fertile terrain for interdisciplinary inquiry.* From various hilltops in the academy, calls for interdisciplinary scholarship ring out. Leaders and institutions in communication studies add their voices to this call in the form of, most recently, the National Communication Association's sponsorship of *Communication and Critical/Cultural Studies,* a journal explicitly devoted to interdisciplinary scholarship. Interdisciplinary from their beginning, public sphere studies forcefully answer the call. More specifically, rhetoric and argumentation scholars in the field of communication studies have both joined and led scholars in allied disciplines such as English, women's studies, political theory, and sociology in testing and clarifying counterpublic theory and employing counterpublic theory to illuminate specific rhetorical engagements. Because of our long-standing and continuing interest in specific discourse practices and expressions of dissent, rhetorical scholars are well positioned to continue to be leaders in the interdisciplinary realm of counterpublic studies.

Related to but distinct from my claim about counterpublic's interdisciplinary richness is its openness to what Miriam Hansen calls "disciplinary promiscuity" (1972/1993, p. xi). I argue that although counterpublic theory clearly bears its origins in the critical theory of the Frankfurt School, it retains conceptual utility even as it comes into congress with erotic agents of disparate, even dissonant, theoretical realms. In pursuit of this argument, I distinguish between two modes of counterpublic critique. This first mode of critique might be called (generic, not Kantian) immanent critique. Recall that Negt and Kluge's discussion of counterpublics and experience was in direct response to Habermas's treatise on the bourgeois public sphere. As such, Negt and Kluge engaged public sphere theory on its own terms, offering a critique of its heralding of Enlightenment principles, its valorization of critical rationality, its presumption of an essentially sovereign subject exercising reason, and more. Negt and Kluge's and others' critiques of Habermas's narrative challenged, among other things, the universality of bourgeois subjectivity and the public sphere's self-correcting *telos* toward greater inclusivity, even as they affirmed the value of the concept of the public sphere. Exemplifying a counterpublic mode of critique on the public sphere's own terms, Rita Felski notes how feminist literature "reappropriates some of the concerns first addressed by bourgeois subjectivity while rejecting both its individualism and its belief in the universality of male bourgeois experience" (1989, p. 155).

This specific insight and this mode of critique generally are valuable and necessary, but they are not the mode of critique that I have in mind when I suggest "disciplinary promiscuity." A second mode of critique might be called incongruous. For example, one might conjoin counterpublic critique of bourgeois subjectivity with poststructuralist accounts of the discursive conditions of emergence of particular forms of subjectivity (under the influence of Foucault, for example) or with poststructuralist/postmodern insights about appropriation and citation (via Judith Butler) or difference and repetition (via Deleuze and Guattari). Nothing about counterpublic's key features of *oppositionality, constitution of a discursive arena,* and *dialectic of retreat and engagement with other publics* prohibits outright counterpublic's promiscuous encounters with other, potentially mutually animating, concepts.

As an illustration, note that while Phillips (1999) has used Foucauldian concepts to indict certain features of public sphere theory and has briefly teased out the potential constraints of the counterpublic concept, others have conjoined counterpublic with Foucault's *heterotopia* (Kohn, 2001) and *governmentality* (Chay-Nemeth, 2001) in analyses of European socialist Houses of the People and HIV/AIDS political activity in Thailand. In this vein, future studies might employ a Foucauldian understanding of resistance as unintelligibility (Biesecker, 1992, p. 357) to offer more precise characterizations of certain practices of counterpublicity. These examples demonstrate that counterpublic's couplings are possible and potentially fertile; they also anticipate Ono's (2003) concern that counterpublic inhibits its fertility and its reach through excessive devotion to germinal figures and concepts from public sphere theory. A final note about promiscuity: because, in the field of communication studies, those who have taken up counterpublic most vigorously have been rhetoricians, counterpublic scholarship in the field has been dominated by rhetorical methods and approaches. Multiplication of the methods and approaches of the study of counterpublics would be a welcome addition: Pezzullo's (2003) rhetorical and ethnographic study of breast cancer activism, with its conversation between performance and counterpublic theory, is an exemplar of this approach.

Coda

Through its facilitation of critical study of various types of protest, the use of vernacular and cultural idioms, the creation of oppositional discursive arenas, oppositional modes of organizing, the experience of communication as embodied, and more, counterpublic has much to offer not only rhetorical theory, but also performance studies, media studies, critical/cultural studies, intercultural communication, and organizational communication.[7] This is not to say that its utility is foreclosed to other subdisciplines of communication studies; indeed, studies of code switching in interpersonal or small-group encounters might be read as acts of counterpublicity, for example. Still, those subdisciplines that view communication as constituted by structures and practices within a politically charged field are those that are most likely to find counterpublic useful and illuminating.

Its virtues to rhetorical and communication theory elaborated, counterpublic faces several challenges to its utility and fertility. I mention four of these challenges here in the spirit of generating continued interest in and scrutiny of the concept. First, Carabas notes that the authors represented in the *Counterpublics and the State* collection "use mostly Western concepts and employ the tools of liberal democracy as the default mode of thinking about the relationship between the state and marginalized communities"

(2003, p. 170). She cautions against presuming and utilizing such concepts and tools in studies of non-Western cultures. Hirschkind's (2001) essay on the emergence of an Islamic counterpublic in Egypt might offer a provisional response to this concern, but it is worth pursuing further. Second, although I promote promiscuity between counterpublic and other, dissonant concepts, such couplings are not necessarily easy. While promiscuous couplings might produce creative juxtapositions or curious pastiches, they might also produce theoretical incoherence. Third, future counterpublic studies must carefully account for translation and efficacy. The means and outcomes of translations between counterpublics and dominant public idioms—and between different counterpublic idioms—must be interrogated as must the subject positions of agents who serve as translators (activists, public officials, scholars).

Finally, while counterpublic seems to have reinvigorated the study of social movements by shifting the terrain of such studies, the precise contours of that shifted terrain have yet to be thoroughly elaborated.[8] That is, scholars have yet to systematically interrogate differences between counterpublics and social movements (for an exception, see Palczewski, 2001). Such distinctions are important if communication scholarship on counterpublics wants to do more than simply repeat the once robust debates about definition and methodology that occupied social movement scholars. Indeed, in more cynical moments, one might decide that counterpublic theory is appealing simply because it allows scholars to conduct studies of social movement and social movements without being obligated to slog through the dense accumulation of social movement scholarship. More earnestly, one might ponder Warner's (2002, p. 124) claim that counterpublics become recognizable as social movements when they take a stance toward the state and speak in its rational-critical idiom. One need not agree with this distinction. More important, communication scholars interested in counterpublics should not let this distinction stand as the final word.

Notes

1. See Michael Dawson (1995) for an exploration of the utility of counterpublic to contemporary black politics.

2. Fraser (1990, p. 67) defines subaltern counterpublics as "parallel discursive arenas where members of subordinated social groups invent and circulate counterdiscourses"; these publics emerge "in response to exclusions within dominant publics, [and] they help expand discursive space."

3. Zulick and Laffoon (1991) do not specifically cite the term *counterpublic* in this essay; thus, they do not amplify Fraser's contrast between formally *enclaved,* or isolated, publics and *counter*publics, which exhibit a dialectic of withdraw and engagement with wider publics. Nevertheless, the authors provide a keen and fruitful elaboration of the significance of such publics.

4. Minutes of ACT UP/New York's meetings and documents related to Tell It to ACT UP are available from the Manuscripts and Archives Division of the New York Public Library. For March 19, 1990, minutes of the meeting, see Box 4, Folder 10. For November 15, 1993, minutes of the meeting, see Box 6, Folder 2.

5. Of course, one should avoid a reductive conflation between collectives and counterpublics. That is, the concept of counterpublic is not reducible to particular groups of people (Asen, 2000, pp. 430–432).

6. I think it worth noting here that most counterpublic scholarship drops the "subaltern" qualifier that Nancy Fraser included in her 1990 elaboration of counterpublics. For Fraser, subaltern described a general relation of subordination. Yet, for Gayatri Spivak ([1988] from whom Fraser explicitly derives the term), subaltern described social positions radically delimited by material conditions. While counterpublic studies need not necessarily be studies of subaltern counterpublics, I suggest that Fraser's attenuation of subaltern and other scholars' frequent elision of subaltern might promote unfortunate scholarly neglect of resource disparity.

7. I do not mean to suggest that counterpublic theory has been completely neglected by communication scholars other than rhetoricians. Indeed, for example, Mariangela Maguire and Laila Mohtar (1994) have suggested the potential utility of counterpublic theory to performance studies, and John Downey and Natalie Fenton (2003) have discussed the relationships between new media and public and counterpublic spheres.

8. Anecdotally, Catherine H. Palczewksi, Dana L. Cloud, Valeria Fabj, and Matthew J. Sobnosky are among those who have voiced claims about the potential for counterpublic to stimulate social movement studies.

Additional Readings

Asen, R., & Brouwer, D. C. (Eds.). (2001). *Counterpublics and the state.* Albany: SUNY Press.

Dewey, J. (1954). *The public and its problems* (Rev. ed.). Athens, OH: Swallow Press.

Felski, R. (1989). *Beyond feminist aesthetics: Feminist literature and social change.* Cambridge, MA: Harvard University Press.

Hill, M., & Montag, W. (Eds.). (2000). *Masses, classes, and the public sphere.* London: Verso.

Warner, M. (2002). *Publics and counterpublics.* New York: Zone Books.

References

Anderson, B. (1991). *Imagined communities: Reflections on the origin and spread of nationalism* (Rev. ed.). London: Verso.

Asen, R. (2000). Seeking the "counter" in counterpublics. *Communication Theory, 10,* 424–446.

Asen, R., & Brouwer, D. C. (2001). Introduction: Reconfigurations of the public sphere. In R. Asen & D. C. Brouwer (Eds.), *Counterpublics and the state* (pp. 1–32). Albany: SUNY Press.

Biesecker, B. (1992). Michel Foucault and the question of rhetoric. *Philosophy and Rhetoric, 25,* 351–364.

Carabas, T. (2003). [Review of the book *Counterpublics and the state*]. *Southern Communication Journal, 68,* 169–170.

Chay-Nemeth, C. (2001). Revisiting publics: A critical archaeology of publics in the Thai HIV/AIDS issue. *Journal of Public Relations Research, 13,* 127–161.

Dawson, M. C. (1995). A black counterpublic? Economic earthquakes, racial agenda(s), and black politics. In Black Public Sphere Collective (Eds.), *The black public sphere* (pp. 199–227). Chicago: University of Chicago Press.

Deem, M. (2002). Stranger sociability, public hope, and the limits of political transformation. *Quarterly Journal of Speech, 88,* 444–454.

Dow, B. J. (1992). Performance of feminine discourse in Designing Women. *Text and Performance Quarterly, 12,* 125–145.

Downey, J., & Fenton, N. (2003). New media, counter publicity and the public sphere. *New Media & Society, 5,* 185–202.

Doxtader, E. (2001). In the name of reconciliation: The faith and works of counterpublicity. In R. Asen & D. C. Brouwer (Eds.), *Counterpublics and the state* (pp. 59–85). Albany: SUNY Press.

Felski, R. (1989). *Beyond feminist aesthetics: Feminist literature and social change.* Cambridge, MA: Harvard University Press.

Fraser, N. (1990). Rethinking the public sphere: A contribution to the critique of actually existing democracy. *Social Text, 25/26,* 56–80.

Gates, H. L., Jr. (Ed.). (1988). The signifying monkey and the language of signifyin(g): Rhetorical difference and the orders of meaning. In *The signifying monkey: A theory of Afro-American literary criticism* (pp. 44–88). New York: Oxford University Press.

Greene, R. W. (2002). Rhetorical pedagogy as a postal system: Circulating subjects through Michael Warner's "Publics and Counterpublics." *Quarterly Journal of Speech, 88,* 434–443.

Habermas, J. (1989). *The structural transformation of the public sphere: An inquiry into a category of bourgeois society* (T. Burger & F. Lawrence, Trans.). Cambridge: MIT Press. (Original work published 1962)

Hansen, M. (1993). Foreword. In O. Negt & A. Kluge, *Public sphere and experience: Toward an analysis of the bourgeois and proletarian public sphere* (pp. ix–xii; P. Labanyi, J. O. Daniel, & A. Oksiloff, Trans.). Minneapolis: University of Minnesota Press. (Original work published 1972)

Hirschkind, C. (2001). Civic virtue and religious reason: An Islamic counterpublic. *Cultural Anthropology, 16,* 3–34.

Hoberman, R. (2002). Women in the British Museum Reading Room during the late-nineteenth and early-twentieth centuries: From quasi- to counterpublic. *Feminist Studies, 28,* 489–512.

Kohn, M. (2001). The power of place: The House of the People as counterpublic. *Polity, 33,* 503–526.

Lowney, J. (2000). Langston Hughes and the "nonsense" of bebop. *American Literature, 72,* 357–385.

Maguire, M., & Mohtar, L. F. (1994). Performance and the celebration of a subaltern counterpublic. *Text and Performance Quarterly, 14,* 238–252.

Mansbridge, J. (1996). Using power/fighting power: The polity. In S. Benhabib (Ed.), *Democracy and difference: Contesting the boundaries of the political* (pp. 46–66). Princeton, NJ: Princeton University Press.

McDorman, T. (2001). Crafting a virtual counterpublic: Right-to-die advocates on the Internet. In R. B. Asen & D. C. Brouwer (Eds.), *Counterpublics and the state* (pp. 187–209). Albany: SUNY Press.

Negt, O., & Kluge, A. (1993). *Public sphere and experience: Toward an analysis of the bourgeois and proletarian public sphere* (P. Labanyi, J. O. Daniel, & A. Oksiloff, Trans.). Minneapolis: University of Minnesota Press.

Ono, K. A. (2003). [Review of the book *Counterpublics and the state*]. *Argumentation and Advocacy, 39,* 61–64.

Palczewski, C. H. (2001). Cyber-movements, new social movements, and counterpublics. In R. Asen & D. C. Brouwer (Eds.), *Counterpublics and the state* (pp. 161–186). Albany: SUNY Press.

Pezzullo, P. C. (2003). Resisting 'National Breast Cancer Awareness Month': The rhetoric of counterpublics and their cultural performances. *Quarterly Journal of Speech, 89,* 345–365.

Phillips, K. R. (1999). A rhetoric of controversy. *Western Journal of Communication, 63,* 488–510.

Ramsey, R. E. (1998). Suffering wonder: Wooing and courting in the public sphere. *Communication Theory, 8,* 455–475.

Scott, J. C. (1990). *Domination and the arts of resistance: Hidden transcripts.* New Haven, CT: Yale University Press.

Spivak, G. C. (1988). Can the subaltern speak? In C. Nelson & L. Grossberg (Eds.), *Marxism and the interpretation of culture* (pp. 271–313). Urbana: University of Illinois Press.

Squires, C. R. (2002). Rethinking the black public sphere: An alternative vocabulary for multiple public spheres. *Communication Theory, 12,* 446–468.

Stephenson, M. (2002). Forging an indigenous counterpublic sphere: The taller de historia oral andina in Bolivia. *Latin American Research Review, 37,* 99–118.

Warner, M. (1992). The mass public and the mass subject. In C. Calhoun (Ed.), *Habermas and the public sphere* (pp. 377–401). Cambridge: MIT Press.

Warner, M. (Ed.). (2002). Publics and counterpublics. In *Publics and counterpublics* (pp. 65–124). New York: Zone Books.

Wittenberg, D. (2002). Going out in public: Visibility and anonymity in Michael Warner's "Publics and Counterpublics." *Quarterly Journal of Speech, 88,* 426–433.

Zulick, M. D., & Laffoon, E. A. (1991). Enclaved publics as inventional resources: An essay in generative rhetoric. In D. W. Parson (Ed.), *Argument in controversy: Proceedings of the Seventh SCA/AFA Conference on Argumentation* (pp. 249–255). Annandale, VA: Speech Communication Association.

PART V

Questioning

23

Communication as Dissemination

John Durham Peters

The one who scatters abroad has much; the one who gathers in has little.

—Tao Te Ching

Whatever "communication" means, it is neither a single thing nor all things. It is a few things. Communication has neither a Platonic essence that underlies all its forms, nor is it a nominalistic vacuum into which any old notion can be sucked. Between the tyranny of monism and the vertigo of pluralism, communication theory is most fruitfully advanced by looking for the few families of ideas and axes of argument without which it is impossible to think of communication (such as sign, time, space, body, turn, or interpretation). In choosing *dissemination,* I do not intend to bring one more pet concept to the scrimmage of brands. As in the marketplace today, so in communication theory: many brands, few real alternatives. Rather, dissemination is a lens—sometimes a usefully distorting one—that helps us tackle basic issues such as interaction, presence, and space and time that are destined to appear, in some form, on the agenda of any future communication theory *in general.* Such a theory would encompass communication acts from all creatures, human or not—computers, animals, extraterrestrials, and even our cousins the whales and dolphins.

Seedtime and Harvest

Dissemination descends from Latin roots that indicate the scattering of seeds. The act of sowing has long stood for acts of communication, commerce, and sexual reproduction. In Plato's masculinist metaphors, explored at length by scholars such as Jacques Derrida and Jesper Svenbro, seed = word = voice = semen = offspring. Agriculture is one of civilization's central achievements and has been widely viewed in patriarchal terms (father seed, mother earth), and yet dissemination need not have an exclusively macho overtone: the metaphor of broadcasting seed occurs in most of the world's wisdom literature. "You reap what you sow" is one of life's fundamental lessons—and one of the most difficult to master. Seedtime and harvest are linked, but so much can happen in the interim—drought, frost, hail, flood, fire, pests. Making a public offering is perhaps the most basic of all communicative acts, but once the seeds are cast, their harvest is never assured. There is always a delay between sowing and reaping during which diverse mischief can occur. The metaphor of dissemination points to the contingency of all words and deeds, their uncertain consequences, and their governance by probabilities rather than certainties. The harvest of meaning always waits in the future.

Dissemination also downplays exchange or reciprocity as the defining criterion of communication. Dissemination reminds us of the relative autonomy of sending and receiving, the liberty of combination possessed by all speakers and hearers. The other to whom we speak is never fully known; neither are the consequences of our words. Broadcasting—address to an open-ended destination—is a feature of all speech. The metaphor of dissemination directs our attention to those vast continents of signification that are not directly interactive. Much of what we speaking animals do in person and in public is not desirous of an immediate or even long-term response—church bells, royal decrees, movie marquees, the Congressional Record, university lectures, blogs, or everyday conversation. (Face-to-face speech genres are not always dialogic—think of interrogations or scoldings.) Once you stop looking for symbolic tit-for-tat, an entire kingdom of forms and formats involving suspended interaction signs comes into view. The sustained interaction that is usually called dialogue is an important art form for humans in philosophy, plays, novels, and some close relationships, but it is relatively rare among the diverse and perverse things we do with words. Most speech compared with a standard of philosophical dialogue looks like dereliction.

Accenting dissemination reconfigures the object of communication. Theorists have been prone to take symbolic events that occur in one time and space as the unmarked norm. Using one of the great tools of modern social science, the two-by-two table, we can make a rough diagram of communicative relations in time and space. (A third variable, population size, ought to be added on the z-axis, and could be defined dichotomously thus: small enough to sustain mutual interaction or not.)

Table 23.1   Relations Among Participants in Communication

	One Space	Many Spaces
One time	I. Dialogue	II. Broadcasting
Many times	III. Attendance	IV. Dissemination

When participants communicate in the same space and time, we may call this dialogue. Perhaps a less loaded name would be better, because not all social intercourse, as I just suggested, involves sustained turn taking with the aim of mutual understanding, but "dialogue" can do provisionally for chats, interviews, gossip, and everything else that occurs when two or more people come together in the flesh and the word. When the number of participants in the same space and time exceeds a certain threshold (determined by the physics and symbolics of a given context), discourse tends to take on the features of broadcasting—oratory, lecture, sermon (many people = many spaces).

Cell II represents forms of communication in which participants are present in time but remote or dispersed in space. The epitome is radio or television broadcasting, which can arrange people into virtual assemblies the size of a region or nation, if not the entire world—assemblies so large that any mutual interaction is impossible. For smaller population sizes, cell II suggests that even in face-to-face settings, broadcasting is an apt description of much discourse, inasmuch as individuals are always in different "spaces." Modern physics has shown that proximity in space and time is a convenience of approximation, not a strict mathematical or scientific fact. It is hardly unusual for people to speak into the air at each other—just as it is hardly unusual for broadcast personae on radio and television to adopt the tone and style of intimate talk as they address unseen multitudes. Some might object to my mixing of geographic and metaphorical conceptions of space. Fair enough: the space covered by a prime-time TV broadcast is of a different order than the "space" implied by personal history and consciousness. But crossing categories is highly profitable for thinking about communication. (Daniel Dayan and Elihu Katz, in their work on media events as "the live broadcasting of history," for instance, interpret cell II in terms of cell III, just as I like to treat cell I in terms of cells II, III, and IV). Why should we take cell I as the normative category—especially when proximity in space and time may be a rarity or downright impossibility?

Cell III consists of forms of communication that have one space and many times. Broadcasting is tight in time and loose in space, and what I call attendance here (for lack of a better word) refers to settings that arrange participants along a temporal rather than spatial axis. Shrines, graves, places of pilgrimage, and museums, for instance, typically accommodate only small numbers at a given time, but cumulatively, mass communication can occur here as much as in cell II. (Cell III typically deals in the sacred, as cell II deals in the profane.) We might see Notre Dame Cathedral in Paris as a medium of mass communication whose audience spreads over centuries. Shakespeare's *Hamlet* may have a relatively small number of people attending to it at any given moment, but it has certainly attracted a mass audience over the past 4 centuries. There is broadcasting over time as well as space. The Internet marks this kind of communicative relation with its geographic metaphors of travel, visiting, and "sites." A single website may accumulate millions of hits even though the participants only ever show up one by one. One space/many times is, of course, the norm for smaller collectivities— families, congregations, sports fans, bar patrons, and all others who have what Martin Heidegger called a "dwelling" to which they return habitually.

Cell IV consists of forms of communication that distantiate participants in space and time. Most of what we call civilization, the human record found in libraries, universities, and museums, is available as dissemination. Most of the human world comes from other times and places than the present moment: broadcasting, attendance, and dissemination are just as crucial sorts of communication as dialogue. Strictly speaking, no act of communication is ever received in the same space or time as its origin. Even in conversation, there is an infinitesimal if imperceptible delay between utterance and audition as the sound waves carry through the air. Chances are that nothing significant will happen, but much mischief could happen in the microsecond between speech and hearing. Most tragedy and comedy takes place in the gap between sending and receiving. (Romeo and Juliet died because of the delays of the medieval post.) In strict science, there is no presence in time or space, just slivers of approximation. Presence is an effect of clumsy sense organs. Distances and delays are not obstacles to communication; they are its sum and substance.

By letting cell IV infect the other three, by taking it as the norm, we can see dialogue as a practice that suppresses communicative distances in time and space. Cells II, III, and IV are not deformed dialogue; they, like dialogue itself, are kinds of dissemination. Cell I suppresses gaps; cell II suppresses temporal gaps and cultivates spatial ones as cell III cultivates temporal gaps and suppresses spatial ones. Cell IV is the zone in which we word-breathing animals mostly swim, the sea of signs at large.

Advantages of Dissemination as Model

Communication theory should connect with other inquiries that concern the human estate (and beyond). The ability to talk to other fields—communicability, indeed—is one test of any model of communication.

1. *Economics.* Loose coupling between work and money is a blessing. Only in the most abusive zones of the economy (such as sweatshops and piecework) are payment and labor aligned in a one-to-one relationship. Even wage labor allows for loose fit between labor and reward: one gets the hourly rate if one does the job within a wide range of acceptable variation. A salary, by distancing work and payment, is a privilege that insulates the recipient from the insult of service for cash (and everyone in the salariate knows the slight or negative correlations between productivity and payment that routinely prevail). Pride and care in one's work always transcend pay. In the most fortunate of economic niches, one need do nothing besides be born to receive significant wealth. (Inheritance still accounts for a major percentage of the wealthy in the United States and elsewhere.) Durkheim and Weber both noted that modern capitalism would be impossible without the legacy of older cultural, especially religious, practices: discipline, honesty, impersonal sociability, and so on. Business people socialize, do favors, dress up, call customers by name, spend time cultivating big prospects that may never pay off, and engage in all kinds of irrational exuberance. Tracking profit and loss is the most abstract and least natural part of business—something routinely shunted off to the unglamorous class of accountants (despite Weber's and Foucault's efforts to rescue them from their obscurity by treating them—quite rightly—as the symptomatic figures of modernity). For the more fortunate among us, balancing income and outgo is a periodic chore rather than the central task of housekeeping; for the poor it can be a daily terror. In a just world, the tie between work and payment would be completely severed; such a world would find ways to make everyone wealthy without exploiting humanity or nature. Work would stem from pride, play, or joy; payment would stem from need (yes, I know . . .). The point is not to celebrate the rich or conjure utopian improbabilities; rather, it is to show the substantial normative and explanatory power of the suspension of tit-for-tat relationships. Exchange— whether in economics or communication—is not just reciprocal but full of

delays and differences, as in gifts, loans, refusals, stalls, and barters. Just as the gift illuminates much of economics, so dissemination illuminates much of communication: neither acts without the promise of a return gift or response. It is more blessed to give than to receive. Those who give are rich; those who receive are poor.

2. *Education.* From the teacher's point of view, almost everything is wasted effort: the problem is, we rarely know exactly what is the twenty, or the two, percent that redeems (let us hope) the rest. Parents spend thousands of kisses and commands, dollars and diapers, never quite knowing what works and doesn't work to produce a human being. So much happens in the first two years of life—when a child is hardly capable of dialogue in any sense, and is learning, quite precisely, what interaction is. Feeding, holding, and changing an infant are hardly dialogic practices, but they are immensely communicative. If dialogue is defined as the sharing of being and time, rather than the conjoint effort at mutual understanding, then of course such practices are dialogic, but the asymmetrical nature of the interaction—helpless and unabashed love exchanged for care and sustenance—makes dissemination an apter model.

Anyone who has taught at a university knows that there is a huge difference between how the minds of freshmen and seniors work, and yet most university students apparently retain very little from the classes they take. Something succeeds in the aggregate that seems to fail in the particular. The majority, in my experience, study sporadically, cram for tests, miss class occasionally, resell their textbooks, toss their notebooks—and somehow learn to think or at least talk in new ways (perhaps they just learn to perform for professors). Forgetting is part of learning. Revelation is relatively rare. We can all remember our favorite teachers and moments of epiphany, but cascades of words go out without apparent result. Perhaps those sometimes endless hours and minutes in the classroom are all somehow necessary for the epiphanies. Indeed, most of what we experience in any context doesn't even register in consciousness: the present moment provides enough sensation to exhaust a lifetime of analysis. Most of the blooming, buzzing confusion around us never is even noticed or is chunked into perceptual habits. It took painters to discover that, if you really look, grass is yellow and clouds are purple. We constantly and massively reproduce our own ignorance of the true shape of things—and this ignorance appears to us as the taken-for-granted world that we assume to be stable. Learning lies less in gathering in (facts, information) than throwing away (prejudice, habit). Often knowledge consists of dumping, not acquiring, information. If we could not purge the sensory data of almost everything we experience, imagination and thought would never occur. What a meager harvest we reap from the phenomenal (in both senses) riches the world offers. The most erudite among us have perhaps simply forgotten more and better than anyone else. We educators are as spendthrift as nature in dropping seeds into the world, most of which will never take root or amount to anything at all. Some, however, will grow into oaks and fish, and such dissemination seems the best way we, or nature, know to ensure onward growth.

3. *Public Space.* Someone said that publishing a book of poetry is like dropping a rose petal in the Grand Canyon and waiting to hear an echo. (This might also be true of an academic article.) We all know that most of what is printed is read by very few, and yet somehow having it out there (wherever "there" is) feels like it makes an important difference. This is a central tenet of liberal free expression theory: the mere dissemination of ideas, regardless of their effect or audience, is itself a powerful political and moral potion. Václav Havel, one of the most incisive analysts of censorship in our time, thought that truth was a "bacteriological weapon": Once it found an opening, it could spread like a virus. We may not share his optimism in a time when market and state collaborate in the design of messages (rather different from the posttotalitarian societies he was analyzing, whose public propaganda had to make do with the state alone), but somehow, having diverse doctrines in public dissemination does seem to matter. Albert Schweitzer apparently discovered his calling to serve the people of Africa while reading a Paris tabloid. The free press may bring us scandal, comics, and box scores, and yet it still seems to perform some greater office. The notion of being tried by a jury of one's peers, also central to liberal political theory, rests on the proposition that any citizen can testify of the truth and bear witness of his or her experience. In such a system, there is no privileged center point of truth, no royal power that knows everything; truth is scattered openly and within the grasp of anyone. Science's confidence in basic research is moved by a similar faith: we cannot know what the future will value, and today's flotsam or folly may turn out to be tomorrow's cure for cancer. In publishing, First Amendment law, and science, dissemination is already the implicit doctrine and policy of public life. Being established does not make something good, of course, but dissemination has proved fruitful as a model for a society that seeks to respect the open-endedness of the future and the quirky contingency of individual life projects. I am glad to live in a society whose public spaces are mostly ruled by devil-may-care oblivion rather than solicitous interactions with neighbors or the state about what I am writing, reading, and thinking. Though we should be careful about confusing free societies with free trade (I have no interest in enlisting

"dissemination" in the already oversubscribed neoliberal ideological army), dissemination remains one of the great political ideas of the modern world.

4. *Ethics*. Dissemination provides a vision of communication for incomplete or damaged people. Most dialogic philosophy—from Buber's existentialism and Dewey or Mead's pragmatism to Gadamer's hermeneutics and Habermas's communicative action—invokes an implicit or explicit picture of the human subject as integrated, whole, and self-mastered. Stable ego-identity is taken as a prerequisite for dialogical interaction, or sometimes as its outcome. In the conviction that dialogue means an encounter between full-fledged consciousnesses, dialogical theorists usually want to defend humanity against the onslaughts of a cruel modernity. Dissemination, in contrast, models communication for creatures that emit weak, pathetic signals—infants, pets, the dead, most of us, most of the time. It gives us no counsel of perfection, and, in its acknowledgment of our lacks, is more humane. We need not share consciousness: a gesture, a reach, or a brief bridge across the chasm is enough for the humble ambitions favored by dissemination. Integrated egos can be great things, but there is no such price of admission to the dissemination party.

I need hardly mention the ancient ethical maxim, found in the New Testament and *Bhagavad-Gita*, among many other sources, that the best action is done without regard for the consequences, as one more support for the ethics of dissemination.

5. *Art and Nature*. Art does not communicate in the sense of moving information or messages about; it uplifts and delights, depresses and alarms sooner than it informs or teaches. Feelings are usually faster and more condensed in their reasons than are thoughts. Birds sing, as Charles Hartshorne argues, not only because they have a territory to defend, but because they have a sense of play and beauty that they broadcast to whomever it may concern. Play is one of the chief means by which the universe evolves: play accounts for the random variation so central to evolutionary theory. Sporting, in the full sense of that pun (play and genetic mutation) makes the universe grow. This drive to share, to scatter, to generalize is far greater than any person, society, or organism: its fierce metabolism lies at the heart of life as we know it. Like Charles Sanders Peirce, whose ideas I am cribbing here, I do not believe in pure randomness in evolution: variations are too fast, smart, and efficient to be simple rolls of the dice. In the same way, scientific inquiry is just an accelerated version of evolution itself: the making of intelligent leaps beyond the given. A philosophy of science that made us test every possible hypothesis before we could conclude anything would make

science stupid and dull. Intelligence and nature grow in chunks. (Nature does make leaps.) The universe itself has an aesthetic imperative. Evolution need not be the brutal survival of the fittest, but the urge to generalize, to grow, to sympathize and connect. Humans may dialogue, but the slime mold, the frogs, the sturgeon and oak trees, the comets and galaxies all disseminate.

Beyond Human Communication

Communication theory should not be afraid to depart the human scale. *Human communication* as a term has an aura of special pleading about it. When it first came into use in the 1950s, it was in part a rearguard action designed to allay the suspicion that there was something inhuman about communication as it was then emerging. Indeed, we talk of communication among bees, birds, primates, extraterrestrials, and computers. As a field, we have been rather incurious what the *human* means. An unexamined human-ism can clog the theoretical imagination. (By humanism, I mean both an unreflective human point of view and the doctrine that emerged from the European middle classes since the Renaissance.) Naturalism gives us all that humanism does, a sense of our place in the order of things, without the hubris and self-satisfaction. The choice of dialogue as the best or central kind of communication owes to this legacy. If communication theory is to encom-pass all creatures, dissemination is a much more hospitable term.

Human experience of the universe is doled out in minute sample sizes whose data are subject to severe degradation. A life of 70 years will see about one 200 millionth of the history of our universe. What one person can know is a thimbleful of the ocean. Moreover, for intelligent beings even to exist who are capable of observing the universe, the universe has to be old and cold enough to possess the large chemical elements that sustain intelligent life as we know it. Human knowers are latecomers to the universe, and their rela-tion to it will always be belated and partial. Communication has typically been studied within a very narrow anthropocentric spectrum of time, from the split seconds of perception up to the millennia of time-binding messages sent across civilizations. And yet, communication can occur on all kinds of scales and speeds, small and large. Computers thrive in the ecological niches of nanoseconds (10^{-9} s) and picoseconds (10^{-12} s), and laser research is explor-ing the realm of the attosecond (10^{-18} s), a time span during which light travels a bit farther than the width of a water molecule. Similarly, super-slow and super-old communications are of interest. Historians are receivers of communications from old time, but they are outstripped by archaeologists (thousands of years), paleontologists (millions of years), geologists (hundreds of millions of years), cosmologists (billions of years), and theologians (before the beginning of time—if you can even say that). No dialogue is possible with the older or infinitesimally small sorts of messages. For communication theory on the grandest (nonhuman) scale to be possible, dissemination is the most fruitful model. Stretching the ends of our analytic scale makes clear things about the human level as well: dialogue fits beings for whom time and space are in short supply.

In conclusion, let us once again visit the cetaceans—porpoises, dolphins, and whales, our kindred mammals who took to the water instead of the land millions of years ago. There is no reason to think that such obviously intelligent and sociable creatures do not have highly developed forms of communication—and if they do not, our conjecturing does no harm to them. Cetacean communication would be obviously different from the human. If work and the resulting world of durable objects are a key part of the human condition, as Hannah Arendt suggests, it is no part of the cetacean condition. Their lack of an equivalent to our hands means the lack of writing or any other kind of permanence of record, making memory the sole archive of cetacean history. The enveloping water medium also has several curious effects. Up and down, day and night, the pull of gravity and the diurnal rhythm of wake and sleep are much less dictatorial. The sea is a relatively homogeneous environment compared to the earth's surface, one that suppresses the visual sense and enhances the auditory sense. In most creatures, the eye is excellent at spatial discrimination and poor at temporal discrimination (one reason why movies work); the ear is poor at spatial discrimination and excellent at temporal discrimination. Trained studio engineers can supposedly discern sound intervals up to one microsecond (10^{-3} s), and most people can discriminate sound intervals smaller than a hundredth of a second. In an aqueous environment, the evolutionary incentive for loading communicative intelligence on the acoustic channel would be tremendous. (For humans too, sound is the chief medium of oceanographic exploration.) Cetaceans have a complex vocal apparatus and well-developed neural auditory processing centers that may allow them to send and receive something like auditory images through the water. They also seemingly have acute powers of spatial location. No wonder human efforts to "communicate" with them have largely failed: we might as well try to understand the squeaks a modem makes with our ears or transmit pictures, sounds, and data by talking to a modem. Our air-tested ears and voices simply lack the bandwidth; our neural baud rate may be too slow. Like computers, they can perhaps pack much more data into subsecond slices of time. Cetaceans seem to prefer human music to speech, and who knows what pictures, maps, or data they decode from our musical transmissions. They also may be able to do ultrasounds of living matter, scoping out potential prey or the well-being of their kind. What sort of communication would occur if we could see sympathetically into each other's bodies?

Most curious of all is what would happen under water to real-time inter-action, so central to many dialogic takes on communication. Sound travels much faster under water (with variations for temperature, depth, and salin-ity) than through the air. The loudest noises in the atmosphere dissipate within about 10 kilometers, but ocean sounds can travel 20 thousand kilo-meters, given the right kind of underwater sound channel. Half the circum-ference of the earth can be covered in more than 4 hours. We know that humpback whale songs off the coast of Mexico, for instance, can be heard off the coast of Alaska. Given their gregarious nature, we can assume that cetaceans do engage in rapid-fire exchanges when swimming in groups. But what happens when distant voices speak or sing in different places of the sea to each other and it takes minutes or even hours for the sound to carry? Just as different observers located at different points in the cosmos will see dif-ferent star constellations, so intelligent creatures in different spots of the sea will each hear a distinct sonic constellation, receiving distant messages in an order determined not by the time when it was sent but by the proximity of the sender. Thus the sequence of turns in distant ocean discourse would lack what conversation analysts call "adjacency turns" and "implicature" or could have these only in the loosest sense. If whale music is a conversational art, like jazz, one singer might respond to a riff that had already (if you can say that) been answered by some other singer closer who heard it first. Einstein discovered relativity while pondering the finite speed of light, and our large briny friends face the same problem with the speed of sound: they have no universal standpoint that could set all clocks simultaneously to the same time. (Einstein spoke of the relativity of the observer, and perhaps some dolphin collective has discovered the relativity of the listener.) The nighttime stars appear to us in our present moment, though they mingle huge differences in their times of origin. For distant underwater communi-cation, there may be no single "now" that can serve as the fulcrum of turn taking. Perhaps the whales live in what the medieval mystics called the time of the now—a plural now in which many different times cross and recur. Since the songs persist as sound in the water, arriving to different ears at dif-ferent times, perhaps singing cetaceans identify the voices of the singers and retroactively reconstruct who must have been responding to whom, in the same way that one can read an Internet discussion group and piece together the various threads of discussion. The ocean is a medium that is not cursed and blessed by the instant dissipation of sound, and perhaps smart ocean mammals can and do listen, tune, and sing on many channels. But perhaps our maritime siblings are less worried about sequence and response, and are content to speak into the water, making music for anyone to enjoy, any time, all the time.

Additional Readings

Arendt, H. (1958). *The human condition.* Chicago: University of Chicago Press.

Derrida, J. (1981). *Dissemination.* Chicago: University of Chicago Press.

Hartshorne, C. (Ed.). (1970). The aesthetic matrix of value. In *Creative synthesis and philosophic method* (pp. 301–321). LaSalle, IL: Open Court.

Peters, J. D. (1999). *Speaking into the air: A history of the idea of communication.* Chicago: University of Chicago Press.

Stappers, J. G. (1983). Mass communication as public communication. *Journal of Communication, 33,* 141–145.

24

Communication as Articulation

Jennifer Daryl Slack

After years of reading and critiquing myriad definitions of communication, I feel the need to come clean. Let me get this out into the open: communication *is* the process of transmitting messages from sender to receiver, it *is* the process of encoding and decoding, it *is* the effect of a message on a receiver, it *is* the negotiation of shared meaning, it *is* community, it *is* ritual, it *is* . . . please feel free to fill in the ellipsis with your favored definition. Although I'll grant the significance of any sense of communication you desire, don't settle on or quote any part of that sentiment without this coda: communication is not *in essence* any of these, and it is not any of these *exclusively*. If the past two decades of communication scholarship have stumbled onto anything significant at all, it is the reality that there is no single, absolute essence of communication that adequately explains the phenomena we study. Such a definition does not exist; neither is it merely awaiting the next brightest communication scholar to nail it down once and for all.

To my mind—that is, thinking with articulation—this is not an undesirable state of affairs. Quite the opposite: liberated from the need to *be* any one thing, communication gives us permission to look long and hard at the world in order to explore how it works and how to change it. Thinking about communication *with* the idea of articulation gives us just that: permission to explore the workings of a complex world, figure out how it works, and propose changes to make it better. This is not to say that communication *is* articulation, although it is that, too. However, my argument here resists the strategy adopted by most communication textbooks, which, in performing a huge disservice at this point in the history of the field, begin with a brief discussion of different definitions of communication yet settle on one. I want to resist opening the door merely to close it and thereby to close down thought that might accompany the copresence of multiple definitions before we've even gotten started. Indeed, thinking with articulation necessarily involves understanding that definitions of communication themselves respond to and perform articulating work and thereby contribute to shaping the world we set out to study and change. But let me work this through in something like a logical manner. In what follows, I first develop the argument that thinking with articulation helps us to understand the work definitions of communication perform. Embedded in this discussion is something like a definition of articulation. However, the manner in which I make my argument about the work of definitions of communication better demonstrates the principle of thinking communication as articulation than my asserting any particular definition. Then, I address the claim that thinking communication as articulation opens up a whole new way of looking at the world. Finally, I make a plea for respecting the political component of thinking with articulation, so that we might get on with understanding and changing the world: what I consider the real work and contribution of communication study.

Articulating Communication

Rejecting the idea of an imperial definition of communication does not necessitate rejecting simultaneously the importance of definitions that have been posed as such. Indeed, without imperial definitions of communication, we might not have a field from which to venture forth. Such is the articulated reality of intellectual, institutional, and political life. With Harold Lasswell's 1948 definition of communication as "*Who* says *what* in *which channel* to *whom* with *what effects*," (Lasswell, 1948) and Wilbur Schramm's 1954 landmark book divided into sections that isolate messages, channels, audiences, and effects (Schramm, 1954), a field of study was given shape, a stage was set. Upon that stage, Lasswell, Schramm, and a host of others positioned themselves, and years later we position ourselves, to play a part in the ongoing drama: we certify ourselves as communication scholars, apply for grants, offer consulting services, develop departments, proselytize, offer degrees, and argue about the correctness of various characterizations of the field—surely a sign of the establishment of a field. Thank you, Harold, Wilbur, and others, of course, for opening that door.

What is most critical to remember about their foundational work, however, is that it occurred in a particular place, at a particular time, in a particular set of relations: in, as it were, the articulation of a real historical moment—something often referred to as a conjuncture. But before going any further, let me take a detour to explore my use of this term, *articulation*.

Typically, the term articulation denotes enunciation: if you articulate well, you state your case clearly. But articulation as used by cultural theorists takes on a slightly different inflection. Articulation, for cultural theorists, suggests two critical dynamics: a contingent joining of parts to make a unity or identity that constitutes a context, and the empowerment and disempowerment of certain ways of imagining and acting within that context.

With regard to the first dynamic, articulation refers to the way that different things (values, feelings, beliefs, practices, structures, organizations, ideologies, and so on) come into connection or relation at a particular historical conjuncture. These articulations are contingent, meaning that these different things might have come together differently. But given historical forces, relations, and accidents, things have come together in this particular way. Just as a joint articulates bones to make, for example, an arm, a conjuncture is the articulation of social and cultural forces and relations that similarly constitute a particular historical moment as a kind of unity—for example, an antiterrorist climate in the United States after the September 11 attack on the Trade Towers in New York City. An arm might have been articulated differently: it might, for example, have been articulated to bend backward as well as forward. Similarly, the antiterrorist climate might have been articulated differently: with, for example, more emphasis on the forces within the United States that contributed to the terrorism against this country.

With regard to the second dynamic, an articulated sociocultural conjuncture does the work of empowering ways of thinking, being, and acting in the world as possible or not. Just as an arm renders some sorts of movements possible and others unlikely or impossible, so, too, do sociocultural conjunctures render some sorts of movement possible and others unlikely or impossible. An articulated sociocultural conjuncture thus necessarily will have particular and significant effects, creating a sort of map of what is possible and what is not, who or what is valued and who or what is not, who or what benefits and who or what does not. For example, since September 11 in the United States, it has become very easy to violate once-accepted practices of personal privacy and very difficult to challenge increases in defense spending. Likewise, it has become difficult for most Americans even to imagine a kind of patriotism that does not blindly wave the flag and support whatever is proposed by President George W. Bush.

Neither the character of an articulated conjuncture nor the possibilities thus empowered are guaranteed. In other words, a conjuncture never is "sewn up," or an absolutely fixed unity, but a web of articulating, dynamic movements among variously homogeneous and heterogeneous forces and relations. Consequently, articulation is an ongoing process of disconnecting, reconnecting, reinforcing, and contradicting movements. So, unlike an articulated arm, an example that conveys a sense of fixity, an articulated conjuncture is always more supple, variously open to possibilities for change, given the particular play of social antagonisms and tensions, the efforts of real people to foster new connections, the effects of new forms of organization, and the important role of accident. Thus, the post–September 11 antiterrorist climate in the United States is variously open to possibilities for change given what people imagine they can and should do, and given what forces, antagonisms, and tensions are possible to develop or exploit.

As scholars of communication who think with articulation, we do not read the history of communication theory as the process of discovering what communication *is*. Rather we read it as articulating—that is, connecting, bringing together, unifying, inventing, contributing to—a sort of force field of relations within which it made sense to talk about communication in a particular way: for the most part as the sending and receiving of messages, the goal of which was persuasion. As the history of communication theory reveals, some of the articulating forces that contributed to this conjuncture include the state of social theory, the development of media technologies, the promises of marketing, the fear of propaganda, and the disciplinary nature of the university. The version of communication that emerged has been persistent and popular, due to both the persistence and development of relations that have sustained it: among them, the acceleration of a commercial culture using techniques of persuasion; the mainstreaming of marketing and propaganda techniques in the politics of everyday life; the increasing tendency to situate people-as-receivers in relation to the development of new media technologies; the enactment of governmental policies built on this model of communication; and the establishment of educational programs and consulting services that continue to infiltrate the culture with this particular version of communication.

Something I learned from the philosopher Louis Althusser (1970, 1971) long ago in his elaborations on ideology is relevant here: a belief (more correctly, an ideology, in Althusser's terms) does not have to be true to be powerful in its effects, and therefore, for all practical purposes, real. Circulating definitions and concomitant practices of communication are real in their effects, hence real and worthy of analysis. Thinking with articulation is a way to comprehend the power of a concept, the work it performs, its reality, without being seduced into accepting it as an absolute truth or as an unchanging essence. Thinking with articulation also encourages a certain distance that permits a reading of the force field, set of relations, or context within which a world takes shape and within which (sometimes against which) we give it shape. As Karl Marx has taught us, we make the world, but we do not do so under conditions of our own making. Thinking with the concept of articulation, we map the conditions we inherit as well as envision how we might move on from there.

Communication as Articulation

If we envision communication as articulation, my second point, our attention is most obviously drawn to the contingent relations that constitute competing effective definitions and practices of communication. But beyond that, and far more significantly, envisioning communication as articulation, as seen though the work of Ernesto Laclau (1977) and Stuart Hall (see, for example, 1986), opens up a whole new way of looking at the world. It demands a broader, more encompassing acknowledgment and exploration of how the world works as a matter of multiple, contingent, articulating relations among forms of expression, the content of expression, materiality, economics, politics, and power. It insists, as early communication theory did not, that communication cannot be studied apart from, as Hall has argued "(a) a general social theory, (b) a developed cultural theory, and (c) a properly historicized model of social formations" (Hall, 1989, p. 43).

The gift that communication has bestowed, beyond the designation of a legitimate field of study, is precisely the historical proposition that communication *is* about expression: of how we understand the world, of how our understandings of and responses to the world shape individual actions and give shape to society. When that legacy is articulated to the broader insight that contingent sociocultural conjunctures more generally constitute meaningful reality in ways that differentially empower possibility and therefore unequal relations of power, the study of communication becomes a critical site from which to interrogate and celebrate what is interesting, liberating, and life-giving. At the same time, it becomes a powerful site from which to interrogate and challenge what is stultifying, oppressive, and life destroying. It is as though communication has become the site where we are allowed to address—unfettered by disciplinary and methodological limitations of earlier ways of studying communication—what really matters, and consider how we might make life better.

Though communication scholars and students may be freer than most to shake off disciplinary limitations, we also are encouraged to draw on disciplinary insights to craft a necessarily interdisciplinary story of the world. To explain phenomena that matter—whether we begin with more traditional communication studies topics such as the meanings of television programs or the significance of images of romance, or more far-reaching matters such as the significance of new biotechnologies or the cultural context of war—the approach to communication as articulation requires looking at the far-ranging contingent articulations that constitute those phenomena. So, for example, a message can be seen as having an effect; given a particular configuration of the sociocultural conjuncture, talking about the effect of the message on an audience might makes sense. However, what matters about a message is never *just* that. There may be a component of ritual involved in the reception. There may be significant community building involved in the transmission. There will be a political-economic context within which the message is produced, delivered, and received. There will be differential privileging of certain ways of being in the world over others: some possibilities empowered, others disempowered; some cultural groups empowered, others disempowered. Many kinds of articulations will matter, depending on the phenomena under consideration: political-economic relations; the work of ideological assumptions; forces of globalism, capitalism, and consumerism; material components of technology; biological components; the sense of what it means to be human; the experience of affect; and so on. This list is neither exhaustive nor constituted by mutually exclusive categories. Communication as articulation does not provide a neatly wrapped method with which to hammer the world into a predetermined form. It offers instead a vantage point from which creatively to engage a richly constituted world, to offer explanations and interventions that make sense in a particular historical conjuncture.

Had I been able to title this essay to my liking, rather than to the demand for consistency among contributions, I would have called it "Articulating Communication: A Position Just Shy of Communication as Articulation." The assertion of "a position just shy of communication as articulation" is meant to resist substituting communication as articulation as *the* metaphor or definition that most accurately describes communication. Rather, as I have tried to make clear above, thinking with the concept of articulation allows me to acknowledge—regardless of the object of analysis—the vast articulation of relations within which some beliefs and behaviors are valued and encouraged over others and certain structures of privilege and discrimination are maintained. The communication scholar or student who thinks with articulation undertakes the daunting task of mapping the multiple articulations of a sociocultural conjuncture. Her or his purpose in doing so is to expand understanding outward into the complex reality of the world rather than to restrict vision to a misleadingly limited, albeit more comfortable, perspective—either for the sake of being manageable or for the sake of avoiding uncomfortable political realities. No researcher can do everything, hence the challenge for the communication researcher who thinks with articulation: how to draw the map with attention sufficiently outward to see and say something significant about the complex articulations, without getting so lost in the complexity as to say nothing at all? This is art, just as science at its best is art. But this is also clearly politics.

A Plea for Politics

My third and final point, a plea really, is to argue that thinking with articulation—regardless of the object of analysis in communication with which we begin—leads us to what matters most in the sociocultural conjuncture: the work of politics and power in the structure and experience of life, to the tendencies, trajectories, and affects within which the world is given shape. When found wanting, we ought to have at least understood the conjuncture well enough to begin to suggest ways of rearticulating or reorganizing contingent articulations in ways that might change the world for the better.

There are, of course, no guarantees that the recognition of communication as articulation will be used in this way, for it is simply too easy to adopt articulation as a method that permits the isolation of particular articulations of interest while turning a Dantean blind eye to matters of politics and power. As Hall warned long ago, "articulation contains the danger of a high formalism" (Hall, 1980, p. 69). By this, he means that articulation can be applied in a formulaic manner, so as to point to the fact that one thing is articulated to another while ignoring the unexpected and rich complexity of the real world as well as the complex relations of power that occur in any conjuncture. Communication scholars typically make too little of communication with the retreat into formalism. When communication means, almost by rote, nothing more than effective writing or speaking, the rhetorical analysis of content, the effect of this particular message on that particular behavior, the celebration of difference, the expression of community, the enactment of ritual, the implementation of new media, or even merely the point that one thing is articulated to another, it has been hijacked by Dante's neutrals, deprived of exercising the historical muscle that has been laid at our feet. Dante's neutrals, who occupy the first circle in Hell, are those whose refusal to act when given the opportunity supports de facto political oppression (see Canto III in Dante's Inferno, 1994).

Repeatedly, when I read studies in communication that find comfort—indeed, mastery—in a restricted "scientistic" version of method, I am astonished that so many competent scholars seem content with the neatness of their work, the conformity of their method and approach, to the detriment of reaching critical insights about the world they are studying. When Stuart Hall (1992, p. 280) states that "the only theory worth having is that which you have to fight off, not that which you speak with profound fluency," he warns us away from taking any theory, including articulation, and reifying it into a paper cutout with which to withdraw from the unexpected richness and complexity of the real world as well as to the political realities of oppression. If indeed communication is articulation, a position which demands the exploration of the range and effects of articulating relations in sociocultural conjunctures, then to study communication ought to be nothing less than the search to liberate human potential while honoring the richly articulated life-giving interconnections that sustain the world of which we are part.

Additional Readings

Hall, S. (1996). On postmodernism and articulation: An interview with Stuart Hall. In D. Morley & K.-H. Chen (Eds.), *Critical dialogues in cultural studies* (pp. 131–173). London: Routledge. (Reprinted from *Journal of Communication Inquiry 10*[2], 450–460, 1986)

Laclau, E. (1977). *Politics and ideology in Marxist theory*. London: New Left Books.

Latour, B. (2002). How to talk about the body? The normative dimension of science studies. Retrieved December 18, 2004, from www.ensmp.fr/~latour/articles/article/077.html

Mouffe, C. (1979). Hegemony and ideology in Gramsci (D. Derome, Trans.). In C. Mouffe (Ed.), *Gramsci and Marxist theory* (pp. 168–204). London: Routledge & Kegan Paul.

Slack, J. D. (1996). The theory and method of articulation in cultural studies. In D. Morley & K.-H. Chen (Eds.), *Stuart Hall: Critical dialogues in cultural studies* (pp. 112–127). New York: Routledge.

References

Althusser, L. (1970). *For Marx* (B. Brewster, Trans.). New York: Vintage Books.

Althusser, L. (1971). Ideology and ideological state apparatuses: Notes towards an investigation. In L. Althusser (Ed.) & B. Brewster (Trans.), *Lenin and philosophy and other essays* (pp. 127–186). New York: Monthly Review Press.

Dante, A. (1994). The inferno of Dante (R. Pinsky, Trans.). New York: Farrar, Straus and Giroux.

Hall, S. (1980). Cultural studies: Two paradigms. *Media, Culture and Society, 2*(1), 57–72.

Hall, S. (1989). Ideology and communication theory. In B. Dervin, L. Grossberg, B. J. O'Keefe, & E. Wartella (Eds.), *Rethinking communication: Vol. 1. Paradigm issues* (pp. 40–52). Newbury Park, CA: Sage.

Hall, S. (1992). Cultural studies and its theoretical legacies. In L. Grossberg, C. Nelson, & P. Treichler (Eds.), *Cultural studies* (pp. 277–294). New York: Routledge.

Hall, S. (1996). On postmodernism and articulation: An interview with Stuart Hall. In D. Morley & K.-H. Chen (Eds.), *Critical dialogues in cultural studies* (pp. 131–173). London: Routledge. (Reprinted from *Journal of Communication Inquiry, 10*[2], 450–460, 1986)

Laclau, E. (1977). *Politics and ideology in Marxist theory.* London: New Left Books.

Lasswell, H. (1948). The structure and function of communication in society. In L. Bryson (Ed.), *The communication of ideas: A series of addresses* (pp. 37–51). New York: Harper.

Schramm, W. L. (1954). *The process and effects of mass communication.* Urbana: University of Illinois Press.

25

Communication as Translation

Ted Striphas

*Infected by the entrenched prejudice that through speech we
understand each other, we make our remarks and listen in such
good faith that we inevitably misunderstand each other much
more than if we had remained silent and had guessed.*

—José Ortega y Gassett, *The Misery and the Splendor
of Translation* (1937/2000, p. 55)

B
y the end of this chapter, I hope to have persuaded you that what
we commonly refer to as "communication"—the process, the product,
or both—is understood best from the standpoint of translation. This may,
admittedly, require some counterintuitive thinking, because imagining communication as translation raises serious questions about some of our most
basic assumptions regarding language and language use: How and why do
we draw boundaries between languages? Can people ever speak the same
language? And, as suggested by the epigraph above, do we ever truly understand one another? With these questions in mind, my plan for this chapter is
to use the term *translation* very broadly, to encompass a range of what we

---

I am grateful to Phaedra C. Pezzullo, Gregory J. Shepherd, and Jeffrey St. John for
reading and responding to earlier drafts of this chapter. I also would like to thank
Meaghan Morris for introducing me to the compelling world of translation studies.

traditionally think about as communicative activities. I want you to imagine translation as something that occurs not only between people who seem to speak different languages but, perhaps more important, as a process that takes place constantly—and necessarily—between those who appear to share a common language as well. Furthermore, I want to argue that the concept of translation offers more than just another viewpoint from which to understand the nature of human communication; it also suggests an ethics, or a way for you to live your life more responsibly and compassionately in relationship to those around you.

Whatever Happened to Translation?

In 1923, C. K. Ogden and I. A. Richards (1923/2001), arguably two of the most influential voices in 20th century communication theory, wrote in their groundbreaking book *The Meaning of Meaning,* "With an understanding of the function of language and of its technical resources the criticism of translations provides a particularly fascinating and instructive method of language study" (p. 235). In helping lay the early theoretical foundations of the communication discipline, Ogden and Richards recognized how both the practice and critical analysis of translation might serve as resources for scholars interested in language, language use, and issues related to communication more broadly. They saw how translation crystallized many of the very same questions about the nature of human communication that had motivated them to develop their "science of symbolism," questions that continue to animate communication research and theory to this day: How do signs (words, phrases, sentences, etc. that stand for specific objects or ideas) generate meaning? How and why do misunderstandings occur, and how might they be mitigated? How can one understand what another person means, particularly when she or he seems to be using different signs?

Despite Ogden and Richards' suggestion that the study of translation might enrich communication theory, and despite other, more or less explicit, attempts by Edward Sapir (1921, pp. 90–119), Benjamin Lee Whorf (1956), and other early communication theorists to think communication through translation, translation, unfortunately, does not seem to have gained much traction in the discipline. Where it has been taken up, translation generally has served as little more than an instrument for determining what someone from another culture "really" means, given perceived differences in worldview and communication style. Why translation has faded from the discipline's repertoire of key concepts remains a mystery, though it's worth offering a few speculations as to why. For starters, translation often is dismissed as an exceptional case (as in, for example, what people may do when they travel abroad), rather than an appropriate beginning from which to theorize communication in everyday life. Second, translations often are imagined to be degraded copies of "original" expressions rather than unique in their own right, condemning them unfairly to an inferior, derivative status. Closely related is the historically marginal status of the translator, a figure who generally has been perceived to be subordinate or secondary to those for whom she or he is translating (Bassnett, 2002, pp. 4–5). Finally, as both a practice and a theoretical problem, translation has tended to engage scholars in comparative literature far more than their counterparts in communication. This unevenness of interest may flow from the urgencies of translating written literature in the former discipline, as compared to the latter discipline's bias toward speech. In any event, despite some early opportunities, translation and communication have had little to "say" directly to one another.

The Tasks of the Translator

As the volume you're now reading and as numerous other publications no doubt demonstrate, *communication* is, and long has been, a fraught term for scholars at work in this discipline. I say this recognizing that contest and argumentation may be damaging, yet they may be highly productive activities as well. Indeed, struggles over the term *communication* have yielded dozens, perhaps hundreds, of different definitions, resulting in a remarkable plurality of perspectives regarding what "it" is and inspiring a healthy array of research and thinking. Without smoothing over important differences, I want to suggest that many of these definitions share at least three common attributes. First, most proceed from the assumption that symbols or signs are the primary media through which communication occurs. Second, they tend to privilege meaning and shared understanding as the desired outcomes of communication. Finally, and relatedly, these definitions tend to be biased toward mutuality, or the sense in which "successful" communication necessarily demands various forms of psychological, moral, social, and/or metaphysical entanglement. Thus, I want to put forth the following definition of communication, which I hope captures some sense of the discipline's normative assumptions regarding the term: Communication is the intersubjective coconstruction and sharing of meaning, value, and experience, a process made possible by various forms of symbolic exchange.

Translation, I want to suggest, cuts against the grain of this definition, and thus should prompt us to redefine communication. To do this, I want to begin by considering linguist Roman Jakobson's (1959/2000) useful distinction between two forms of translation. *Inter*lingual translation refers to *transposing* and/or interpreting signs *across* one or more languages or sign systems. This is perhaps the most commonsense understanding of translation, denoting the deliberate activities in which one might engage to communicate with someone who's using an unfamiliar language. *Intra*lingual translation, in contrast, refers to *substituting* apparently comparable signs *within* a specific language or sign system. Rewording is one example of this type of translation, as in when we use synonyms, euphemisms, and/or circumlocutions to say what we mean to say by way of alternative signs (p. 114).

All that makes translation sound reasonably straightforward, as though it were just a matter of finding equivalent signs either across or within sign systems. As any seasoned translator will attest, however, translation never is as simple as that. On the one hand, extralinguistic elements like sense, mood, and tone pose serious challenges when translating *inter*lingually, which may explain why humor tends to fall flat when it's rendered from one language into another. In other cases, words, concepts, and even entire verb tenses may exist in one language but not in another, as in the French future past, which has no direct English correlate (roughly, they *will have succeeded*); the English perfect and imperfect tenses (e.g., I *have gone;* she *was hoping*), which have no counterpart in the Hopi language; or the definite and indefinite articles that exist in many Indo-European languages (*the* tire, *a* house), which must be inferred from the Chinese language. Finally, there's the challenge of translating "nonsense" words and neologisms, as in the term *Muggle* from the popular *Harry Potter* book series.[1] Because *Muggle* was fabricated by author J. K. Rowling and sounds vaguely English but has no correlate in another language, translators have had to concoct words that approximate its feel and function in non-English languages. In French, for instance, the term is translated either as *Moldus* or *Moldue*, depending on whether one is referring to a male or female Muggle (Jentsch, 2002, p. 296).

The fact that signs gain their meanings contextually, or in relation to other signs, further complicates interlingual translation, for even signs that seem to have clear and obvious interlingual equivalents may in fact signify or connote quite different things. Consider the challenges involved in translating a word as apparently simple as *butter*:

When translating *butter* into Italian there is a straightforward word-for-word substitution: butter—*burro*. Both *butter* and *burro* describe the product made from milk and marketed as a creamy-coloured slab of edible grease for human consumption. And yet within their separate cultural contexts *butter* and *burro* cannot be considered as signifying the same. In Italy, *burro*, normally light coloured and unsalted, is used primarily for cooking, and carries no association of high status, whilst in Britain *butter,* most often bright yellow and salted, is used for spreading on bread and less frequently in cooking. . . . So there is a distinction both between the *objects* signified by *butter* and *burro* and between the *function and value* of those objects in their cultural context. (Bassnett, 2002, p. 26; emphasis in original)

Almost every translated text contains some sort of translator's note to this effect, and with good reason: translators struggle to find words, phrases, and so forth that capture some sense of what the authors whom they're translating are trying to convey. The difficulty of interlingual translation consists not merely of translating signs from one system into another, but also of expressing a whole host of connotations that may be difficult, if not impossible, to translate directly.

At first glance, *intra*lingual translation also might seem relatively uncomplicated but, like *inter*lingual translation, it, too, poses a number of quandaries. If you agree that signs gain their meaning in relationship to other signs, then you're already on your way to seeing why translating intralingually, or communicating with someone whom you perceive to share the same language, also may be a challenge. Owing to myriad differences in background, upbringing, environment, and so forth, it seems reasonable to surmise that rarely, if ever, do those who seem to speak "your" language share exactly your associations with a given sign. For example, I recently asked students in my introductory communication theory class to define the word *justice,* hoping to prompt them to see how signs have varied and ambiguous meanings. Many responded with words and phrases such as "the courts," "fairness," "equality," "impartiality," "a reasonable punishment," "what goes around comes around," and "what someone deserves," which I thought represented a fairly disparate range of interpretations. Much to my surprise, however, another student responded by saying, "baseball." Puzzled, I asked, "Baseball?" "Yeah, you know," he replied, "Dave Justice? He plays for the Oakland A's." What this anecdote begins to suggest, I hope, are the profoundly different associations each and every one of us maintains with many, perhaps even most, signs, and how those idiosyncrasies may forestall understanding—the intersubjective synthesis or "communion"—implied etymologically in the word *communication.*

Recently, linguist Geoffrey Nunberg (2003) reported on a series of English language words and idiomatic expressions whose meanings many of us take for granted, often without realizing that others very well may understand something radically different, even opposite, from what we intend. Consider the phrase "on the up and up," which, Nunberg discovered, could signify both "on the level" (as in, what's expected) and "on the increase."

Nunberg shared his findings with a colleague, who expressed dismay upon hearing that "on the up and up" could mean "on the increase." Nunberg states:

> But when [my colleague] asked his wife about it, she said that for her, that was the only thing it could mean. She didn't know it could mean "on the level." And what made it odder still was that they'd been married for twenty years, and both grew up in southern California. I had this image of the two of them sitting at the breakfast table. He asks, "Is your brother's new business on the up and up?" And she says, "No, but he's making do." And they go on like that, with neither of them ever realizing that they're talking at cross-purposes. (n.p.)

Similarly, Nunberg found that the expression "that gives me heartburn" could mean "that makes me worried" or "that makes me furious"—a substantial difference in one's degree of consternation, to be sure! Even a word as apparently straightforward as "minimal," he discovered, could send us into a communicative tailspin, because it can signify both "a small amount" and "nothing at all" (n.p.). Imagine telling your passenger before leaving on a car trip, "The gas tank has a minimal amount of fuel in it." Are you stuck in the driveway, empty, or is there just enough gas left to get you to the filling station? Thus, Nunberg concludes: "We can never be sure we're understanding each other. . . . But maybe the wonder of it all is that we manage to muddle through even so" (n.p.). Another, less tentative, way of putting this would be to say that perhaps we never really manage to communicate in the sense in which I defined it at the beginning of this section, yet still we manage to coordinate with one another. The question remains, how?

Communication as Translation

In the preceding section, I suggested that we never speak the same language as someone else, even when common sense may be telling us otherwise, nor do we ever quite communicate with someone, even when it may appear as though another genuinely has understood us. Even if you're not persuaded by these arguments, I hope that you at least will entertain their possibility. (You can treat them as working hypotheses rather than as statements of fact, if you prefer.) Either way, these arguments probably fly in the face of most of what you've learned about the nature of communication. Why might they seem so counterintuitive?

The difficulty may stem in part from our taken-for-granted assumptions about language, language use, and communication, or better yet how we *represent* these aspects in both theory and practice. Naoki Sakai (1997) has pointed out, for instance, that the idea of communication—by which, echoing the definition above, he refers to an "unruffled empathetic transference" of meaning and understanding (p. 4)—is premised on a series of embedded and potentially flawed suppositions, beginning with a tension that inheres in the very concept itself. Communication refers simultaneously to both a process ("they're communicating about it right now") and an outcome ("she communicated her ideas to me"). The idea of communication thus typically depends on and continually reaffirms an oddly circular logic, so that the former sense of the term seems to presume, even guarantee, the latter sense ("if we're communicating [process] then by definition we must be communicating" [outcome]) (p. 4). In simpler terms, Sakai wants us to recognize how the term *communication* cannot account for those apparently communicative acts, such as those I discussed in the preceding section, in which understanding and synthesis are far from assured.

How, then, can we describe what we ordinarily take to be the processual sense of communication without presuming that it must indeed end in shared understanding and/or some transcendent form of connection? Sakai recommends that we begin by introducing a new word, *address,* to get us out of the dilemma (1997, p. 4). Address denotes the act of giving off an utterance or expression, with no guarantee that it will be understood and/or reciprocated in kind. Address thus is a more theoretically nuanced term than is communication, for it presumes no necessary outcome from the activities it refers to. Address "precludes the description of what it accomplishes . . . whereas [communication] anticipates its accomplishment" (p. 4). The term *address* might be an appropriate name, in fact, for what John Durham Peters (1999) has described as the profoundly humble and humbling experience of "speaking into the air," or the act of expressing ourselves without ever expecting those expressions to result in understanding or common union.[2]

Taking address as a starting point raises a difficult question about how people interact and coordinate with one another, for if in most, perhaps all, cases we don't communicate in the old sense, then how in the world do we ever manage to get by? The answer is, in a word, *translation.* The sense of translation that I am proposing here is premised on twin assumptions: (a) there are no simple correspondences between languages or sign systems (as in *inter*lingual translation); and (b) people never, ever speak the same language (as in *intra*lingual translation). Translation, in fact, challenges any simple notion of language as a symbol system shared by, and thus uniting, a more or less coherent social group. From the standpoint of translation, "you are always confronted . . . with foreigners" (Sakai, 1997, p. 9), which implies that we shouldn't allow ourselves ever to presume that anyone actually speaks "our" language and/or understands us. Translation, indeed, is a must. As understood from the standpoint of translation, communication refers to the processes by which we first interpolate another's address into, and then interpret it using, our own unique sign systems. This process by no means assures understanding, much less a neatly ordered and organized social world, but provides instead for our everyday ability to improvise imperfectly and haphazardly with others.

From Communication Theory to an Ethics of Translation

Clearly, translation calls for a fundamental shift in our attitudes toward forms of symbolic expression, the practice of communication, and those whom we perceive to be more or less the same as or different from ourselves. With this proposition in mind, I want to conclude briefly by saying a word or two about what the concept of translation might hold for communication theory. As I hope to have shown, communication and translation might appear to be at odds with one another conceptually, especially given how the idea of communication has been wedded to notions of meaning, understanding, reciprocation, and an almost supernatural belief in the possibility of synthesis. These attributes, indeed, seem contrary to translation's emphasis on making do, misunderstanding, contingency, and difference. Given the opportunity for an encounter, however, communication and translation actually have much to "say" to one another. Both concepts attempt to explain how humans, despite our differences, manage to coordinate our affairs and activities, and thus they share, at least initially, some important common ground. Their encounter shows us, moreover, that as a discipline we need to challenge—or perhaps it would be more accurate to say translate—the very concept of communication, to account better for the awkwardness, imperfection, and fissures intrinsic to the complex pantomime by which we reach out to and interact with others. Their encounter shows us, finally, that the object that both interests and unites our discipline—communication—can be startlingly consistent with that of the burgeoning field of translation studies, assuming that we push ourselves to further unwork embedded assumptions that, for too long, have constrained our thinking about this foundational concept.

After having presented earlier versions of some of the essays collected in this volume at an academic conference, my copanelists and I were asked by an astute audience member to clarify whether we were proposing theories, analytical frameworks, or metaphors by which to imagine human communication. I recall thinking at the time how much I wanted my work on translation to be included in the theory camp, because, after all, what scholar wouldn't want to come up with an Original Theory? I also remember my disappointment upon hearing that audience member suggest that most of the papers, mine included, did not offer a theory per se. I realize now that he was right, and in retrospect I couldn't be more pleased that he was. Translation is not a theory; its aims are far more modest, its goals are far more humble, than those demanded by the grand project of Theory Building. Throughout this essay, I've referred to translation using a linguistic shorthand, "concept," but really it denotes a pragmatics, or better yet an ethics, of social life. Translation should be a disposition and a way for you to live your life, not an abstract idea or a system of thought for you to apply. For only when we realize that we are always confronted by foreigners can we begin to embrace both the joys and the responsibilities—the ethics—of getting lost in translation.

Notes

1. *Muggle,* in *Harry Potter,* serves as both a noun and an adjective. The noun form refers to persons without magic, and the adjectival to the objects associated with those belonging to that group.

2. Several scholars have proposed alternative terms by which to designate roughly what Sakai means by "address." These include Erving Goffman (1959), who put forth the highly suggestive idea of "expressions" in his *Presentation of Self in Everyday Life.* I've incorporated Goffman's language into my definition of address above. John Durham Peters' (1999) notion of "dissemination" also gets at what Sakai seems to mean by "address," though I must confess to feeling somewhat uneasy with its masculine/procreative overtones. I want to add that although I mention the word *utterance* in my definition of "address," I do not mean to suggest that speech is the only, much less a privileged, means through which to address one another. Likewise, I do not mean to imply that we should resuscitate old models of "public address," where "great speakers" are presumed to enlighten a more or less passive audience with their "great ideas" and artful modes of delivery. I am attempting, rather, to reappropriate the term *address* through my use of it here.

Additional Readings

Bassnett, S. (2002). *Translation studies* (3rd ed.). London: Routledge.

Benjamin, W. (1968). The task of the translator. In H. Arendt (Ed.) & H. Zohn (Trans.), *Illuminations: Essays and reflections* (pp. 69–82). New York: Shocken Books.

Derrida, J. (1998). *Monolingualism of the other, or, the prosthesis of origin* (P. Mensah, Trans.). Stanford, CA: Stanford University Press.

Sommer, D. (2004). *Bilingual aesthetics: A new sentimental education*. Durham, NC: Duke University Press.

Venuti, L. (Ed.). (2004). *The translation studies reader* (2nd ed.). New York: Routledge.

References

Bassnett, S. (2002). *Translation studies* (3rd ed.). London: Routledge.

Goffman, E. (1959). *The presentation of self in everyday life*. New York: Anchor Books.

Jakobson, R. (2000). On linguistic aspects of translation. In L. Venuti (Ed.), *The translation studies reader* (pp. 113–118). London: Routledge. (Original work published 1959)

Jentsch, N. K. (2002). Harry Potter and the tower of Babel: Translating the magic. In L. A. Whited (Ed.), *The ivory tower and Harry Potter: Perspectives on a literary phenomenon* (pp. 285–301). Columbia: University of Missouri Press.

Nunberg, G. (2003, November 12). [Digital audio recording of radio program]. On *Fresh air*. National Public Radio. Available online at http://freshair.npr.org/day_fa.jhtml?display=day&todayDate=11/12/2003

Ogden, C. K., & Richards, I. A. (2001). *The meaning of meaning: A study of the influence of language upon thought and of the science of symbolism*. London: Routledge. (Original work published 1923)

Ortega y Gasset, J. (2000). The misery and the splendor of translation (E. G. Miller, Trans.). In L. Venuti (Ed.), *The translation studies reader* (pp. 49–63). London: Routledge. (Original work published 1937)

Peters, J. D. (1999). *Speaking into the air: A history of the idea of communication*. Chicago: University of Chicago Press.

Sakai, N. (1997). *Translation and subjectivity: On "Japan" and cultural nationalism*. Minneapolis: University of Minnesota Press.

Sapir, E. (1921). *Language: An introduction to the study of speech*. New York: Harvest Books.

Whorf, B. L. (1956). *Language, thought, and reality: Selected writings of Benjamin Lee Whorf* (J. B. Carroll, Ed.). Cambridge: MIT Press.

26

Communication as Communicability

Briankle G. Chang

H ow does one begin to question "communication"? More fundamentally, can one not not begin? Certainly, in writing and reading about communication, has one not already begun doing and affirming in some way what is being questioned? Moreover, in questioning communication, shouldn't the very fact of this questioning speak back, if only obliquely, to what is being questioned as well as to what the act of questioning is permitted to say? If so, how does one parse out what can be or ought to be questioned from what is to remain unquestioned? In any case, there seems to be a demand in this effort to question communication that one be reflexive and self-critical, an imperative that opens the topic and structures our inquiry by the force of a hermeneutical circle.

Because there is no beginning from the beginning, as what we are now doing indicates that we have already begun, we have no choice but to begin in the middle, to begin, again, where we already are. So instead of trying to square the logical circle that appears to frustrate our inquiry, let me begin by proposing a simple observation as my starting point: "One thing is said but another heard." In the few pages that follow, I wish to examine briefly the implications of this statement as they bear upon some of our received notions about communication and to demonstrate how and to what extent these notions can be read as symptoms of an identifiable conceptual naïveté. My objective is to return to where I begin and to shed light, through this returning, on the enigma of communication that makes our analysis interminable.

One thing is said but another heard. In the saying, something happens; in the hearing, something happens, too. However, from the saying to the hearing, something fails to take place, for one thing is said but another heard. There is a failure because what is said is not (the same as) what is heard, because there seems to be a nonequivalence or mismatch between what is sent and what is received, for whatever reason. The lack of correspondence that becomes manifest at the moment of reception allows us to describe what happens as a failure of communication, a failure not because nothing has come to pass but because what has transpired amounts to "misunderstanding."

To speak of failure, of misunderstanding, in this connection, however, implies that things could be different, that what is heard could sometime succeed in corresponding to what is said. There would be no failure, in other words, if what is given at one end by the addresser is taken by the addressee at the other end as the former intends it, if decoding echoes encoding, that is, if the receiver "understands" the sender.

To understand an other! Isn't this what communication is all about? Since understanding is always sutured to communication through what is called "message," let me make a few preliminary remarks about this relation. Regardless of what happens when, on claims to understand someone else, understanding requires the presence of what is to be understood. Short of telepathy or grace of divine intervention, to understand an other requires that he or she be present, even if indirectly; it requires, at a minimum, that a sign of the other be given, a sign given both as the thing (*res*) to be interpreted and as the cause (*causa*) for interpretation.[1] This *res causente* constitutes what we call the message, something semiotic that is capable of representing the self-sender to the other-receiver in that it stands between them. Because a message of an other must be given when one speaks of understanding him or her, understanding is essentially a response to the coming of the other, to his or her expression as it comes; it is to answer the call of the other from whom the message originates. Viewed in this way, communication begins with the coming of the other, a coming mediated by his or her message, and it ends or culminates in the moment when "one understands what the other means," if only momentarily, when, that is, the message is "shared" by the one to whom it is addressed.[2]

That "mutual understanding," achieved through sharing the message, functions as the telos, or end, of communication has been one of the well-entrenched assumptions in communication theories. According to this assumption, communication (*com-munis*) reflects not only the condition of cobeing (being-with, being-together) among disparate individuals but also, and more important, the presence of something *in common* that sustains their cobeing, their communion, their community, across space and time and helps differentiate one form of being-together from another. Against this romantic image of communication as "message sharing," variously articulated as "transsubstantiation," "fusion of horizons," and the like, I wish to make two observations. First, if the other is represented by his or her message, if his or her presence is mediated by what gives and is given by him or her, then, strictly speaking, the other cannot be said to be fully present to the self in any communicative exchange. Through his or her message, the other comes, but coming through the message in which he or she is given, the other appears in the encounter only to the degree that he or she permits himself or herself to be embodied semiotically. Paradoxically, becoming present in this way amounts to a kind of absence, because presence is made possible by and represented in the disembodied message.

In saying that the other is absently present (or presently absent) vis-à-vis the self, I don't mean to invoke anything transcendent, for example, the Levinasian alterity, that, infinite in its being relative to the self, resists objectification or appropriative knowing in principle. In fact, the ethico-ontological issues stemming from the problem of the other are irrelevant here. My point is much more straightforward: to the extent that the other comes to meet the self *through* his or her message, the other, although speaking first, should be considered in this instance as no more than an effect or, rather, a retroactively constituted agent, of what is being said, because his or her appearance in the encounter, to repeat, is contingent upon, or, as I argued elsewhere, *conditioned by*, the message he or she *sends*.[3] That being the case, "sharing the message" should be understood precisely as sharing *the message*, and "understanding (the message of) an other," by extension, should be understood strictly as grasping that the other *says*. If communication necessarily involves exchange of some sort, it is an exchange of signs or messages, not of mental content or any element of what is called one's inner life.

Second, I just suggested that sharing a message should mean sharing *the message* because, as indicated above, the other *as such* does not really partake in the verbal exchange. But can something like a message be *shared*? Let me make a quick point about the message before taking on the issue of sharing. A message must assume identity. Like anything that carries meaning, it must be capable of remaining selfsame across various and varying contexts. It is this capacity of keeping itself as itself, regardless of who uses it as well as where and when it is used, that enables a message, say, M, to mean what it means, say, *a,* rather than something else. If *M* means *a* here and now and also means *b* there one second later, then *M* would not be able to mean anything at all, if only because one would have no idea as to how to use it. In fact, lacking identity, *X* cannot even be said to exist, let alone to carry meaning, since one would have no anchor by which to refer to it, still less any way of making it mean what it is supposed to mean.

Now the question raised earlier can be reformulated as follows: Can a message, which must keep its identity to function as such, be shared? Looked at from a different angle, can the act of sharing avoid compromising the identity of the thing that is (sent to be) shared? To share is to divide. Something can be shared if and only if it is divided or divides itself. To the extent that there is no sharing without division, what can be shared is of necessity already divided; conversely, since what is shared must be divided, only that which is divided can be extended by one to share with an other. Put simply, what is shared shares, which is to say, what shares (itself) is thus shared by the act of sharing.

Accordingly, the notion of communication based on the image of "sharing the message" ought to be complicated. When someone says something, the message is given; it is given to be shared. However, because something can be shared only on the condition that it is divided, the message must suffer a certain loss of identity before it is imparted and thus be internally split before it can be shared. In other words, because sharing implies differentiation, separation, and distribution, so must the message undergo the ordeal of self-partitioning in order to be shared. In fact, because the message both shares and is shared, it embodies the very splitting that makes itself and exchange possible. Self-splitting, the message offers itself as sharable, bringing the sender and the receiver together when offered. However, splitting itself, the message disqualifies itself as a message *in common.* Self-splitting and splitting itself, the message, I contend, separates the sender and the receiver as much as it ties them; yet it ties them by the very division it establishes.

Someone, a stranger, says something as he approaches me; hearing what he says, I turn toward him. Through this turning, he and I become a "we," because in this instance I recognize what he is doing. In this instance, he and I begin to have something in common, something that does not exist before he comes. As this happens, I may say something in return. The ensuing exchange suggests that indeed we have much in common; we share, for example, the same interests, and perhaps much more. But because, as I suggested earlier, what is shared is what divides, isn't what we have in common also what keeps us apart? Isn't what we share, an interest in soccer, for instance, exactly what separates us, keeping us apart so that we discuss the game last night as long as we want to? In this scenario, what is being communicated? What am I communicating, or what could I communicate, to him, this stranger I just met, and vice versa? Perhaps only this: communication is "not of something held in *common* but of a *communicability*," that when communication takes place, what is communicated, first and foremost, is not the sense or meaning that the sender and receiver claim to have but the fact "*that there is communication*" at all.[4]

Struggling to articulate what I want to say in this short essay, I thought about a well-known painting by Jan Vermeer, *Woman Reading a Letter* (c. 1663–1664). Looking at the picture, we see what the woman is doing: reading. But who sends the letter? What does it say? What is she thinking as she reads the letter? Standing by the window and holding what is sent to her from afar, the woman, engrossed in one of the most solitary of all acts, crosses without motion the divide between the inside and outside. Poised like a voyeur, the viewer can easily imagine the woman, despite her solitude or perhaps because of it, taking flight momentarily from her tranquil domesticity, exchanging hearts with someone through the private act of reading. However, by not disclosing to the spectators what they are thus made curious about but do not and cannot see, the picture reveals as much as it conceals; it does so precisely by keeping secret what the painted scene nonetheless puts on display. In fact, all the things rendered visible by Vermeer work to lure the gaze of the viewers toward what remains invisible, thus making the painted surface all the more mysterious and, for this very reason, all the more communicative.

I mention this painting not because I am always impressed with Vermeer's painterly genius; rather, it is because this painting communicates quietly the truth of communication I am trying to articulate: like the letter in the woman's hands, which we see and do not see because it is only partly seen, every message is at once both visible and invisible, both open and closed, both private and public. As the painting subtly suggests, all communicative acts are essentially *publicly intimate* and, for this very reason, *intimately public* as well. Indeed, communication communicates, first and foremost, the fact that there is communication. Possible interpretations of this statement aside, what I hear in it is this: when all is said and done, there remains something occult (*occultus*: private, concealed) in the event of communication. This in turn reaffirms the statement that I have repeated several times now: when one thing is said, another may be heard. There is a truth in this painting—a truth of communication that is veiled and unveiled simultaneously by what is apparently communicated, a truth that communicates to us what will always remain invisible, and perhaps forever enigmatic, precisely because the divided message is all that is available.

One thing is said but another heard. To the extent that this is the case, what I have been saying may be taken to mean something different from what I intend it to mean. This can happen because, as I have been suggesting, what is said, the message, is in itself *de-cisive*. It is precisely this possibility of a message going astray, a possibility grounded in the message's very own division, that causes something *decisive* as well to take place when it is sent, whether or not what takes place reflects what is usually called "mutual understanding." My strong impression is that much of the writing on communication today is still mortgaged to the normative assumption that communicative processes unfold toward the end of understanding between individuals, toward, that is, a condition where the message in question is shared by them. To this assumption, let me simply end in response by saying: "Communication happens on the side—or in some cases does not happen: then the sound of the voice fades away, or the text is left there."[5]

Notes

1. I should interject here that when one sees an other, as Freud, among others, has pointed out, the other is divided into two parts: (a) one part that is liable to change, such as with gestures or facial expressions and (b) another part that remains the same across perceptions, such as the face itself, a part that is recognized without being understood. A gesture, an expression, may convey meaning; the face is either recognized or not. I should also note that the Latin word *res* for "thing," to which words such as *causa, casa, chose,* or *Ding* are associated, is also linked to *reus,* meaning the accused. The judicial, political root of the meaning of *res,* thing, is clearly significant.

2. It is worth mentioning that concepts often invoked in the literature of inter-personal communication to explain the dynamic of social interaction should be regarded as metaphorical. An example is "perspective taking," which is based on the practice of pictorial representation. As such, it is at best descriptive and has little explanatory power, as it presupposes what it seeks to explain. For how can I take the perspective of an other if I did not already know what that perspective is? In fact, I already must have understood what perspective the other takes before I can take it myself.

3. See Chang (1996).

4. See Nancy (1977).

5. See Frey (1996).

Additional Readings

Agamben, G. (2000). *Means without end: Notes on politics.* Minneapolis: University of Minnesota Press.

Chang, B. G. (1996). *Deconstructing communication: Subject, representation, and economies of exchange.* Minneapolis: University of Minnesota Press.

Derrida, J. (1988). *Limited, Inc.* Evanston, IL: Northwestern University Press.

Fenves, P. (2001). *Arresting language: From Leibniz to Benjamin.* Stanford, CA: Stanford University Press.

Frey, H.-R. (1996). *Interruptions.* Albany: SUNY Press.

Marion, J.-C. (2004). *The crossing of the visible.* Stanford, CA: Stanford University Press.

Nancy, J.-L. (1977). *The sense of the world.* Minneapolis: University of Minnesota Press.

Nancy, L.-C. (1993). *The birth to presence.* Stanford, CA: Stanford University Press.

27

Communication as Failure

Jeffrey St. John

M y essay begins not with communication theory, but with American literature. I want to discuss the New York–based writer William Gaddis, who between 1955 and his death at age 75, in 1998, penned five novels (1955, 1975, 1985, 1994, 2002a). In my reading, Gaddis's books collectively posit one darkly comic claim, bitter but brilliant: that communication is best understood as failure. I think that a wealth of clues in his books suggest two main reasons why he held this view. First, I believe he was convinced that the average person in our society fears failure intensely. Second, I think he also thought that because we tend to avoid what we fear, we are doubly distanced from a serious and open engagement of failure as a lived dimension of life. We thus tend not to be very adept at keeping failure in view. What I mean, and what I think Gaddis meant, is that failure is neither a common nor salutary subject of self-scrutiny, at least not outside the painfully dispiriting context of our forced encounters with it. How often do we walk down the street calmly asking ourselves, "I wonder whether I will face failure today?" Put another way, my claim is that we do not regularly and lucidly appraise the possibility of failure's appearance in our lives, *as a fact of life,* in a clear-sighted way. After all, who would want to?

Gaddis himself was not distanced from failure. Conversely, his personal and professional lives were riddled with it. He endured three failed marriages; he was often on the verge of insolvency; and his books, in addition to selling poorly, were panned by critics who had not bothered to read them. (In a colorful diatribe called *Fire the Bastards!* the pseudonymous "Jack Green"

[1962/1992], a fervent admirer of Gaddis's first novel, *The Recognitions*, examined 55 reviews published in newspapers and magazines throughout the United States. By Green's count, all but two of them contained substantive errors about the novel, its author, or both.)

I lack the space to paint a fuller picture of the miseries that befell Gaddis, but my point is this: Gaddis engaged failure not as an abstract exercise or an empty concept, but as a lived communicative *experience,* one both raw and unpredictable in its interpersonal effects. While struggling to support himself, Gaddis for many years taught a course at Bard College. Its theme? Failure in American literature. Without question, he believed we could learn much from a study of failure in its imaginative forms. "The real marvel in our complex technological world, given the frustration implicit in Murphy's law," Gaddis observed, "is not that if anything can go wrong it will go wrong[,] but that anything goes right at all" (2002b, p. 49).

Like Gaddis, I believe literature can teach us something important about communication that we have not learned from communication itself. I also believe that because *what* literature offers is disturbing, unflattering, indifferent to the rules of empirical science, and (consequently) a threat to more than a few theoretical models of communication, we tend to ignore it. I used the word *brilliant* above to describe Gaddis's novels. I believe they are brilliant because I believe they shine on communication a light dismissed by many communication theorists, one that reveals how an *imaginative* confrontation with the realities of failure may strengthen our understanding of why, and with what effects, humans do or do not communicate with one another.

So then: I claim that communication is best understood as failure. I ground that claim on two assertions. First, I think that humans fail to communicate far more often than they succeed. Second, I think that there is no implicit contradiction or irony attached to my holding the view that communication should be understood as failure, and my own daily, genuine efforts to communicate with people in spite of that view. In other words, I am claiming that the rarity of communication belies neither the ubiquity nor the stunning persistence of our efforts to communicate. In fact, I think it is precisely the omnipresence and endlessness of those efforts that underscore the unrivaled allure of their object. We pan harder and longer for gold than for any other stone; its scarcity, and the concomitant trouble we have obtaining it, are the surest measures of its worth. I believe the quest for communication is analogous to the quest for gold in just this way.

Beginning with the claim that humans fail to communicate far more often than they succeed, I think that many of our efforts toward theory construction in the field of communication have disregarded the explanatory powers of literature, and that they have done so for one reason. Literature is an accounting of the human experience as undergirded by one tremendously unsettling theme: the failure of persons to communicate with each other in all sorts of ways, for all kinds of reasons, in every conceivable context, and with devastating results. That formulation may seem exaggerated, yet I believe it is substantially defensible.

Here is a polite challenge. Take any period, any nation, any genre of literary fiction, or even any one well-reputed writer. Upon investigation, you will find that a significant thematic current running through that period, nation, genre, or writer is failure. The theme in world literature that has been universally viewed by writers and readers as worthy of the most exacting and eloquent exploration is failure. The evidence is abundant; it germinates across the spectrum of literary modes: poetry, novels, plays, and modernist experimental venues such as comics and graphic novels. Failures of honor, marriage, love, war, faith, truth, nation, community, identity, duty, and family are the oldest themes of world literature, and continue to be mined more deeply than any others.

It has been said by someone that time, love, and memory are the three pillars of literature, and I agree. Yet isn't each of those in some sense a manifestation of a deeper, unifying theme? I think so, and I think the theme that anchors those pillars is failure. Consider time. We cherish time because we know that it fails us: we lose it, it flees, it runs out, we wonder where it has gone. Consider love. We exalt it, and for four millennia have sung its manifold praises; but, and without contradiction, it is also incontestably true that the world's poets, novelists, and playwrights are far better known (and praised) for their depictions of love's failures: star-crossed lovers, love cheated by death, a love denied, a love in flames, the love that dare not speak its name. Finally, consider memory. It is treasured for its ability to offer us a recollection of what we can never really, fully experience again: the portion of life that we have already lived. In this sense, memory is less a material good than a kind of tropological substitute for something lost. Its mere presence confirms the sharpest of absences; memory delusively guards what we have failed, often to our lasting regret, to hold on to.

Perhaps this line of argument is too abstract, so here is a concrete example. Arguably the most famous novel of the last century is Marcel Proust's (1932/1981, 1993) largely autobiographical tale of his life as a lonely urbanite searching for social validation in Parisian high society. The novel's first English translator wrongly titled the book *Remembrance of Things Past*. Subsequent translators have settled upon the now standard *In Search of Lost Time*. I offer both titles to underscore a point. Proust's novel is mammoth, running to more than 3,000 pages, and is filled with lost loves, misdirected lusts, fleeting moments of grace, unrecoverable emotions, and, above all else, the sheer pain of life's failures as reflected in the inexorable passage of time. Time, love, and memory, rooted in failure; this was somehow the chemistry for a widely praised masterpiece. But why? What is it about that mixture that has attracted so many readers to a story that unflinchingly immerses itself in misery and loss?

I think the answer to this question may be found in the context of something I wrote earlier. Recall my claim that we tend not to sit around thinking about our prospects for failure. At the same time, I believe we recognize failure almost instinctively, and that we see it nearly everywhere we look. I also think that we embrace, or at the very least accept, failure in the realm of imaginative literature in ways that we do not and cannot accept it in our own lives. Literature provides us with strangely clarifying yet unreal sites in which to confront, without fear of material consequences, that which we implicitly know pervades our lives: failure.

By way of both defending one claim and introducing another, I want to be as reflective as possible about the kind of language I have been using so far. I have used collective nouns—*we* and *us*—and have addressed my claims to "you" (the reader) in what I hope has been a lucid way. Yet, I have been arguing all along that communication is mostly about failing to communicate—or, more pointedly, that we fail to communicate far more often than we succeed. You might therefore question how I can presume to write confidently of what "we" experience, or of what "you" might say in response to my claims, when my assessment of communication is so bleak. Why should you be persuaded by my view at all if beneath it rests the belief that humans fail to communicate more often than not?

I want to answer by way of making another claim. I believe that much of what we define empirically and qualitatively as "communication" cannot be demonstrated as such; should not be evaluated as such; and can only with difficulty, and through the application of a set of subtly compensatory symbols and gestures, be defended as such. Think, for example, about the use of the word *we* in expository writing—in other words, in essays like the one you are reading right now. This word is often used to suggest a warm party of two, some vital solidarity established between writer and reader. "I" (the writer) make a claim, or tell a story, or declare a truth, and if "you" (the reader) agree, or feel a kind of bond, or even merely offer mental assent, then a reciprocally communicative "we" is thought to have formed.

As uncomplicated as that might seem, I believe that the assumptions on which it rests are unsupportable. No such "we" exists or ever will exist. How could it? While I was writing the last three sentences of the preceding paragraph, I was thinking at the same time about what I would like to have for lunch in an hour or so. I was also momentarily interrupted by a graduate student who stopped by my office to show me his new Indonesian green python, which had just arrived via express mail from the island of Aru (I am not making this up). He explained that while it is now only a "baby," his snake will eventually grow to 5 feet in length and will consume entire rats. Then he left, and, having lost all interest in lunch, I began to write the paragraph that is now coming to an end.

My point is that the "I" who is (or, more truthfully, *was*) writing the essay you are now reading is a selective, artificial, and generally unrevealing "I." This is more or less true of all writing, even the self-confessional kind that purports to expose the core of the writer's being. It is an "I" separated from "you" (whoever you are; I don't know you, and probably never will) in limitless respects. For example, our bodies are not present, so we cannot draw from the remarkable fund of nonverbal gestures that speakers count on all the time to compensate for what they do not understand about the words they are hearing in face-to-face conversation. Similarly, you have no entry to my thoughts beyond what I put down on this page—which, again, severely constrains your understanding—and I have no access at all to yours. I could change my mind two minutes after completing this essay, and you would be left with a "stance on communication theory" written by someone who no longer holds that view or anything remotely like it. Also, you are not able to ask what I mean by this word or that one, so the collective bedevilments of solecism, slippage, and syntax, upon which so much of human communication stands or falls, may (or may not) play havoc with either the meaning I intend or the meaning you derive. In short, I believe we can scarcely begin to number the ways you or I could show how easy it is to distort or even kill the communication putatively occurring between us at this moment—and even the success of *that* communication would be a meager achievement within the broader scope of this essay.

If you feel betrayed at this point, I can only imagine that you were hoping for a more successful or firm solution to the problem of communication's many failings. If you find yourself moved by my claims about those shortcomings, I can only imagine that you have experienced enough communicative failure to appreciate what I am driving at. And if you do not understand what I am arguing, I can only imagine that I have, in some sense, inadvertently proven my point. But please recognize that no matter what you are thinking or feeling, *I can only imagine.* I have no credible knowledge of what your response to my stance might be. As I hope to have shown, the many environmental and semantic vagaries of written communication often ensure that such exchanges produce no real communication at all.

I realize that my efforts to answer my own question until now may appear only to have further diminished the chance that a satisfactory explanation is on the horizon. But I think I must extend a line of questioning before coming to a conclusion. My last question to you is, Why did I write this essay at all, if neither the illusory "we"—as real communicators—nor the medium itself— as a mode of transmission—is, to my thinking, viable?

The answer is this: Our hopes for communication are *enormous*. As John Durham Peters (1999) has observed, there is almost no element of modern human life into which we have sunk as much hope and as many expectations as we have in the promise of communication. All that a nonexistent "we" *cannot* communicate pales in comparison to all that it *can*, or at least all that we *imagine* it can. Most people who write something for public consumption appear to take on faith the notion that a "we" is imminent (or immanent): that mutual edification will issue from the meeting of writer's words and reader's mind. I do not disparage that hope, but I do not for a moment believe that it is a reasonable one.

I have already described some of the weaknesses inhering in written communication, so I turn now to spoken communication. For all of our optimism about the spoken word, we routinely face what the philosopher David Carr has called the "dark and looming outer limit" of human experience (1986, p. 88). We use words like *ineffable* and *sublime* and *unutterable* to describe those moments when we have reached the edge of speech, yet these words paradoxically tell us next to nothing about the unsayable. It is worth noting that while communication theory and rhetoric—two fertile realms of inquiry in contemporary communication studies—are both deeply indebted to the work of Aristotle, scant attention is paid to how Aristotle himself ranked speech in relation to the other humane arts. As the political theorist Hannah Arendt usefully reminds us, *contemplation,* not speech, occupies the Hellenic seat of honor, and is distinguished from the lesser arts chiefly by the fact that "its contents cannot be rendered in speech" (1958, p. 27). For Aristotle, the highest rung of achievement in the liberal arts is one that not only deposits a speaker beyond spoken language altogether, but does so deliberately. On this logic, to communicate in words, whether written or spoken, is to reach something lower than the summit of classical education. Seen this way, communication theory emerges from an intellectual tradition which views human speech as less than a complete rhetorical success; the need to speak reflects at least a partial failure to communicate.

I argued earlier that memory tends to function as a trope, a rhetorical proxy for the real experiences we have lost to time and cannot recapture. I want to extend that claim to include the communicative landscape in which, and for which, I think our failures of memory, time, and love have their central meanings: imagination itself. I believe that the key to understanding communication as failure lies neither in communication itself nor in moments of failure. Rather, I believe the key lies in the role that imagination plays in transforming our unreal encounters with unreal failure into rhetorical resources serviceable for our real grapplings with real failure.

I also argued earlier that literature has explanatory powers that communication theorists have ignored. While literature has been dismissed from many quarters as a means of escape from the pressures of life, I think its persistent engagement with exactly the kinds of subjects that it would never address if it were merely a diversion from real problems is enormously instructive. Why do people, as readers, run from real-world troubles straight into the arms of the *same* troubles dressed in imaginary guise? They do so because to confront failure in the world of imagination is to begin to learn how to confront failure in the world of lived experience. On this view, imagination succeeds in ways that communication never has and probably never will. Communication theorists, almost by definition, think of failure as a distraction, of imagination as irrelevant, and therefore of communication as the only one of those three phenomena meriting formal inquiry. For all the reasons adduced in this essay, I disagree with them. I side with Gaddis. We should be studying failure, not communication. If we were, we might learn something about communication that can be fathomed in no other way.

In asserting that we recognize failure instinctively, I claimed that we accept failure in literature in ways that we do not and cannot accept it in our real lives. Why? Because failure imagined is infinitely more tolerable than failure experienced. There is a remarkable contrast between what we expect from communication in our real lives and what we expect from it in our imaginative lives. We *expect* to communicate with one another in real life; we assume we will, we count on being able to do so, in all the ways I have mentioned and in far more that I have not. But we expect to find something fundamentally different in literature. There we find failure, there we confront it, and there we teach ourselves how to resolve it. If the same could be said of our encounters with communication theory, we might know more than we do presently about its successes—and its failures.

Additional Readings

Davidson, D. (1984). *Inquiries into truth and interpretation*. Oxford, UK: Clarendon Press.

Jones, D. (2003). *In parenthesis*. New York: NYRB Books. (Original work published 1937)

Levinas, E. (1961). *Totality and infinity*. Pittsburgh, PA: Duquesne University Press.
Sebald, W. (2001). *Austerlitz*. New York: Modern Library.
Stevens, W. (1942). *The necessary angel: Essays on reality and imagination*. New York: Vintage.

References

Arendt, H. (1958). *The human condition*. Chicago: University of Chicago Press.
Aristotle. (2003). *The Nichomachean ethics* (J. A. K. Thomson & J. Barnes, Trans.). New York: Penguin Classics.
Carr, D. (1986). *Time, narrative, and memory*. Bloomington: Indiana University Press.
Gaddis, W. (1955). *The recognitions*. New York: Harcourt, Brace.
Gaddis, W. (1975). *JR*. New York: Knopf.
Gaddis, W. (1985). *Carpenter's gothic*. New York: Viking.
Gaddis, W. (1994). *A frolic of his own*. New York: Poseidon Press.
Gaddis, W. (2002a). *Agape agape*. New York: Viking Penguin.
Gaddis, W. (2002b). *The rush for second place: Essays and occasional writings*. New York: Viking Penguin.
Green, J. (1992). *Fire the bastards!* Normal, IL: Dalkey Archive Press. (Original work published 1962)
Peters, J. D. (1999). *Speaking into the air: A history of the idea of communication*. Chicago and London: University of Chicago Press.
Proust, M. (1981). *Remembrance of things past* (C. K. Scott Moncrieff & T. Kilmartin, Trans.). New York: Random House. (Original work published 1932)
Proust, M. (1993). *In search of lost time* (D. J. Enright, Trans.; a revision of the Moncrieff-Kilmartin translation). New York: Modern Library.

Index

mundane/common experience
approach to storytelling, 124
phatic function of
communication, 127
poetic function in communication,
125, 127–128
productivity of communication, 128
referential function of communication,
126–127
relevance, 128–129
semiotic/phenomenological research,
124–125
summary/conclusions, 129–130
See also Autoethnography,
communication as
Structuration theory, 35–36
Structure of communication
networks/social system and
communication as diffusion, 178
Structuring, communication as:
advantages of, 148–150
modalities of structuration, 148
moves that interactants make to
appropriate structures, 116–117
organizing/organization, centrality of
communication to, 145–146
overview, 143–144
patterns of interaction in social
systems, 147
structure and structuration, 144–145
Suffering people and communication as
autoethnography, 120
Surveillance and communication as
vision, 61–63
System and structure, distinction
between, 144–145

Tannen, Deborah, 189
Tao Te Ching, 211
Tarde, Gabriel, 179
Taxemic modality of discourse, 134
Techné, communication as:
add technology and stir model of
communication, 96
bodies and technologies, rethinking
relationship between, 94–95
defining techné, 91–93
epistêmê contrasted with techné, 92
historical core of what it means to
communicate, 96–97
media, the, 95

social aspect of, 93–94
summary/conclusions, 97
Technique contextualized within a
relationship by relational
perspective, 9–10
Technology and communication as
collective memory, 55–56
Technology and communication as social
identity, 87
Television and communication as ritual,
15–17
Tell It to ACT UP (TITA), 199
Temple University, 78
Tensionality and communication
as dialogue, 103–104
Texts and communication as complex
organizing, 136–137
Texts that keep bodies at a distance,
67–73
Theology and communication
as deliberation, 170
Theory:
autoethnography, theories/stories
contrasted and communication
as, 116–117
practice and, communication as
practice and transforming
relationship between, 41–44
process of theorizing, xvii
stand on communication, taking a,
xi–xx
See also individual subject headings
Time and communication as
diffusion, 178
Time/space and communication as
dissemination, 212–215
Tools/crafts and communication as
techné, 96–97
Tradition and communication as
collective memory, 55
Transcendence, communication as:
definitional consequences, 25–26
democratic definition of
communication, 28
empowering definition of
communication, 26–27
ennobling definition of
communication, 27–28
experience defined, 22–24
hopeful definition of
communication, 26

About the Editors

Gregory J. Shepherd (PhD, University of Illinois) is Professor and Director of the School of Communication Studies and is currently serving as Interim Dean of the College of Communication at Ohio University. His primary scholarly interests are in communication theory and American pragmatism. He is a winner of the Central States Communication Association Outstanding Young Teacher Award, as well as a W. T. Kemper Fellowship for Teaching Excellence. He is coeditor with Eric Rothenbuhler of *Communication and Community* (2001, Lawrence Erlbaum), and in addition to chapters in various edited volumes, his work has appeared in *Communication Monographs, Human Communication Research, Journal of Communication, Communication Yearbook, Communication Studies, Southern Journal of Communication, Communication Research, Journal of Social Psychology, Management Communication Quarterly, Journal of Research and Development in Education,* and other scholarly publications.

Jeffrey St. John (PhD, University of Washington) is Assistant Professor in the School of Communication Studies at Ohio University. His published work includes essays on legal argument, critical rhetoric, the construction of self at sites of public controversy, and the deployment of contested terms (e.g., *tolerance, civility*) in public culture. He teaches undergraduate courses in public advocacy, free speech, communication theory, and political rhetoric, along with graduate courses in communication theory and public deliberation. His current research projects include a mapping of the rhetorical geography of "moral values" voting patterns (with his colleague Jerry Miller) and a study of mimesis and public memory in contemporary fiction.

Ted Striphas (PhD, University of North Carolina–Chapel Hill) is Assistant Professor in the Department of Communication and Culture, Indiana University. His primary research interests include media historiography, cultural studies, Marxism, and communication theory. At present, he is at work on a cultural history of the U.S. book industry tentatively titled *Equipment for Living: Everyday Book Culture in the Making.* He also is coeditor (with Kembrew McLeod) of a forthcoming special issue of the journal *Cultural Studies* on the politics of intellectual properties. His work has appeared in, among other places, *Critical Studies in Media Communication; Cultural Studies; The Review of Education, Pedagogy, and Cultural Studies; Social Epistemology;* and *Television and New Media.* He is a 2004 recipient of the Gerald R. Miller Outstanding Dissertation Award from the National Communication Association.

About the Contributors

Leslie A. Baxter is F. Wendell Miller Distinguished Professor of Communication Studies at the University of Iowa. She has published 100 articles, book chapters, and books on topics related to communication in relationships, both familial and nonfamilial. Her work on communication and relationships is largely informed by Bakhtin's dialogism.

Carole Blair, Professor of Communication Studies at the University of North Carolina, is coeditor and cotranslator of *Friedrich Nietzsche on Rhetoric and Language* (Oxford), and coeditor of *Critical Questions: Invention, Creativity, and the Criticism of Discourse and Media* (St. Martin's), as well as numerous monographs and anthology articles. Her work has received the National Communication Association's Doctoral Dissertation Award and Golden Anniversary Monographs Award, as well as the annual outstanding article award from the Organization for the Study of Communication, Language and Gender. Her research focuses on the rhetorical and cultural significance of U.S. commemorative places and artworks.

Arthur P. Bochner is Professor of Communication and codirector (with Carolyn Ellis) of the Institute for Interpretive Human Studies at the University of South Florida. He is coeditor (with Carolyn Ellis) of *Composing Ethnography: Alternative Forms of Qualitative Writing* (1996) and *Ethnographically Speaking: Autoethnography, Literature, and Aesthetics* (2002), and the AltaMira book series Ethnographic Alternatives. He has published more than 70 articles and book chapters on communication theory; interpersonal, personal, and family communication; and narrative inquiry.

Franklin J. Boster is Professor in the Department of Communication at Michigan State University. His research focuses on social influences processes and group dynamics. He is corecipient of the Speech Communication Association's Golden Anniversary Award for outstanding scholarly publication (1976), the Charles H. Woolbert Award for scholarship of exceptional originality and influence (Speech Communication Association, 1989), and the John E. Hunter Meta-Analysis Award (Division 1 of the International Communication Association, 1998). In 2003, he received the Distinguished Faculty Award from Michigan State University.

Daniel C. Brouwer is Assistant Professor in the School of Human Communication at Arizona State University. His research and teaching projects include public sphere studies, rhetorical criticism, the rhetoric of social movements, the rhetoric of HIV/AIDS, and cultural performance. What unifies his research and teaching projects is a focus on controversy and conflict and the ways in which various social actors employ cultural, economic, and political resources in the drama of a controversy. He is coeditor of and contributor to the 2001 book, *Counterpublics and the State.* Appearing in *Text and Performance Quarterly, Critical Studies in Media Communication, Rhetoric & Public Affairs, Western Journal of Communication,* and *Argumentation & Advocacy* are his articles on HIV/AIDS tattoos, passing, congressional eulogies, congressional debate about lesbians and gays in the military, and public intellectuals. He is currently working on manuscripts about HIV/AIDS zines and a coedited book project on public modalities.

Briankle G. Chang is Associate Professor of Communication at the University of Massachusetts, Amherst. He is the author of *Deconstructing Communication: Representation, Subject, and Economies of Exchange* (University of Minnesota Press, 1996). His work has been published in journals such as *Cultural Critique, Differences, International Philosophical Quarterly, History of European Ideas,* and *British Journal of Aesthetics.*

Celeste M. Condit, Distinguished Research Professor of Speech Communication, University of Georgia, teaches courses in rhetorical criticism and theory. She is the former coeditor of *Critical Studies in Media Communication,* and author or coauthor of *Decoding Abortion Rhetoric, Crafting Equality: America's Anglo/African Word,* and *The Meanings of the Gene.* She is a National Communication Association Distinguished Scholar.

Robert T. Craig is Professor in the Department of Communication, University of Colorado at Boulder, and a past president of the International Communication Association. His research has addressed a range of topics in communication theory and discourse analysis, including cognitive processes, conversational coherence, goals and strategies in discourse, argumentation, the philosophy and methodology of communication as a practical discipline, and the intellectual structure of communication theory as a field. A primary focus of his work for the last 2 decades has been to conceptualize communication theory as a form of discourse for the cultivation of reflective communication practices in society. Current projects include a book and an anthology of readings on communication theory, and studies of metadiscursive practices in public and group discourse.

James W. Dearing is Professor of Communication and Director of Graduate Studies in the School of Communication Studies at Ohio University. He has been on the faculty of Michigan State University and a visiting faculty member at the University of California, Berkeley, and at the University of Michigan. His primary activity is social science research about the strategic testing of using diffusion of innovation concepts to accelerate the spread of best practice innovations in health, health services, youth development, education, and development. He has been the principal investigator for research sponsored by the U.S. National Science Foundation, the U.S. Environmental Protection Agency, the U.S. Agency for Health Care Policy & Research, the W. K. Kellogg Foundation, and other organizations. He has taught doctoral seminars in diffusion of innovation theory and research, program evaluation theory, the media-public-policy agenda-setting process, mass communication theory, and research methods.

Carolyn Ellis is Professor of Communication and Sociology at the University of South Florida. She is the author of *The Ethnographic I: A Methodological Novel about Autoethnography* (2004) and of *Final Negotiations: A Story of Love, Loss, and Chronic Illness* (1995). She is coeditor (with Arthur Bochner) of *Composing Ethnography: Alternative Forms of Qualitative Writing* (1996), *Ethnographically Speaking: Autoethnography, Literature, and Aesthetics* (2002), and the AltaMira book series Ethnographic Alternatives.

Cara A. Finnegan is Assistant Professor of Rhetorical Studies in the Department of Speech Communication at the University of Illinois at Urbana-Champaign. She is the author of *Picturing Poverty: Print Culture and FSA Photographs* (Smithsonian Books, 2003), which won the National Communication Association's 2004 Diamond Anniversary Book Award for the outstanding scholarly book published in communication in the past two years. Her research on rhetoric, visual culture, photography, and the public sphere has appeared in journals such as *The Quarterly Journal of Speech, Rhetoric & Public Affairs*, and *Argumentation & Advocacy*. She is currently completing a book manuscript titled *Image Vernaculars: Rhetorics of Photography in American Public Culture*.

John Gastil is Associate Professor in the Department of Communication at the University of Washington, where he studies and teaches courses on political deliberation and group decision making. He earned his PhD in communication from the University of Wisconsin-Madison in 1994 and a BA in political science from Swarthmore College in 1989. From 1994 to 1997, he conducted public opinion research at the University of New Mexico Institute for Public Policy. He is the coeditor (with Peter Levine) of *The Deliberative Democracy Handbook: Strategies for Effective Civic Engagement in the Twenty-First Century* (Jossey-Bass, 2005). He is the author of *By Popular Demand: Revitalizing Representative Democracy Through Deliberative Elections* (University of California Press, 2000), *Democracy in Small Groups: Participation, Decision Making, and Communication* (New Society Publishers, 1993), and the Election Day computer simulation game (http://www.election-day.info). Most of his writings and projects are accessible at http://faculty.washington.edu/jgastil.

Jake Harwood is Associate Professor of Communication and chair of the graduate program in Gerontology at the University of Arizona. He received his PhD in Communication from the University of California, Santa Barbara, in 1994 and taught at the University of Kansas before moving to Tucson. His research focuses on intergroup communication, with a particular focus on age groups, and draws on theories of social identity, intergroup behavior, and communication accommodation. He is the editor of *Intergroup Communication: Multiple Perspectives* (Peter Lang, 2005) and has published more than 50 articles in professional journals. His recent publications have appeared in *Personality and Social Psychology Bulletin, Journal of Communication, Journal of Applied Communication Research, Journal of Social and Personal Relationships,* and *Human Communication Research.* He is book review editor for the *Journal of Language and Social Psychology* and currently serves on the editorial boards of the *Journal of Communication, Communication Theory, Communication Research Reports,* and *Communication Studies.*

Todd Kelshaw is Assistant Professor of Communication Studies at Montclair State University, Montclair, New Jersey. His research considers deliberation and dialogue in public meetings, particularly in novel settings that permit the institutional incorporation of public voice in policymaking. These interests in the qualities and potentials of deliberative public participation are shaped by broader concerns about contemporary organizational life as it is influenced by the integral forces of globalization, postmodernity, and democratization. His teaching interests include organizational, group, and interpersonal communication topics, with an emphasis on connections between theory and practice. Along these lines, he is especially interested in experiential and service learning initiatives.

Karen Kroman Myers is a doctoral candidate in the Hugh Downs School of Human Communication at Arizona State University. Her research examines organizational assimilation, organizational knowledge, leadership, and identity in high reliability organizations.

Kristin M. Langellier is Mark and Marcia Bailey Professor at the University of Maine, where she teaches communication, performance studies, and women's studies. Her research interests include narrative performance, family story-telling, and Franco American cultural identity. Her numerous publications include *Storytelling in Daily Life: Performing Narrative* (Temple University Press, 2004), coauthored with Eric E. Peterson. She is former editor of *Text and Performance Quarterly*.

Judith N. Martin is Professor of Communication at Arizona State University. She has taught undergraduate and graduate courses in communication at the University of Minnesota, Pennsylvania State University, and the University of New Mexico. She has published research on ethnic identity and communication, interracial communication, sojourner communication overseas, and research ethics in a variety of social science journals; and served on the editorial boards of *Communication Monographs, International Journal of Intercultural Relations,* and *Western Journal of Communication Journal.* She has coauthored (with Thomas K. Nakayama) *Intercultural Communication in Contexts* and *Experiencing Intercultural Communication* (McGraw-Hill), and coedited *Whiteness: The Communication of Social Identity* (Sage).

Carolyn Marvin is Frances Yates Professor of Communication at the Annenberg School for Communication at the University of Pennsylvania. She is the author of *When Old Technologies Were New, Blood Sacrifice and the Nation: Totem Rituals and the American Flag,* and numerous articles on communication.

Katherine Miller is Professor and Director of Graduate Studies at Texas A&M University. Her research and teaching interests lie at the intersection of organizational and health communication. In particular, she is interested in communication in the lives of health care and human service workers, and has considered topics such as stress and burnout, professional and personal identity, and emotional communication in the workplace. She has published two textbooks and numerous journal articles and book chapters.

Thomas K. Nakayama is Professor of Communication and Director of Asian Pacific American Studies at Arizona State University. He is interested in the critical theory and cultural studies traditions, particularly as they inform the study of intercultural communication. In developing a critical intercultural communication agenda, he has published essays on whiteness, critical race theory, and critical sexualities. He has been on a Fulbright at the Université de Mons-Hainaut (Belgium), and has been Visiting Libra Professor at the

University of Maine. He has served on a number of editorial boards, including *Critical Studies in Media Communication, Communication and Critical/ Cultural Studies, Quarterly Journal of Speech,* and *Women's Studies in Communication.* He is coauthor (with Judith Martin) of "Thinking Dialectically About Culture and Communication" in *Communication Theory.*

John Durham Peters is F. Wendell Miller Distinguished Professor in the Department of Communication Studies at the University of Iowa. He is author of *Speaking into the Air* (1999) and *Courting the Abyss: Free Speech and the Liberal Tradition* (2005), and coeditor of *Canonic Texts in Media Research* (2003) and *Mass Communication and American Social Thought: Key Texts, 1919–1968* (2004). His work has been translated into Bulgarian, Chinese, French, German, Greek, Italian, Lithuanian, and Macedonian.

Eric E. Peterson is Associate Professor at the University of Maine, where he teaches in the Department of Communication and Journalism. His research and teaching interests are in narrative performance, media consumption, non-verbal communication, and communication diversity and identity. He is coauthor (with Kristin M. Langellier) of *Storytelling in Daily Life: Performing Narrative* (Temple University Press, 2004), and coeditor of *Public Broadcasting and the Public Interest* (M. E. Sharpe, 2003).

Eric W. Rothenbuhler is Professor of Communication at Texas A&M University and was previously Director of Graduate Media Studies at New School University (2001–2004) and on the faculty of Communication Studies at the University of Iowa (1985–2001). He earned his doctorate at the Annenberg School for Communication at the University of Southern California in 1985. His research and teaching address communication systems ranging from ritual through community to media industries. He is the coeditor (with Mihai Coman) of *Media Anthropology* (in press, Sage); author of *Ritual Communication: From Everyday Conversation to Mediated Ceremony* (1988), which has been translated into Polish (2004); and coeditor (with Greg Shepherd) of *Communication and Community* (2001, Lawrence Erlbaum). He was Review and Criticism Editor for the *Journal of Communication* (1997–1999) and has authored or coauthored more than 50 articles, chapters, essays, and reviews on media, ritual, community, media industries, popular music, and communication theory.

Robert C. Rowland is Professor and Chair in the Communication Studies Department at the University of Kansas. His research focuses on argumentation, rhetorical criticism, and the Israeli-Palestinian conflict. He is the author of three books: *The Rhetoric of Menachem Begin: The Myth of Redemption*

Through Return, Analyzing Rhetoric, and (with David Frank) *Shared Land/Conflicting Identity: Trajectories of Israeli and Palestinian Symbol Use,* which won the 2004 Kohrs-Campbell prize for rhetorical criticism. Rowland has written numerous journal articles and has won several major teaching awards at the University of Kansas.

David R. Seibold is Professor in the Department of Communication and Director of the Interdisciplinary Graduate Program in Management Practice at the University of California, Santa Barbara. Author of more than 100 publications on organizational communication, innovation and organizational change, group processes, and interpersonal influence, he has received numerous research and teaching awards. He is past editor of the *Journal of Applied Communication Research* and serves on the boards of many other journals. He has served as Chair of the Interpersonal and Small Group Interaction Division of the National Communication Association and is a past Chair of the Organizational Communication Division of the International Communication Association. He also has consulted widely with business, government, and health organizations.

Jennifer Daryl Slack is Professor of Communication and Cultural Studies in the Department of Humanities at Michigan Technological University. She is author of *Communication Technologies and Society* (1984), editor of *The Ideology of the Information Age* (with Fred Fejes, 1987), editor of John Waisanen's posthumous *Thinking Geometrically* (2002), editor of *Animations* (of Deleuze and Guattari, 2003), coauthor of *Culture and Technology: A Primer* (with J. Macgregor Wise, in press), and associate editor of *Communication Theory.*

Jonathan Sterne teaches in the Department of Art History and Communication Studies and the History and Philosophy of Science Program at McGill University. He is author of *The Audible Past: Cultural Origins of Sound Reproduction* (Duke University Press, 2003) and numerous essays on media, technologies, and the politics of culture. He is also an editor of *Bad Subjects: Political Education for Everyday Life,* one of the longest-running publications on the Internet.

James Taylor, author/coauthor of 6 books and some 70 published articles, is Emeritus Professor and recently served as interim chair of the Communication Department, which he founded, at the Université de Montréal. He has pioneered approaches to the study of the role of language in the constitution of human organizations, emphasizing in his work the contrasting roles of conversation and text in the construction of social reality. He is a member of the Board of Directors of the International Communication Association. He is currently working on two new books, and, since 1999, has authored or coauthored two books, *The Emergent Organization* and *The Computerization of Work*, and some 25 articles in peer-reviewed journals and books, and has been the recipient of Best Article and Best Book awards at the International Communication Association and National Communication Association. In 2003, he was the first scholar named to the prestigious Kurt Baschwitz Chair at the University of Amsterdam.